SO-ATQ-415

For my children, Ruby and Mac, and my wife,

Casey, who is no longer a vegetarian.

CONTENTS

UTAH

COLORADO

FOREWORD

There is no delicate way to put this: George Motz is nuts.

Who in his right mind would spend years traveling the country, clogging his arteries, parting with his hard-earned money, and suffering culinary indignities and belt-busting insults, all in pursuit of the perfect burger, something even he admits might not exist?

I first met George when he came to Chicago to visit that subterranean tavern know as the Billy Goat. Being a New Yorker, he knew little of the legend of this venerable spot; I don't think he realized that the *Saturday Night Live* "cheezborger, cheezborger" skits were inspired by this place and its shouting Greek "chefs"; and he'd never heard of Mike Royko and the other journalists who called the place home.

There have been, by my rough calculation, 4,540,762 burgers served at the Billy Goat since it opened on Hubbard Street in 1964, but none was more significant than the one grilled at 12:14 p.m. on April 19, 2003, and consumed seconds later by George.

The Goat's burgers are griddled, but Motz has eaten them deep-fried, steamed, broiled, baked, and raw; eaten them on buns, rolls, and bread; eaten them plain and covered with butter, bacon, chili, peanut butter, pimentos, pastrami, and almost any other topping that can be concocted by a cook's imagination and whatever might be lying around the kitchen.

He did this initially to create the film *Hamburger America*. The documentary gained a robust cult following. It made George proud but it did not make him stop. Rather, the film became the inspiration for and foundation of this book, for George's search for the best hamburgers in the country.

The great television journalist Charles Kuralt once observed, "You can find your way across this country using burger joints the way a navigator uses stars." And George set out to prove him right.

What you hold in your hands is the labor of his travels—a gathering of meat, if you will, but also a celebration of burgers and the people who make them.

Yes, George Motz is nuts.

As nutty as Columbus, or Lewis and Clark, but in his quest to find the best burgers in America, George has found something more important. He has discovered, in the mom-and-pop grills and out-of-the-way diners, an America that most of us probably thought had already vanished, a country of individuality and inventiveness, of people willing to rage, rage against the homogenizing of the land. You should enjoy that as much as what arrives on your plate. It's not just about the meat but the people you will meet.

RICK KOGAN | *CHICAGO TRIBUNE*

INTRODUCTION
TO THE
COMPLETELY REVISED *HAMBURGER AMERICA*

They came at me from every angle and thankfully none of them were angry. The minute the first version of this book hit the shelves, hamburger enthusiasts thumbed through looking for their favorite burger joints. Most found what they were looking for. Others were not so lucky and were kind enough to let me know what I had missed. For those that let me in on where to find their favorite burgers I'm forever grateful.

You see, this book is not really meant to be a "Best Of" by any means. It is only meant to function as a guide to finding great burger experiences in America. There are thousands and thousands of burger joints in this country and there's a good chance that your small town secret is not here. I'm getting a little bit closer, however, as I present to you 52 additions to the Hamburger America family of approved burger joints.

The original book profiled 100 great burger places to visit coast-to-coast. Sadly, since the publication of that book we've lost two hamburger greats, the Yankee Doodle in New Haven and Tookie's in Seabrook, Texas. When I had learned of their demise I did everything to save them but it was not to be. Tookie's suffered a devastating blow from Hurricane Ike and the Doodle had irreparable financial woes. We have bid farewell to the "Double Doodle" and the "Squealer" and are now left only with our memories. The downfall of these two seemingly invincible titans of the All-American hamburger only strengthened my resolve.

In a turn of events befitting a Hollywood survival story, amazingly one of America's great hamburger treasures came back to life. The Wheel Inn Drive-In of Sedalia, Missouri suffered a major setback when it needed to be demolished to make way for highway expansion. The owner had no interest in carrying on at a new location and shut the doors. Soon after, a former employee of the 65-year-old burger destination chose to take on the Herculean task of refiring the engines, and the Wheel Inn was resurrected just a few short blocks from its original location. It returned because the people wanted it to.

One of the questions I'm asked almost on a daily basis now is, "Aren't you sick of burgers?" In all honesty, no, and my appreciation of the hamburger grows exponentially with each new burger experience. The deeper I go into Hamburger America, the better it gets, and I still feel as though I've only scratched the surface.

While gathering new information about

hamburger joints for the revised edition of the book the most famous vegetarian in the burger world, my wife, Casey, decided after 17 years of avoiding meat that she'd like to have a burger. I was overjoyed, and scared. I chose the Bobcat Bite in Santa Fe to be her first, mostly because it's a great burger, she loves spicy foods, and I knew John Eckre would be sensitive to the task at hand. Upon taking her first bite, with the entire restaurant watching, someone yelled out, "What do you think??" She replied, "What's not to love?!" But the best part was that someone sitting next to her at the counter blurted out, "Did you think your husband was making this stuff up?" Needless to say, I'm really enjoying having Casey as a burger companion and, not surprisingly, our tastes are similar.

Speaking of tastes, here again is the all-important list of criteria for being included in *Hamburger America*. To make the list, the burger had to be made from fresh-ground beef (chuck, sirloin, rump—something good from a cow) and never frozen. In most cases age, provenance, and historical context played a factor in deciding what was most relevant for this book. For example, Louis' Lunch in New Haven may or may not have "invented" the hamburger, but it's safe to say that it is, without argument, the oldest continually operating burger joint in America (at well over 100 years), run by the same family for four generations, and they still make a tasty hamburger. And naturally, the burger had to

excite and satisfy this expert's taste buds. Many of the burgers in this book fall into the under $5 category, and I avoided most of the supersized forty-seven-pound burgers and bloated, over-the-top wallet-busters—bigger is not always better, and Kobe beef should be enjoyed in Japan as a steak. Furthermore, I chose places you'd want to visit, and should, before the wrecking ball comes down and replaces all of these wonderful bits of Americana with a Wal-Mart parking lot, or worse, a McDonald's.

Please don't try to be a hero (or a martyr) and eat all of the burgers in this book back to back. One thing that frightened me after the first book was released were the reports I was hearing about people powering through the book, coast-to-coast, in a matter of months. Whoa! Please be careful! During my research, even I, scarfing up to five burgers a day (not recommended), sought out the hotels with exercise equipment so that I might be alive today to bring you this book. My doctor laughed when I told him of my quest to write the Great American Hamburger Book, but then took my expanding waistline seriously, as should you. Embrace moderation.

My primary reason for writing this book was to make sure that the next generation of burger lovers has a starting point for saving the all-American hamburger. The way to do this is to patronize as many of these restaurants as possible. Looking into the not-so-distant future I see the McDonald's hamburger as a reference point for many as to what an American burger should look and taste like. This is not a good thing. A real American hamburger is so much more.

Go forth into America—Hamburger America that is—and meet real people and eat real burgers. Across the nation, regional uniqueness abounds. Using this book as your guide you'll discover the steamed cheeseburger of central Connecticut, the fried-onion burgers indigenous to Oklahoma, and Miami's Cuban Frita. Meet some of the hardest-working Americans you'll ever come across, whose commitment to great burgers will astound you. This book is for you, the burger aficionado. It is also for those who truly appreciate the preservation of a part of America that is threatened by the homogenization of the eating experience in this country. When you can appreciate a burger from a mom-and-pop joint that has found success in feeding people with high quality food for decades, you'll have a much better sense of what this country is really made of.

GEORGE MOTZ | BROOKLYN, NY, 2011

ARKANSAS

COTHAM'S MERCANTILE

5301 HIGHWAY 161 I SCOTT, AR 72142

501-961-9284 I WWW.COTHAMS.COM

MON–THURS 11 AM–2 PM I FRI & SAT 11 AM–8 PM

There's really only one reason to go to Cotham's—for their "Famous Hubcap Burger," so famous that you knew that already. What you may not know is that the Hubcap is made with over a pound of meat. You read that correctly; 17 ounces of fresh ground beef is cooked on a flattop griddle and served on a bun that resembles a small throw cushion. But aside from its frightening proportions, the Hubcap makes a tasty meal. I had no problem finishing one.

Cotham's (pronounced *cot-hams*) is a restaurant that in a previous life served as the local grocery and dry goods store. The place contains the standard country store antiques and collectables that give it a lived-in feel. Original wood and glass cases are still in place, only now they house vintage food boxes, snuff canisters, and some truly bizarre tonics for curing "the chills and malaria."

For all of the attention Cotham's has received nationally, it is still a local place at heart. The restaurant is a major tourist destination, but conversations can still be overheard that start with sentences like, "What church do you go to?" Cotham's is only a few minutes from downtown Little Rock but from the view out the front window you'd think you were in the middle of nowhere. The scene looks straight out of *The Wizard of Oz*—long, telephone pole–lined dirt roads leading out to dusty cotton and soybean fields. There's even a working chicken coop right next door to the restaurant.

In 1999 a new location opened in downtown Little Rock. Be aware, though, that both loca-

tions are open only for lunch during the week (for three hours) and only the original Scott location is open on Saturdays.

The Hubcap comes with mayo, green-leaf lettuce, tomato, onion, and pickles and at $9.75 is a bargain. If the prospect of hefting this Frisbee-sized burger to your lips sounds daunting, ask for the children's "Lug Nut Burger" (get it?) which is much smaller and adds ketchup. But you really need to set your sights on the hefty Hubcap.

President Clinton was no stranger to Cotham's during his time as governor of Arkansas. The old country store made a nice backdrop when the press followed him out to Scott to get a burger. "He loves the Hubcap," waitress Danielle told me. Now that the Clintons live in New York, frequent trips to Cotham's may be a bit difficult.

02

CALIFORNIA

THE APPLE PAN

10801 W. PICO BLVD I LOS ANGELES, CA 90064

310-475-3585 I TUES–THURS 11 AM–MIDNIGHT

FRI & SAT 11 AM–1 AM I CLOSED MONDAY

The Apple Pan may serve the best burgers in America. I say may only because I don't like playing favorites, but believe me, if there were a definitive burger in America this would be it. The synthesis of flavors and textures in their burgers is second to none, and the presentation is entirely Californian with its waxed paper wrapping. And the atmosphere of the place is pure nostalgia, not the kind that is manufactured, but real and enduring. They may serve the best burgers in America because in the 20 years that I have been going there nothing has changed—the burger I ate in the early '90s is exactly the same as the one I ate last week.

The Apple Pan looks completely out of place on Pico Boulevard in the neighborhood of West Los Angeles. The small white-shingled burger cottage is directly across the street from the towering behemoth Westwood Pavilion Mall. All of Westwood has built up around the tiny burger spot but the Apple Pan remains. Where the four-story mall stands was once a pony ride field. If you look directly at the Apple Pan and block out all of the surrounding urban chaos, you will be transported to a burger shack on a quiet country road somewhere in rural America.

Clark Gable used to visit regularly when he was working down the street at Paramount. Jack Nicholson and Barbra Streisand are regulars, as are many other Hollywood stars looking for a late-night burger fix.

The interior looks the same as it did on opening day in 1947 with its scotch plaid wallpaper and now worn terrazzo floor. A horseshoe counter with 26 red leather stools and two clunky old mechanical cash registers surrounds an efficient short-order kitchen. The counter- and grillmen all wear crisp white shirts and paper hats and take your order the minute your pants hit the stool. If you ask for fries, out comes a paper plate and the *thwock-thwock* of a counterman pouring ketchup for you. Ask for milk and you'll receive a metal cup holder with a paper insert. It's almost as if someone forgot to tell them the '50s were over. I hope no one does.

The burger menu consists of only two choices—the "Steakburger" and the "Hickory Burger." Both start as fresh ground beef that is formed into quarter-pound patties in the restaurant daily. "We'll patty up to a thousand a day,"

Sunny Sherman, the owner and granddaughter of the man who started the restaurant told me. The most popular burger at the Apple Pan is the Hickory Burger. What separates this burger from most is a proprietary, tangy hickory sauce that goes on the burger, along with pickles, mayo, and a sizable wedge of crisp iceberg lettuce (no tomato). All of this (and a slice of Tillamook cheddar if desired) is placed on a toasted white squishy bun and served the way most burgers are in Southern California—wrapped in waxed paper, no plate. The Steakburger replaces the hickory sauce with a sweet relish.

Iceberg lettuce on a burger is an LA tradition, but no burger I've met takes this condiment so seriously. "We only use the middle layers of the head, not the core or outside," grillman Lupe told me. "Just the crisp part." A prep chef slices perfect chunks of the crisp lettuce—one head of iceberg can yield only seven to eight chunks. That's a lot of heads of lettuce when you are cranking out up to a thousand burgers a day.

The result of biting into this pile of textures and flavors is pure bliss. The softness of the bun, the tang of the sauce, the warmth of the griddled beef, and the snap of the lettuce and pickle synthesize in that first bite like no other. It's nearly a perfect burger experience.

Walking into the Apple Pan at peak times can be daunting. There's no real order to who sits where. The trick is to position yourself behind someone who looks like they are finishing (look for half-eaten pie). If you are alone, the wait is minimal. For groups of ten—forget it.

Ellen and Allan Baker opened the Apple Pan in 1947. Allan had succeeded with another venture across town called King's Kitchen. From King's he brought the Steakburger. With the Apple Pan he introduced the Hickory Burger.

Allan built the Apple Pan as a business to retire on and had not planned to work there but did anyway. He hired Joe Kelly, his caddy from his golf days in Chicago, to be the general manager. In 1973, when Joe fell ill, Charles Collins took his job. Charles celebrated his fiftieth year of employment at the Apple Pan in 2007 (and retired after 52 years in 2009), but he is not alone. Many of the countermen have been donning paper caps and serving up burgers and pie for decades. Today the Bakers' daughter and granddaughter, Martha Gamble and Sunny Sherman, own the Apple Pan. They are committed to keeping the Los Angeles landmark as vibrant as it has been for 60 years.

The timeless quality of old Los Angeles is a draw that is hard to ignore. The Apple Pan does its part to remind us of what can endure in this town of disposable careers and an ever-changing cityscape. But there's no need to rush down to the Apple Pan. It'll be there forever.

CASSELL'S HAMBURGERS

3266 WEST 6TH ST I LOS ANGELES, CA 90020
213-480-8668 I WWW.CASSELLSHAMBURGER.COM
MON–SAT 10:30AM–4 PM I CLOSED SUNDAY

When a classic burger joint starts to fade, people tend to look the other way and wait for its demise. And when the icons of the burger business move on or sell out, there's always the temptation to jump to the conclusion that "It's just not the same as it was." Cassell's tends to fall into this category for most who see the 62-year-old hamburger restaurant as a has-been. I'm here to tell you that the burger at Cassell's is amazing and this vintage Los Angeles burger cafeteria has most definitely not lost its way.

In 1948, Al Cassell opened a burger joint across from the Bullock's Department store on Wilshire Boulevard in what is now part of Los Angeles's Koreatown. He successfully ran the restaurant until 1984 when he sold the business to Hakbae Kim. Mr. Kim, as he was affectionately known, was smart enough to not change anything. In 1986, he moved the restaurant to its current location on 6th Street, just a few blocks from its original location. Today, Mr. Kim's son, Jon Kim, owns Cassell's and amazingly, the place has stayed true to its roots.

Cassell made a name for himself by employing a unique method for cooking burgers on equipment of his own design. The large, high flattop griddle behind the counter also contains two smaller flattops that slide out from underneath. These smaller, sliding flattops are actually the bottom half of a double broiler. When the patty is placed on this flattop and slid back in, the burger cooks simultaneously from the top as well as the bottom. I'm guessing that Al's invention was designed for speed but he inadvertently invented a method for keeping the burger very moist. When a burger is placed in this contraption, it is not touched until it is placed on a bun. No flipping or pressing is necessary. Manager and Jon Kim's brother-in-law, Tek Kim, explained, "It holds the juice in. That's the difference."

Get in line at the rear of the large, sparse restaurant and grab a tray. Order your burger (the #23, a one-third-pound cheeseburger, is the most popular) and watch the double broiler in action. When your burger is ready, slide down the cafete-ria-style stainless steel rails and prepare to dress the burger yourself. I've become so accustomed to having classic burger joints prepare their signature burger their way that I was lost at the toppings bar. The choices are limited but great. Choose from standards like sliced tomato, sliced raw onion, pickles, and iceberg lettuce, all very fresh, and add mustard, mayo, and ketchup at will. There's also a homemade Thousand Island dressing, a recipe of Al's that you must put on your burger. The amazing mayonnaise is also made in-house and was a recipe of Al's. "We just follow his way," Tek explained. There's no limit to how much you can put on your burger but be sure keep it simple so you can taste the beef.

You'll want to taste the beef at Cassell's because it's unbelievably fresh. Sitting in the front window at Cassell's is a large meat grinder. "We grind it right here," Tek explained, and told me that every morn-

ing they grind chuck steaks for the day's burgers. "That's why we have customers of 30 or 40 years coming back." He then paused and said, "I don't think many other places still do this, do they?"

The burgers come in 2 sizes—one-third-pound and two-thirds-pound. The latter is large and sticks out from the super-wide, soft white bun. Even the one-third-pound burger seems really big since the entire package is wide, soft, and floppy. I'd be happy at Cassell's with a one-third-pound cheeseburger with nothing but Al's home-made Thousand Island on top.

The Kims have introduced fries to the menu, something that Al never offered. One menu item of Al's that remains today is a potato salad like none other. Totally unique, this uncomplicated salad is really just boiled potatoes and horseradish and it blew me away. "Some customers come in just for the potato salad," Tek told me. It's that good.

Don't show up for dinner at Cassell's. The burger restaurant has never been open past its peculiar closing time of 4 p.m. Tek explained that Cassell's is only open for lunch to feed nearby office workers. Incidentally, if you arrive 30 minutes before closing time the double broilers will be shut off. Fear not though, the large upper flattop, used for warming buns, is where your burger will be cooked.

So before you judge a burger joint on how it looks or make assumptions about its new ownership, get your butt there to judge for yourself. Or take it from me and go to Cassell's because this place continues to crank out great burgers. It seems to me that the only thing missing today from Cassell's is Al Cassell himself. "If we are different, the customer won't come," Tek told me, and added, "They come here for the name." I guarantee that Al would be proud of how his place turned out.

★　★　★　★　★

GOTT'S ROADSIDE

933 MAIN ST | ST HELENA, CA 94574

707-963-3486

(2 OTHER LOCATIONS IN SAN FRANCISCO AND NAPA)

WWW.GOTTSROADSIDE.COM

OPEN DAILY 10:30 AM–9 PM

The drive to Gott's takes you right through the heart of the Napa Valley. You'll pass rows and rows of vineyards and welcoming wineries with products to sample. Take a deep breath and smell the dense, pungent odor of freshly pressed grapes. It seems like the last place you'd find a good hamburger joint. That is, of course, until you pull into Gott's Roadside.

Gott's is in the center of it all. Most of the patrons of this updated classic '40s burger drive-in seem to be the buttoned-down wine-tasting types, but the stand does get its fair share of working-class locals as well. A bit of an anomaly in this part of the Napa Valley, Gott's has endured the influx of luxury hotels, inns, and spas, as well as a number of high-end restaurants.

The burger stand opened in 1949 as Taylor's Refresher. In the late '90s, two brothers with a

long family history in winemaking, Duncan and Joel Gott, bought the ailing stand. The structure received a first-class face-lift, but they made sure to maintain the integrity of the original stand. The city of St. Helena allowed the Gott brothers to expand only slightly, as Duncan put it, "for health reasons." He explained, "Before we bought the place, the refrigerators used to be outside, out back." Today's Gott's is a super-clean, contemporary version of the former stand with an upgraded kitchen and menu full of gourmet road food. In 2010, the Gott brothers, proud of the burger stand they had resurrected, decided to change the name from Talyor's to Gott's Roadside.

The hamburgers at Gott's are well thought out, tasty, and like so many quality hamburgers of the Pacific Northwest, socially conscious. Duncan explained, "We spent weeks of testing to come up with the right blend for the burgers." The one-third-pound fresh patties come from naturally raised, hormone-free California cattle. They are cooked on an open-flame grill and served on locally made soft, pillowy buns. A "secret sauce" also goes on all of the burgers at Gott's. It's a creamy, tangy mayo-based sauce, a sort of proprietary version of "Goop," (see page 346) the standard condiment on most burgers of the North-west. "The spices in the sauce we keep secret," manager Dave told me. All of the burgers are served with lettuce, pickle, and tomato in a red-checkered paper basket.

The burger selection at Gott's ranges from the traditional with American cheese to gourmet creations topped with guacamole or blue cheese. The extensive menu also includes healthy options like a chicken club, veggie tacos, and a Cobb salad, but no meal at Gott's would be complete without one of their extraordinary milkshakes. The first time I was there the flavor of the day was mango. The woman in front of me tasted hers and proclaimed, "Oh MAN, that's good!" I had an espresso bean milkshake that I still dream about today.

There's no indoor seating and the carhops are long gone, so find a spot at one of the many large red picnic tables in front, or on the spacious back lawn. Save your wine tasting for Gott's too. There's a separate "bar" here that serves a rotating selection of over 40 local wines and eight small-batch beers like Sierra Nevada and Anchor Steam. I'm not too confident about the pairing of a cheeseburger and a good Cabernet, but I can tell you there's nothing like a great burger and a cold beer. Add Napa Valley to the equation and you'll be in heaven.

I asked Duncan why the offspring of a wine family (his brother is a fifth-generation wine-maker in the region) decided to buy a hamburger stand and he told me, "We have a family love affair with food." They weren't even sure the venture

would work. "The day we opened 500 people showed up, and we thought, 'We could do this . . . we could be successful!'"

HODAD'S

5010 NEWPORT AVE I OCEAN BEACH, CA 92107
619-224-4623 I WWW.HODADIES.COM
SUN–THURS 11 AM–9 PM I FRI & SAT 11 AM–10 PM

Hodad's is exactly what you are looking for in a Southern California burger destination—an open-air restaurant serving enormous, tasty, no-frills burgers wrapped in waxed paper just steps from the beach. The atmosphere is inviting, with its license-plate-covered walls, the front end of a '66 VW Microbus that serves as a two-person booth, a public water bowl for dogs outside, and a sign reading "No shoes, no shirt . . . no problem!"

There are basically three burgers to order here: the Mini, the Single, and the Double. Single burgers start as a one-third pound patty. A Double involves two patties, and after adding cheese, lettuce, tomato, onion, mayo, bacon, and so on, becomes very large. The bacon served at Hodad's is out of this world. Longtime employee Benny invited me into the kitchen to show me how the bacon is prepared. Fortunately for the sake of keeping proprietary secrets safe, I didn't really follow the process. It involved large amounts of special, uncooked bacon in a sieve sitting over a pot of

boiling water. At some point this *bacon boil* is transferred to the grill, cooked to crispy, and married to your burger. The taste is truly unique and adds an intense smokiness to the burger experience. I also got a glimpse of the decades-old cast-iron grill. Needless to say, I can see where a Hodad burger gets its flavor.

The restaurant doesn't grind their own beef anymore, though tattooed 14-year employee Junior told me, "We get a delivery of fresh patties every morning." And don't miss the fries. They are enormous, battered slices of potato that resemble the popular "Jo-Jo," a deep-fried, mid- western truck stop spud specialty.

Like a surprising number of hamburger stands in America, Hodad's has moved locations three times, but all within a few blocks. It is owned by Michael Hardin, whose parents built the first stand in the sand next to the lifeguard tower in 1969. "This location has been great for us," he said of the newer central Ocean Beach spot. "We have crowds all year, even in winter."

And manager Jeremy told me, "We are slammed in the summertime and have a line down the street from 11 a.m. to 10 p.m. There is no down time here!" Because of this, a new Hodad's location is in the works, set to open in downtown San Diego sometime in 2011.

Michael is a true, tattoo-covered, Ocean Beach local. He even has the local surfer's code "1502" tattooed across his back, which in surfer vernacular refers to Ocean Beach. You can see Michael driving around town regularly in his customized, chopped VW Microbus, a great-looking, shortened bus with about six feet missing from its center. "We'll drive it into the O.B. parades unregistered," Michael told me laughing, "and the guys will do donuts and throw fries out the window."

Hodad's still accepts license plate donations, and if you submit a custom plate your meal is free. You really have never seen a collection of plates quite this extensive.

What is a "hodad"? A person who hangs out at the beach and pretends to be a surfer. Hodad or not, I would suggesting eating here *after* surfing, not before . . .

IN-N-OUT BURGER

MANY LOCATIONS THROUGHOUT CALIFORNIA,
ARIZONA, NEVADA, AND UTAH
800-786-1000 | SUN–THU 10:30 AM–1 AM
FRI & SAT 10:30 AM–1:30 AM

Putting a fast food burger with over 250 locations in this book does not really seem like my style. But think of it this way— had McDonald's, White Castle, Burger King, and many others stayed true to their roots, they'd be here too. Their rich histories and their place in the fabric of American food are just as amazing, but at some point they all lost their way. Not In-N-Out. One of the most successful privately-owned burger chains also just happens to make one of the best fresh-beef burgers in the nation.

Harry and Esther Snyder opened the first In-N-Out in Baldwin Park, California in 1948. It was a simple shoebox of a kitchen with drive-up windows on each side. Harry installed 2-way speakers at the ends of each driveway and in doing so revolutionized the business of fast food forever with the first drive-thru. His thinking was that while one order was being filled, the next was being placed. Brilliant.

Over the next 50 years In-N-Out expanded at a very slow and calculated rate. All through the '60s and '70s, the business of selling fast food burgers was in constant flux. Think of the temptation there must have been for In-N-Out to franchise, automate, and sell out. Many of the large chains were expanding at alarming rates, taking their companies public, and switching to a franchise system to sell more burgers to more people. As these places grew, the quality of the fast food burger slowly eroded. Most chains resorted to freezing their patties and shipping them over long distances—whatever it took

to make more money and please more share-holders. It's absolutely mindboggling that Harry and Esther Snyder were persistent in their vision for In-N-Out.

When Harry passed away the future of In-N-Out was secure, thanks to an agreement that only blood relation could run the company. His youngest son Rich took the helm and managed to expand the company greatly without moving away from his parent's core values. Before he died, Harry had expanded the chain to 18 locations limited to Southern California. Before Rich died in 1993, he had expanded the empire to almost 100 stores and today there are over 250 locations in 4 states (with Texas on the horizon). Part of In-N-Out's reluctance to expand nationwide is based on the simple fear that it would dilute the product and ruin the brand. Sound familiar?

The "Double-Double" is the cornerstone of In-N-Out's success. Made from two patties of unfrozen, fresh ground beef, iceberg lettuce, a slice of tomato, a thousand island-type spread, and two slices of American cheese, on a toasted bun and wrapped in waxed paper, the Double-Double is the perfect burger for one-handed driving. In-N-Out declined to tell me the size of the patties, but they seem to be around 2.5 ounces each. They are cooked on specially designed flattop griddles. The fries at In-N-Out start as fresh potatoes that are sent through a French fry cutter as the orders come in. And the shakes, the only thing frozen in the entire restaurant, are excellent. The real winner here, though, is the "Double-Double Animal Style" from In-N-Out's fan-created "secret menu" (see page 27). I have yet to find its equal in the world of fast food hamburgers.

How many times have you seen a McDonald's in a bad area with broken signs and missing light bulbs? You'll never find one single thing out of place at ANY of the In-N-Out stores, ever. The constant upkeep makes each In-N-Out look like new. Management at In-N-Out maintains the company's pristine appearance by doing what most companies should do—they treat their employees, or "associates" as they are referred to at In-N-Out, very well. Incentive programs that have been in place for decades are designed to make the well-compensated people who work at In-N-Out very happy and it shows.

One of the more intriguing aspects to the privately owned burger chain is the often talked about use of hidden Bible passages on the company's packaging. Next time you visit an In-N-Out, flip over your drink cup or spread out the paper that your burger was wrapped in. You'll find a chapter heading to a passage in the Bible (i.e., under the milkshake cup the reference to John 3:16, "For God so loved the world . . . ," is printed). Can you imagine being a public company and doing this? The company's bible-thumping campaign was put in place by former In-N-Out president and son of Harry, Rich Snyder. Just before he died in an awful plane crash, Rich found God and thought everyone else should too. He believed that the popularity of the hamburger was a great way to spread his faith. The use of the semi-hidden passages did little to scare off customers and actually did more to solidify In-N-Out's cult status among its fans. Most of the restaurants in the chain are landscaped with two very tall palm trees that have been planted crossing each other to form an X, further fueling the In-N-Out mystique. In reality, Harry was a big fan of the film *It's a Mad, Mad, Mad, Mad World*, where the final scene involves crossed palms.

Although In-N-Out continues to expand, the core beliefs passed down through the family members over the decades have kept this hamburger phenomenon a mom-and-pop at heart. Hidden bible verses, crossed palm trees, happy grill cooks, and consistently tasty burgers are what the In-N-Out experience is all about. What more could you want from a burger joint?

AN ANIMAL STYLE EPIPHANY AT IN-N-OUT

For years I have made the Double-Double my default order at In-N-Out Burger, the left coast's favorite drive-thru. It's a pretty straightforward burger, two thin patties made from fresh-ground beef on a toasted, white squishy bun served with two slices of American cheese, crisp iceberg lettuce, tomato, and a dollop of Thousand Island dressing. It is presented California-style, wrapped in wax paper, to facilitate one-handed driving.

I could take or leave the Double-Double. There are many other small mom-and-pops in LA and its environs that make a better burger. But this all changed the day I strayed from In-N-Out's modest 5-item menu. That was the day I ate my first Double-Double Animal Style.

Among burger cognoscenti, In-N-Out's secret menu is really no secret. Depending on who you ask, this word-of-mouth menu can add up to 30 additional items to the printed menu. In-N-Out "associates" (employees) are trained to know all of the secret menu items. Ask for a Neapolitan Shake, and you'll get strawberry, vanilla, and chocolate swirled together. Want a burger with the bun replaced by lettuce? You'll need to ask for yours "Protein Style."

I'd been aware of the Double-Double Animal Style for years but had never ordered one. I think I was afraid that a secret menu didn't really exist, that I'd get up to the register and be laughed at for ordering off a rumored menu. I imagined the chuckle of nearby patrons pegging me as a tourist. Eventually, when I overheard others ordering theirs Animal Style, I imagined a burger that was at best an unruly pile of ingredients, too much to handle, something only an animal could consume. It had to be a burger that would most certainly result in instant gastric distress.

Truth is the Double-Double Animal Style is none of this. The cult favorite is a perfectly balanced burger. To a standard Double-Double add grilled onions, extra sauce, and pickles. That's it, but these small additions create a gooey taste explosion. I had heard a rumor once that the burger is also cooked in mustard and after a quick call to In-N-Out headquarters found this to be true. "The patty is spread with mustard as it cooks on the griddle," a very friendly In-N-Out associate told me.

The Double-Double Animal Style should be a standard menu item at In-N-Out, though I'd hate to lose the thrill of asking for a burger that places the customer in a secret club. For those in the know there is no equal.

IRV'S BURGER

8289 SANTA MONICA BLVD

WEST HOLLYWOOD, CA 90046

323-650-2456 | MON–SAT 8 AM–7 PM

CLOSED SUNDAY

rv's was saved, thank God, and Sonia Hong was responsible. When I found a worn leather stool at the ramshackle burger spot 10 feet from the traffic on Santa Monica Boulevard, my first impression was that Sonia was not an Irv. "I am NEW Irv," she said and let out a chuckle.

Korean-Americans Sonia and her brother Sean bought the business, with every penny they had, in 2000 from Irving Gendis, who had flipped burgers there from 1978 to 2000. Before it was Irv's, the tiny stand on old Route 66 opened as Queen's Burgers in 1948. Typical of post–World War II burger ventures along the "Mother Road," Irv's remains as an icon of a quickly vanishing component of the early automobile age in Southern California. Over the decades, many Hollywood stars and musicians became regulars, including Jim Morrison and Janis Joplin, cement-

Linda grabs a bag of chips at Irv's in 1978.

ing the popularity of this burger destination. Irv's also made a great backdrop for the inner sleeve of Linda Ronstadt's *Living in the USA*. Open the record album and you'll see a nighttime snapshot, two feet wide, taken in 1978 at Irv's, with Linda and her band posing.

The most significant event in Irv's nearly 60 years in operation was a day in 2005 when Star-buck's West Coast nemesis Peet's Coffee tried to push Sonia off her little slice of prime real estate in West Hollywood. The regulars were appalled, the neighborhood was empowered, and cute lit-tle Sonia was not going down without a fight. The locals petitioned Peet's. "We were on the

news and received thousands of letters," Sonia told me. The mission to save Irv's became a pub-lic issue. Sonia set up multiple meetings at city hall, and after a year of fighting, Los Angeles County declared Irv's a historical monument.

The burger at Irv's is a California classic: tucked into waxed paper, on a soft, toasted white bun, and served on a paper plate. A wad of fresh ground beef is slapped on the tiny griddle and smashed HARD with a bacon weight once. Somehow Sonia, or whoever is at the grill, manages to whack the ball of meat with just the right amount of force to create the per-fect-sized patty.

Usually three people are hard at work at Irv's, including Mama, Sonia's mother. In all of the craziness that goes on inside the little shack Sonia still has time to write personalized messages on everyone's paper plate. On my last visit she drew, down to the color, the shirt I was wearing and included the message, "Just for George." She positions the burger on the plate so that both the burger and the art can be admired simultaneously. I believe the shirt drawings are her way of matching the burger to the customer—one of the more unique methods of order management.

Opt for a double with cheese because a single thin patty will not sate your appetite. Available condiments are the standard lettuce, tomato, onion, and pickle. Mayo, ketchup, and mustard are also available, and the menu lists a burger that comes with "special sauce." When I asked Sonia what the sauce was, she replied, without pause, "Love! Love is the special sauce."

The next time you visit Irv's, meet Sonia and Mama and feel proud to be an American. Eat your waxed paper–wrapped burger, take in the vibe of old Route 66, and remember the fight that saved this tiny burger spot from the wrecking ball—each bite will taste that much better.

JIM-DENNY'S

816 12TH ST | SACRAMENTO, CA 95814

916-443-9655 | WWW.JIM-DENNYS.COM

TUES–SAT 7 AM–3 PM | CLOSED SUN & MON

For its first 40 years Jim-Denny's was never closed. From 1934 to the late '70s the tiny ten-stool hamburger stand in downtown Sacramento was open 24 hours. Most of those odd late night/early morning hours fed bus drivers from the Trailways depot just across the parking lot and late-night revelers at the long-gone dance hall across the street. The bus depot is no longer active and the restaurant's hours have been reduced, but Jim-Denny's survives thanks to its fourth owner and chef, Patsy Lane. "We call these the ten hottest seats in town," Patsy said referring to the cramped but cozy seating in the burger stand she bought with her daughter and son-in-law in 2005. Upon taking the helm at Jim-Denny's the first order of business was removing decades of grease and grime that had almost rendered the place unusable. "The ceiling had almost caved in, it was caked with so much grease. If you put your hand on the wall it would just stick there!" Patsy told me as she flipped my burger.

Regardless of the rebuild and deep cleansing that the restaurant went through, Patsy still serves beautifully greasy griddled burgers that are slightly larger than those that Jim Van Nort and subsequent owners served for the first 70 years. And with the exception of new curtains on the windows, everything else is pretty much the same.

The wooden candy and cigarette shelves behind the counter labeled with features of the old menu (Fancy Cheeseburgers and a Fancy Cube Steak Sandwich for 25 cents) remain intact. The original red leather swivel stools are still anchored at their spots facing the worn Formica counter. The griddle continues to occupy the same spot just inside the front window.

Jim and a friend Denny started Jim-Denny's just before World War II. After the war, Jim and Denny parted ways and Jim opened a new restaurant with the same name around the corner. That location (also known as #2) is the only one that remains, and thanks to the efforts of Jim in 1988, this classic American burger stand has been designated a historic landmark by the city of Sacramento.

"We use the same butcher for fresh ground beef that Jim used since the early days," Patsy pointed out. The burgers come in two sizes—a smaller three-ounce patty and a larger six-ounce. Both arrive at Jim-Denny's daily as fresh, preformed patties.

The burger menu is extensive. You can order a Megaburger (two half-pound patties), a Superburger (one half-pound patty), or the Five Cent Burger, the original price for the quarter-pound burger. Each is served on locally made fluffy white rolls with lettuce, tomato, onion, pickle, mayo, and mustard standard.

A tradition that disappeared with Jim along with his "my way or no way" attitude was one of the restaurant's most endearing qualities—if you sat at the last seat at the counter you had to answer the phone and take the orders. The rule was created based on the seat's proximity to the phone. Fortunately for lovers of tradition like myself, I was glad to see that Jim's original note to diners at the seat remains, right next to the nonfunctioning pay phone. "If you sit near the phone you must answer it. Take the order, or ask them to hold." This was followed by sample greetings: "Jim-Denny's may I help you?" or "Jim-Denny's, please hold."

★　★　★　★　★

JOE'S CABLE CAR RESTAURANT

4320 MISSION ST | SAN FRANCISCO, CA 94112

415-334-6699 | WWW.JOESCABLECAR.COM

OPEN DAILY 11 AM–11 PM

The meat grinder is in the window— what more can I say? "It's there mostly for dramatic reasons, but it's there so the customer can see what they are getting," says Joe Obegi, owner for over 40 years and the man responsible for some of the freshest burgers on the West Coast. The grinder is only five feet from the huge flattop griddle.

Joe emigrated from Armenia to Brooklyn, NY in the early 1960s and jumped a Greyhound for San Francisco the next day. He found his way to what was at the time a small walk-up diner resembling a cable car. In 1965, after working there for a while, Joe bought the restaurant, added his name to the marquee, and has held court daily since. "I see grandchildren now of customers from way back," Joe told me as I inhaled my burger. Since the early days, Joe has renovated and expanded more than once and continually upgrades the service. Over the decades the restaurant slowly added indoor seating, beer and wine, parking (Joe spends half his day chasing off interlopers), and a larger state-of-the-art kitchen. It's an impressive little empire.

The restaurant décor is an eclectic mix of custom neon, oil paintings of butcher shop scenes, an artist's rendering of retail cuts of beef, and a sea of Polaroids taken of regular customers. The black linoleum floor is polished to an impossible shine and a wall of windows into the kitchen gives you the sense that there's nothing to hide here.

Joe takes his burgers very seriously. Don't look for half-pounders and other fractional designations here. Joe prefers to use what he calls "actual sizes," four-, six-, and eight-ounce "fresh ground beef steaks." The burgers are cooked medium-rare unless specified. The menu explains, "Order your beef steak the way you would like your steak cooked."

About halfway through my "beef steak," Joe made a strange but characteristically brazen

move. He grabbed a fork and delicately pried loose a small portion of meat from the center of my burger. "Eat that, just like that with no bun or other stuff." My burger experience had been altered and I had seen the light—Joe's burgers really were ground steaks.

A butcher dressed in all white with a white paper cap starts the burger-making process by trimming a large chuck steak behind glass, for all the patrons to witness. The meat is coarsely ground, measured, and portioned into balls using ice cream scoops, then gently pressed into patties six at a time with a special press of Joe's design. When the patties hit the griddle they contain 6 to 8 percent fat.

Driving down Mission in the Excelsior neighborhood, it's hard to miss Joe's. A huge sign, larger than the one with the actual name of the restaurant, announces with incredible candor, JOE GRINDS HIS OWN FRESH CHUCK DAILY. He really does and it makes all the difference.

HOW TO BUY HAMBURGER MEAT

Making patties from fresh ground beef at Joe's Cable Car.

OK, I've given you 150 reasons to eat out and you still want to make a burger at home? No problem. All you'll need to do is drop in to your local big-box supermarket and grab a plastic-wrapped wad of ground meat on the Styrofoam tray, right? Wrong. The first step is getting the right meat. Here's a guide to shopping for ground beef:

Go to your local butcher, not the supermarket. Fresh ground beef is the prime ingredient of an excellent burger. Supermarket ground beef is rarely fresh. Also, the origin of the cow (or cows) that is in supermarket beef is usually unknown. If you go to a butcher, chances are the beef comes from one cow and is ground right in front of you.

Depending on your preference, choose a fat-to-lean ratio. The best hamburgers have more fat (surprised?) but lean sirloin is always an option for the health conscious. Most butchers will choose an 80/20 percent ratio of muscle to fat if you don't ask. This is because any more fat will cause the burger to shrink substantially as it cooks. Less than 5 percent fat may cause the burger to stick to the cooking surface.

Ask for chuck shoulder. This is the most common part of the cow used for hamburger meat because of its high fat content. Some butchers will blend fatty chuck with sirloin in the grinder to increase the leanness of the mix.

Ask your butcher to grind the chuck "twice" or ask for a "number two grind." This means he'll put it through the grinder twice to ensure that the fat and muscle fibers are blended well.

Use the ground beef the day you purchase it. After the first day, refrigeration causes the juices to separate from the meat. These are the juices you need to create the perfect burger.

MARTY'S

10558 WEST PICO BLVD | LOS ANGELES, CA 90064

310-836-6944 | OPEN DAILY 6 AM–6PM

In a town where finding old, established anything is getting harder and harder, look for this tiny burger stand in West LA for a genuine blast from LA's past. What's more, Marty's has been serving up quality fast food made with fresh ingredients and has never succumbed to the temptation to serve processed frozen food. For nearly five decades almost nothing has changed. "Nothing," Vicki Bassman told me. "Never will." Vicki is the daughter-in-law of Marty himself. She told me without pause, "There's nothing like fresh meat."

Marty's is the "Home of the Combo" and this fact is proudly displayed on a sign on the roof of the stand. The combo is so basic you'll wonder why more restaurants have not followed suit. Invented in the 1950s, the combo at Marty's is a hamburger with a hot dog on top. It's a great-tasting way to be indecisive and order both fast-food icons together.

Both meats for the combo come from high-quality ingredients. The hot dogs are Vienna Beef foot-longs and the burgers are pattied on the premises everyday from fresh ground chuck. Longtime grillman Geraldo told me, "We take a three-and-a-half ounce measured scoop of fresh ground beef and press each patty by hand." They use a single press that produces an almost paper-thin patty, one at a time. On the original, perfectly seasoned griddle, the combo is cooked separately, then wed. The foot-long is halved lengthwise, flattened, and then halved again, resembling a small square red raft. The burger is cooked for less than a minute on each side before the hot dog raft is placed on top. The stack of America's two favorite fast foods piggybacked on

the griddle and separated by a square of yellow cheese is a sight both absurd and beautiful, a sight that makes you proud to be an American.

Burgers come standard with mayonnaise, ketchup, lettuce, onion, and a tomato slice (which Angel slices as your burger comes off the griddle). Mustard and pickles need to be requested. One time a guy on line in front of me asked for his combo "my way," which naturally sounded very folksy and personal, but he told me, "That just means extra mustard, extra mayo."

Marty Bassman opened the roadside stand in 1958 and worked the griddle until the late 1960s when operations were handed over to his son, Howard. At the time Howard assumed the business, he was only 17 years old. Today, Howard and his wife run the stand, as well as a successful catering business that focuses on supplying local schools with high-quality lunches and private barbecues around Los Angeles.

I never would have discovered Marty's had it not been for my LA cousin Dan Appel. The tiny blue and orange burger stand is a blur to most as they speed down Pico. Wedged between a gas station and a fire department, and down the street from popular Rancho Park, the stand is a daily lunch spot for firefighters. "They have a gym upstairs," former manager Angel told me, "they have nothing to worry about." The hardworking crew at Marty's takes orders without writing a single thing down. "I can remember up to 25 orders at a time, in my head," Angel told me once, tapping his temple.

A throwback to simpler times, the stand offers walk-up service and a few outdoor stools and narrow counters along the sides of the structure. A patio behind the stand (that I only discovered recently) has enough seating for 50.

Howard told me, "When I was a kid, there were mom-and-pop hamburger stands like Marty's all over Los Angeles. They've all disappeared." Across the street from Marty's stands the ubiquitous golden arches of a popular American burger chain. Its garish presence, though, doesn't seem to affect the brisk business being conducted at Marty's. It seems that the waiting customers are smarter than that. They know where to find a real burger.

PIE 'N BURGER

913 E. CALIFORNIA BLVD | PASADENA, CA 91106
626-795-1123 | WWW.PIENBURGER.COM
MON–FRI 6 AM–10 PM
SAT 7 AM–10 PM | SUN 7 AM–9 PM

"That was the last slice of butterscotch pie. Hope you didn't want one," the waitress said to me on my first visit to this forty-plus-year-old burger counter. The customer I had just been speaking to, who had told me he was visiting from London, said he was not leaving California without a slice of butterscotch pie from Pie 'n Burger. No big deal. I didn't know what I was missing. Then I visited two more times and ran into the same problem (one time I showed up on a day they were not even offering the fabled pie). Finally, on my fourth visit, I got my slice. This pie is not to be missed. Their pie motto (written on the pie safe): "Take home one of our famous homemade pies for that special occasion or just when you want to live it up."

But the obvious reason to visit Pie 'n Burger is for their incredible hamburgers. Since 1963, the long, faux-wood-grain Formica countertop has seen its share of burger perfection. The burger they made in the '60s is the same one that is served today. Even the local retail butcher that supplies the ground chuck has not changed in over 35 years. Longtime employee and owner Michael Osborne told me, "The beef we use is top quality and ground coarse. That's why they taste so good."

Two other important factors that go into the great-tasting burgers are the original, well-seasoned, flattop griddle, and the homemade Thousand Island dressing. "We go through about 100 pounds of dressing a week," Michael told me. The recipe came directly from Kraft in the '30s. Original owners Benny and Florence Foote were in the restaurant business long before opening Pie 'n Burger. According to Michael, Benny contacted Kraft and they gave him the recipe. "We still make it the same exact way, using Kraft mayonnaise."

A burger with Thousand Island dressing may sound familiar. California's own burger phenomenon, In-N-Out, also uses the dressing on their burgers. If you order a double-double at Pie 'n Burger, you basically get the same

burger, only much better. Both burgers are made with fresh ground beef that has been griddled, served on toasted white buns with iceberg lettuce and the dressing, wrapped in waxed paper. Pie 'n Burger takes a giant leap forward by doubling the quantity of the beef to a quarter-pound per patty. The burgers at Pie 'n Burger are also somewhat hand formed. Quarter-pound balls of fresh beef are measured with an ice cream scoop then smashed flat with a huge can of tomato juice.

The system for cooking and assembling the burgers is all about efficiency. One person flips the burgers while another preps buns with a wedge of lettuce and dressing. The grillmen are seasoned professionals—one, Franciso, told me enthusiastically, "I've been here for 37 years!"

Michael started working at the restaurant in 1972, flipping burgers and going to USC full time. When he graduated, he continued to work at the restaurant, gradually helping out with managerial duties. In the late '70s, Michael bought a piece of the business and in 1992 the Foote family, in search of retirement, sold the remainder of the shares to him.

Pie 'n Burger looks exactly as it did in 1963 (with some obvious wear and tear). The wood-paneled walls and plaid wallpaper look beautifully out of date, as does the hand-painted wall menu. A cup of buttermilk is still offered with the usual diner fare of tuna sandwiches and chicken pot pie.

I asked Michael why he had stuck with the burger counter for so long and he told me, "I took the job because it was fun working here. To me, life is about having fun." Michael also feels like he has been entrusted to Pie 'n Burger's survival. "I feel like a caretaker to the business for the community."

VAL'S BURGERS

2115 KELLY ST | HAYWARD, CA 94541

510-889-8257 | TUE–SAT 6:30 AM–10 PM

CLOSED MONDAY

Many diners across America attempt to re-create the '50s malt shop experience but few offer an authentic experience. It's not easy to bottle that feeling unless you happen to have been able to survive the last five decades with your values intact. Val's was created to be exactly what it is today—a perfect example of a mid-century West Coast hangout that still cranks out some of the best shakes and burgers in America.

Val's is always busy. At dinnertime, every red leather booth is taken and you'd be hard pressed to find a stool at the long counter that runs the entire length of the diner. There is a constant stream of take-out orders leaving through a side door and the wide indoor flame grill is loaded with sizzling patties. A Little League team had taken over the three booths in the center of the restaurant and a young couple was sharing a hot

fudge sundae in the corner. In the center of all of this ordered chaos I spotted a tall, lanky man with a bushy black moustache sweeping up around a booth. The busboy? Nope, this was none other than owner of 28 years George Nickolopoulos. I asked him why he was sweeping and he replied flatly, "I never stop." I soon realized that after nearly three decades of ownership he still does everyone's job, making rounds of tables, the grill, the register, constantly checking and making sure the dinner rush is going smoothly.

Before the arched wood ceiling diner with its large windows was built in 1958, Val's was a small barbershop across the parking lot. The original Val's eventually morphed into a variety store and post office run by George's aunt and uncle, Carmen and Al Valenzuela (hence the name Val). At some point Al decided to start selling "charcoal burgers," and they quickly became the core of his business. Building a larger building with the focus on burgers and shakes was a foregone conclusion.

The burgers at Val's come in three sizes—the one-third-pound Baby Burger, the half-pound Mama Burger, and the one-pound Papa Burger. On my first visit I was drawn to the Papa Burger mostly because of its absurd size sporting two half-pound patties on a toasted bun. I tried to

The Papa Burger at Val's, actual size

compress the burger to fit into my face but still could not ram it in. I actually finished the mountain of meat-and-cheese and was amazed to find that even though the burger was cartoonish in size it was still exploding with flavor and juiciness. It seemed from looking around that the Mama Burger was the way to go.

I asked George how many burgers he could sell on a busy day and he quickly replied, "If you have time to count you are not doing enough." Other questions about how he runs the business were met with similar responses. I had nothing but respect for this icon of the burger world and was enjoying his caginess. He did however offer one nugget of advice: "I'll tell you this. Our meat is far superior than anyone else's. It's also in the way you prepare the burgers that separates the men from the boys. No one would ever consider putting as much time as we put into these."

Don't miss out on the shakes at Val's. Long-time counterperson Valerie told me, "The best milkshake I've ever had is the Root Beer Banana shake. It's like milkshake crack." She wasn't kidding. The signature shake, also know to regulars as the Rootanana, has only three ingredients—vanilla ice cream, root beer syrup, and an entire banana. A friend of mine along for the trip took a sip of his and shouted, "That's insane!" I agree.

Val's is a Bay Area must on a hamburger tour of America and not just for its great burgers, shakes, and easy-going atmosphere. Go to Val's knowing that it is a family place—not only are generations of regulars still enjoying Val's,

George's entire family works there in some capacity. It takes a family to run a true family restaurant.

WESTERN STEAKBURGER

2730 UNIVERSITY AVE | SAN DIEGO, CA 92104

619-296-7058 | MON–SAT 10 AM–9 PM

On a trip to San Diego to film a TV show, I made plans to visit one of my favorite burger stands in America, Hodad's in Ocean Beach. But a crew member of mine alerted me to another nearby out-of-the-way burger spot that I had to try.

Western Steakburger sits on the edge of the up-and-coming San Diego neighborhood of North Park. Opened in 1983 by Greek immigrant "Gus" Constantinos Anastasiu and his effervescent wife, Maria, the Greek-influenced restaurant kept burgers and gyros separate for the first year. But sometime in 1984, Gus piled a wad of sliced gyro meat on a finished burger and the Western Steakburger was born.

The restaurant is set back from the street, fronted by a large palm tree. If you sit on the small front patio, the soundtrack for your meal is the rustling of palm fronds and the occasional thump-thump of a passing urban party-on-wheels. Members of the San Diego police department make regular stops at this burger restaurant and have been for decades (cops always know where the good burgers are). But before you plan to sit beneath the palm fronds on University Avenue, plan on taking the afternoon off—this burger is a beast.

The menu lists many "steakburgers" and their toppings (e.g., pastrami, bacon, and chili) but there's no mention of the burger that made them famous. The gyro-topped burger is listed simply as the half-pound "Western Steakburger." "Gus never wanted to list the contents of the Western, he always says 'let them ask,'" Maria told me.

The burgers are cooked over an open flame in full view of waiting patrons. Oval-shaped patties of fresh-ground beef are grilled to perfection and placed on toasted white, squishy buns. Grillman Ricky then places a one-third-pound pile of the salty gyro meat on the patty and delivers the burger with mustard, ketchup, mayonnaise, lettuce, tomato, pickles, and onion.

After my first bite, I was in heaven. The familiar spice of the gyro meat complemented the burger well and somehow the pound of ingredients managed to stay neatly tucked into the soft bun. About 20 minutes after ingesting this glorious grease-bomb, I had to pull over in my rental car because I was having food coma hallucinations. My advice to you—do not operate heavy machinery or a motor vehicle after enjoying this burger.

Maria was working the counter when I visited. "You have to love what you do. Mom-and-pops are a dying breed." Western Steakburger was the first burger available to resi-

dents of North Park. Today, the tiny family-owned burger joint feels the heat from a McDonald's, Wendy's, and a Burger King only a few blocks away. But thanks to recent development in the neighborhood (a condo just went up across the street), people are starting to take notice of Western Steakburger and their flair for coupling Greek and American foods. Maria told me, laughing, "How come after 28 years people are just starting to come? Why couldn't they come when we were younger and had more energy!"

★ ★ ★

03

COLORADO

BUD'S BAR

5453 MANHART ST I SEDALIA, CO 80135

303-688-9967

MON–SAT 10 AM–10 PM I SUN 11 AM–7 PM

Bud's Bar is not in Denver. On a map, the town of Sedalia, Colorado, looks like it could be a suburb of the Mile High City, but in person, the tiny town, surrounded by cattle farms, feels as remote as any town on the Kansas Plain.

Bud's is one of only a few businesses in the small downtown of Sedalia. The 63-year-old bar sits between two busy railroad rights-of-way that are only a few hundred feet apart. It's not uncommon to be stuck at either crossing for longer than 20 minutes waiting for a long coal train to pass. "Some guys walk out, see the train, and say 'Oh well!' and head back inside for another beer," Mike Steerman told me. Mike should know. He owns the place.

Mike is only the third owner of Bud's since Calixte "Bud" Hebert converted an auto shop into a bar in 1948. In the 1960s, Bud became a local judge and decided that judges shouldn't own bars. He sold his tavern to an employee, Thurman Thompson. In the 1980s, current owner Mike started tending the bar part-time to relieve stress from his job as a salesman. When Thurman decided to sell the bar, he set his sights on Mike, knowing that he would change little about the place.

The one thing I'll bet most people were afraid he would change was the burger. Rest assured that Mike has kept it the same. With a name like Steerman, it would be stupid to question his Colorado heritage or his affinity for fresh beef. The burger at Bud's is a classic griddled quarter-pounder with American cheese on a white squishy bun. It's absolutely amazing and transcends the standard notion of bar food. The burger bursts with flavor and is one of the juiciest griddled burgers I have ever eaten.

People go to Bud's for two reasons—because they know everyone in the bar and for the burgers. Outside of drinks at the bar, Bud's has served only burgers since the beginning. "It's simple," Mike explained, "we don't offer lettuce, we don't offer tomato, and we only use one kind of cheese." Fries? Nope. Chips will have to do. But trust me, you'll be focusing on this burger and nothing else.

The burgers start as 80/20 chuck hand pressed in a single patty maker. They are cooked on a smallish flattop griddle in a bright, clean kitchen next to the bar. As a burger nears doneness, both halves of a bun are placed on the burger and covered with a lid to steam the bun to softness. Your order is served with a bag of chips and a slice of onion in a plastic mesh basket lined with waxed paper. "That's it," Mike told me, proud of the simplicity of his product. Locals in the know request jalapeño slices that Mike has stashed in a small jar in the kitchen.

Sunday is the busiest at Bud's, a day where the griddle can see up to 500 burgers. "That griddle stays full for six hours on Sunday," Mike told me.

Mike seems to be one of the newer members of the Bud's family, and the only male in an all-female staff. Amiable bartender Nancy has been serving drinks for two decades and I'm told that Judy, the head grill cook, has been at Bud's since Neil Armstrong first set foot on the moon.

Bud's interior is cozy and simple. One side is lined with vintage stools, there are booths on the other side, and a few tables in the middle. An original jukebox sits just inside the front door and one wall displays a unique item—the branding board.

Of course, being from New York I was very intrigued by the branding board, something that probably seems mundane to a ranching community. The idea is simple—it's a long piece of wood attached to one wall of the bar that displays actual cattle brands of the local ranchers. To me, it was a viable piece of "bar art." One glance at the board and you are reminded of just how close you are to fresh beef.

Despite its roadhouse appearance, Bud's has become a place for family and friends. Since smoking in bars was banned in 2006 Mike has seen an increase in business. "A little while ago we had an entire Little League team in here."

4

CONNECTICUT

CLAMP'S HAMBURGER STAND

ROUTE 202 (NEAR MARBLEDALE, CT)

NEW MILFORD, CT 06776 | NO PHONE

OPEN LATE APRIL TO LABOR DAY

11 AM–2 PM, 5 PM–8 PM DAILY

Way up in the northwest corner of Connecticut is a tiny burger stand that is definitely worth the drive. It has no real address and no phone but doesn't need these things. If you show up on a summer day at lunchtime, you'll find a crowd that somehow found its way there regardless of its off-the-grid status.

I asked owner Tom Mendell why, after all these years, there still was no phone at Clamp's. He told me, smiling, "It's always been that way and I don't see any reason to change it." Tom's great-uncle Edwin Clamp opened the little white-shingled stand in 1939 because he had tired of his job as a door-to-door hardware salesman. "I think he came up with this idea because he didn't like to work," Tom told me. The stand is still open only during the warmer months, which gave Edwin the winter off.

When World War II started, meat rationing caused Clamp's to shut down temporarily. During that time, Edwin used the tiny stand to manufacture a faucet washer that he had patented. After his death, Edwin's wife, Sylvia, ran Clamp's and worked there into her late eighties. "She was a worker," Tom told me.

Tom, who lives in Baltimore in the winter and assumed the business 13 years ago at the young age of 30, has changed very little about Clamp's. He expanded ever so slightly the tiny kitchen, but the structure still remains under 450 square feet. Tom himself mans the griddle at the front of the stand and spends most of his day flipping patties to perfection. And like most great keepers of the lunchtime grill, Tom stays focused and politely refused to answer my questions as he managed the incoming orders.

Clamp's gets a daily delivery of fresh ground beef from a local butcher, delivered as quarter-pound patties. Tom is very serious about the quality of the ingredients that go into his roadside fare. Everything is fresh, and he makes his own coleslaw and the chili that goes on the hot dogs and hamburgers.

Somewhat recently, the griddle was replaced. Tom wasn't exactly sure but he thinks it happened around 20 years ago because the original finally gave up. Janine, on staff for 15 years at the stand, told me, "The old griddle had a big slope in the middle from being cleaned so much."

Clamp's is an outdoor place. The stand is basically a kitchen with walk-up order windows. You place an order at one of the windows, find a table (made from those huge industrial wire spools) in the grassy grove on either side of the stand, and wait for your name to be called. Don't expect a loudspeaker to summon you back for pickup. The girls that take your order literally shout your name, sort of like your mom calling you for dinner.

The cheeseburgers are served on white squishy buns with the traditional Yankee white American cheese. Locals know to order theirs topped with a Clamp's specialty—a pile of sweet, slow-cooked, caramelized onions.

The drive to Clamp's is half the fun. If you are coming up from the quaint, historic town of New Milford, Clamp's is exactly 5.9 miles north on Route 202 from the gazebo on the town's square. Trust me, you'll need this info as you pass farm after farm, nearly hit a deer (as I did), and wonder if you've gone too far. Look for the small white building tucked into the trees with an American flag tacked to its side. The only identification the building offers is a postcard-sized sign just over a side door: a small plaque that reads CLAMP'S EST. 1939.

Tom told me, "Most of the time I'm as busy as I can possibly handle." The only break he gets is when it rains, but even then, some like to show up for his famous burgers. "I think we have a cult of people who like to show up during thunderstorms," Tom told me. "It's funny. They sit in their cars, eat burgers, and watch the rain."

LOUIS' LUNCH

261–263 CROWN ST | NEW HAVEN, CT 06510

203-562-5507 | WWW.LOUISLUNCH.COM

TUE & WED 11 AM–3:45 PM

THU–SAT 12 PM–2:30 AM

CLOSED SUN & MON | CLOSED DURING AUGUST

There are many claims to the origin of the first hamburgers in America. One of them is Louis' Lunch (pronounced LEW-EEZ). Even if the claim here can be disputed, it is without a doubt the oldest continuously operating hamburger restaurant in the country. What's more, one family, the Lassens, has owned and operated the tiny burger haven since 1895—four generations of passionate hamburger making. Operating Louis' today are the third and fourth generations: Ken Lassen, his wife, Leona, and their two sons, Jeff and Ken Jr. My wife likes to call Louis' "hamburger church"—there is no excessive banter or typical diner orders being barked, just the clanking sound of the upright flame broilers opening and closing and the crinkling of wrapped burgers going into paper bags. People stand at the counter waiting patiently for their order to be handed to them.

The structure that houses Louis' Lunch is a tiny box with 100-year-old Victorian flair. Small as it seems, it's the largest it's ever been. The original Louis' was a tiny-wheeled lunch cart that eventually went terrestrial as a three-sided cube attached to one side of a large downtown New Haven tannery. When the tannery was torn down in the early 1970s, the three sides were salvaged, dragged four blocks, and an expanded fourth wall was constructed, along with a basement.

A burger at Louis' starts with fresh-ground lean beef, ground daily in the spotless basement. Every morning Ken Jr. rolls the meat into small balls. Two balls are pressed together to make a patty, which is placed vertically in a metal grate and then slid into an ancient upright broiler. The grill cooks from both sides and juices drip into a pan below. The burgers are then placed on Pepperidge Farm white toast, simply because when Louis Lassen invented the "hamburger sandwich" in 1900 there were no buns (in fact buns didn't come around for almost another 20 years). In the 1970s, Ken felt the pressure to add cheese to his famous sandwich. If you ask for cheese, you'll get a cheese spread that seems Velveetaesque. Due to the unique method for cooking the burgers, cheese slices take a back seat to the spread. Fresh-cut tomatoes and onions are standard, but don't ask for ketchup or you may be shown the door. As Jeff Lassen explains, "We honestly believe you don't need ketchup because it's the best burger there is." And Ken told me, "Ketchup is a strong flavor. If we gave you that, it would destroy everything we are trying to give you." Jeff also pointed out that students from nearby Yale frequently try to sneak in small packets of ketchup only to be told that

Louis Lassen in his lunchwagon, 1907.

the burger they wanted to sit down and eat is now a to-go order.

It's not uncommon to walk into Louis' and find matriarch Leona, or "Lee" Lassen operating the vintage burger broilers at a fever pitch. For over 50 years Lee has grilled burgers to perfection for the lunch crowd. In 2006, she was hospitalized with a heart condition, and after only a few months rest, she surprised us all by returning to her spot at the grill.

The Lassens are salt-of-the-earth burger royalty, and they are quite aware of their status in American food history. Regardless of the provenance that surrounds Louis', the prices are fair and the burgers are always fresh and tasty.

SHADY GLEN

840 EAST MIDDLE TRNPK | MANCHESTER, CT 06040

860-649-4245 | MON–SAT 7 AM–10:30 PM

SUN 10:30 AM–10:30 PM

The inside of the Shady Glen looks like a cheeseburger. The yellow-striped wallpaper, warm lighting, and low brown Formica countertops mimic the colors of their famous cheeseburger concoction. Ice cream may be the number-one seller at this Manchester, Connecticut institution, but the cheeseburger is what has made them famous. In 1949, Bernice Rieg invented the "Bernice Original," which became an immediate success and still accounts for 80 percent of their sandwich sales today. The

four-ounce cheeseburger comes with four slices of cheese. The cheese is not just stacked atop the burger; it is symmetrically placed, centered on the burger as it cooks on the hot griddle. An understandably large portion of this cheese makes direct contact with the griddle. When the cheese cooks through it is curled skyward by the deft grillman until it resembles a cheese crown. Amazingly, I watched burger after burger leave the grill with the same dramatic cheese. The same burger, over and over, since 1949.

"It's a special cheese, but that's all I can tell you," Michael the manager smiled. Michael started working at the Shady Glen over two decades ago as a dishwasher. "At 22 years, I'm still the new kid on the block." Shady Glen is a very busy place. There are more than 15 employees in constant motion, waitresses in little ruffled aprons and grillmen in paper caps and black bow-ties. This is the real deal, not a mock-up like Johnny Rockets.

There are no menus at the Shady Glen, just wall menus, and they are basic. You can order a "cheeseburger" or a "big cheeseburger;" the latter comes with the four slices of cheese. The smaller "cheeseburger" comes with only three slices. It's

The Bernice Original

served on a white squishy bun and delivered to your spot at the counter with your own personal condiment tray of relish, raw onion, mustard, and ketchup. The Shady Glen can sell up to 4,000 Bernice Originals on a busy week. That's a lot of cheese sculpture.

I stood by the grill and watched closely—the cheese, which looked like a house-sliced mild cheddar, really does not stick. One of the grill men offered some shaky science. "The carbon, uh, buildup on the griddle over the years acts sort of like Teflon." I think he's right. I had a hard time trying to figure out what do with my cheese wings once I had my burger in front of me. Two guys sitting near me at the counter had opposing views. One told me, "Fold the crisps onto the burger and eat it that way." "Not me," said the other, "I like to break them off and eat them separately." A girl sitting on the other side of me was chewing on some cheese crown crisps with no burger in sight. "This is an order of Crispy Cheese," she told me. This guilty pleasure is served on a bed of lettuce and is not on the menu.

In 2008 Bernice passed away and a longtime employee Bill Hoch and his wife, Annette, became owners of the 62-year-old restaurant. They did not change a single thing about the place, probably because Bill started working at Shady Glen in 1954. He told me with a chuckle, "I've been a lifer here."

At first I was concerned about the large mural that spans the entire west end of the restaurant. It depicts strange elves having a picnic of burgers,

hot dogs, and ice cream. As I left the restaurant I looked again at the mural and fully understood its significance—the Shady Glen is a necessary fantasy. I hope it never goes away.

TED'S RESTAURANT

1044 BROAD ST I MERIDEN, CT 06450

203-237-6660 I WWW.TEDSRESTAURANT.COM

MON–SAT 11 AM–10 PM I SUN 11 AM–8 PM

If you are looking for a truly unique hamburger experience, go to Ted's. If you are looking for a potentially healthy burger, go to Ted's. If you are looking for a char-grilled cheeseburger, don't go to Ted's. Ted's Restaurant is the epicenter of the steamed cheeseburger world—a burger that only exists in central Connecticut. A former owner of Ted's Restaurant, Ted's son, Paul Duberek, once told me, "Within 25 miles of here there are about seven steamed cheeseburger places, but we're the only ones that make ten hot dogs a week and 800 steamed cheeseburgs."

The steamed "cheeseburg," as it's referred to at Ted's, is just what you'd think it would be—a steamed patty of ground beef on a bun. What you wouldn't expect is that the cheese is steamed too, steamed to a molten goo. The process starts with a steaming cabinet that holds 20 small stainless steel trays. Specially ground fresh chuck is pressed into the trays and these are placed in the cabinet. The meat cooks through but stays

amazingly moist and unfortunately, looks like gray matter. The result is a burger that loses most of its fat content (it gets poured off) and retains a truly beefy flavor. A "secret" cheese (Paul told me it's an aged Vermont cheddar, but that's as far as he'd go) is also placed in the small trays in a separate steamer. Once gooey, the cheese is poured onto the burger, served with tomato, ketchup or mustard (or both), lettuce, and a slice of onion, and placed on a soft kaiser roll.

The origins of the steamed cheeseburger are a bit murky, but it's believed to have originated at Jack's Lunch in Middletown sometime in the '30s. Ted Duberek opened his restaurant in 1959 to feed the immense local factory worker popu-lation. For over 100 years, that area of Connecti-cut was home to some of the largest silverware manufacturers and they had shifts around the clock. Ted's used to stay open until 4 a.m., but started closing earlier as the factories moved their business overseas.

In 2007, suffering from back trouble, Paul Duberek decided to leave the business and sold Ted's to his nephew Bill Cally. Bill was no stranger to the steamed cheeseburg and had worked at Ted's on and off during high school and college. Not surprisingly Bill did not change much about the place and plans to own Ted's for a very long time. He told me, "I count my lucky stars everyday."

5

DELAWARE

CHARCOAL PIT

2600 CONCORD PK I N. WILMINGTON, DE 19803

302-478-2165

(2 OTHER LOCATIONS AROUND WILMINGTON)

WWW.CHARCOALPIT.NET

MON–THU 11 AM–MIDNIGHT

FRI & SAT 11 AM–1 AM I SUN 11 AM–MIDNIGHT

When Charcoal Pit opened in 1956, it was way out on the Concord Pike surrounded by fields and very few other businesses. "It was all farmland and nothing but a two-lane road," manager of 42 years Frank Kucharski said, looking out the window of this time-warp diner. "Hard to imagine now." Yes, it is. Concord Pike today is a densely packed commercial strip. It's a wonder this burger gem is still standing.

From the outside, Charcoal Pit looks virtually unchanged since the 1950s. The restaurant's boomerang-inspired marquee with its pudgy pink neon lettering is authentically retro. The interior has seen a few upgrades and design changes over the years and blends styles from the past five decades. If you're lucky, you'll be seated at a booth with a tabletop jukebox. These are not props. They actually work. Holly Moore, Philadelphia area food writer and a man who knows where to find the best greasy food anywhere, told me, "Think Richie, Potsie, and Ralph Malph in a corner booth and Al flipping burgers behind the counter. There's something unmistakably genuine about eating at Charcoal Pit that needs to be experienced."

The burgers are cooked over an open flame, as the restaurant's name implies. The large gas grill, in full view of the dining room, is outfitted with a bed of lava rocks that help to evenly distribute the heat. Grillman of 19 years, Lupe spends hours inches from the flames, flipping hundreds of burgers a day.

For some reason, for the first time in all of my burger exploits I did not order the burger suggested by my host. A burger at Charcoal Pit comes in two sizes, a thick half-pounder and a thinner quarter-pounder. He said to get the big one; I opted for the smaller. The thing about flame-grilling burgers is this—thicker burgers taste much better when cooked on an open flame because all of the moisture stays inside the burger. Thin patties have a hard time retaining that moisture. It's much easier to cook a thin burger on a flattop griddle because the burger stays moist and tasty no matter what you do. I found myself eyeing a neighboring booth's half-pound burger dripping with juices, cooked to temperature, and realized I should have listened to Frank.

The half-pound burger is served on a kaiser roll and the quarter pounder comes on a seeded, toasted white bun. Seems as though someone was paying attention to burger physics when bun decisions were being made. The fresh Angus patties are delivered daily to Charcoal Pit from a local supplier. "We probably go through over a thousand pounds of meat a week," Frank told me, "and it's always fresh."

Not only are the burgers fresh, other items on the menu are house made, like their crab cakes, soups, and coleslaw. The first time I visited Charcoal Pit I found Frank and another employee in the kitchen straining what looked to be about 10 gallons of homemade vegetable beef soup. "We're hands-on here," Frank said as he hoisted the steaming vat of soup.

Outside of burgers, Charcoal Pit is ice cream nirvana. A sign out front proclaims simply, ICE CREAM CREATIONS and they are not kidding. The menu is heavy on ice cream and there is a sundae named after each of the nine local high schools. The thick, hand-dipped milkshakes are enormous and not to be missed.

Every year as the local high schools are letting out for the summer, Charcoal Pit can count on one thing—the prom. "It's total chaos in here," manager Joseph Grabowski told me, "They're really into the Kitchen Sink." For a minute I imagined a burger with enough embellishment to fill a sink, but Joe explained, "It's 20 scoops of ice cream, whipped cream, nuts, etc., and two bananas." Whoa.

DISTRICT OF COLUMBIA

BEN'S CHILI BOWL

1213 U ST NW | WASHINGTON, DC 20009

202-667-0909 | WWW.BENSCHILIBOWL.COM

MON–THU 6 AM–2 AM | FRI 6 AM–4 AM

SAT 7 AM–4 AM | SUN 11 AM–11 PM

"Most people don't want to eat with a lot of loud music. It's just part of our culture," a regular for four decades named Marshall Brown told me as we sat at the counter of this 50-year-old Washington, DC, landmark chili restaurant. Marshall was referring to the sounds of Bob Marley and Luther Vandross that were oozing out of the jukebox, not necessarily loud, but definitely present. One time when I was enjoying a breakfast chili cheeseburger, the guy next to me at the counter was eating his eggs, so consumed by the music that he started dancing in his seat. I'm positive that moving to the music made the food taste that much better.

Ben's was opened in 1958 by Ben and Virginia Ali in a former silent movie theater known as the Minnehaha. Ben, who had emigrated from Trinidad, met his wife at the bank just down the street. "She was a bank teller," the couple's son Nizam told me. Ben passed away in 2009 and Virginia has retired, but two of their sons, Nizam and Kamal, run the restaurant today.

Ben's is known for its tasty chili that gloriously adorns hot dogs, half smokes, and hamburgers. The bright, airy, neighborhood restaurant, with its incredibly colorful façade, also serves a memorable breakfast, but many return from all corners of the country for their chili dogs and burgers. Over the years it also became known for the role it has played in Black American history. Ben's fed many celebrities performing at the clubs along the U Street corridor in the '50s and '60s, including Ella Fitzgerald, Miles Davis, and Cab Calloway.

The 1968 riots sparked by the assassination of Martin Luther King started just a block away when someone threw a brick through a drugstore window. The riots devastated the neighborhood, a curfew was imposed, and the city shut down while attempting to restore order. But Ben's remained open by special police permission to feed firefighters, police, and members of the Student Nonviolent Coordinating Committee located just across the street. When they did close for the night, Ben stayed behind to protect the business from looters. "He kissed my mom goodnight, sent her home, and sat inside with a gun all night," Nizam told me. To identify the restaurant as a black business Ben painted the words SOUL BROTHER across the front window.

Ben's survived the riots, the crack hell of the '70s and '80s, then the construction of a Metro extension that cut off traffic on U Street for almost five years. "We had two employees and were making only about $200 a day during that time," Nizam told me. "The construction was more devastating than the drugs." Massive publicity from Bill Cosby and other black luminaries kept the business alive during the bad times.

Cosby and his wife had many dates there while he was stationed in the Navy nearby.

Today Ben's thrives. Even the Clintons are fans. Nizam told me, "We sent a lot of takeout over to the White House when they were in office." President Obama paid a visit in 2009 and indulged in their famous chili dog (and humorously complained when he noticed that the guy sitting next to him had cheese and he didn't). The U Street corridor is in the midst of a revival and the new Metro stop is directly across the street. There must be twelve people behind the counter and the atmosphere is lively and fun, with all of the employees joking and flirting with each other. The large front room with its long counter and booths gives way to two more rooms that are somewhat hidden from view. The enormous dining room in the back has a projector and screen and the walls are lined with adoring photos of a virtual who's-who in Black America. One great photo shows Cosby and Al Green smiling, the front window of Ben's as their background.

The burgers are quarter-pound patties and arrive fresh daily from a supplier in Baltimore. The chili that goes onto the burger is a simple family recipe that contains only finely ground meat in a dark red, tangy sauce. The burger comes on a toasted bun in a plastic basket with a side of potato chips. If you need more, go for a chili dog, or better yet, the sublime chili cheese fries.

Ben's is a successful family business that has endured incredibly hard times. "We've gotten

the most ridiculous amount of press, more than we could ever dream of," Nizam pointed out. Then, remembering the importance of having a fan like Bill Cosby, he said "this place is a big part of his history." I'm sure Ben's is also a big part of the collective histories of all of the diners who have passed through its doors, and the future stories that have yet to be written there.

TUNE INN

331½ PENNSYLVANIA AVE SE
WASHINGTON, DC 20003
202-543-2725 | SUN–THU 8 AM–2 AM
FRI & SAT 8 AM–3 AM

Johnny Cash on the jukebox, cheap beer on tap, and copious amounts of taxidermy on the walls . . . sounds like a recipe for your favorite country crossroads bar. But the bar is the Tune Inn and it's only steps from the Library of Congress and the Capitol Building in our nation's capital. It'd be easy to assume the country bar trappings are an urban design choice, but all of the stuffed game was bagged by the three generations of the Nardellis, owners of the Capitol Hill watering hole since 1955. This place is the real deal—a comfortable neighborhood dive bar with an excellent burger on the menu.

"I shot that one. That's my first doe," Lisa Nardelli told me, pointing to a stuffed deer head directly over the bar. Lisa is young and

pretty and doesn't strike you as the hunting type. Her grandfather, Joe Nardelli, hunted most of the stuffed game, ranging from deer to squirrels to pheasant. "They would get drunk and shoot at anything," Lisa said of her father, Tony, and grandfather hunting together. Mounted over the bathroom doors in the rear of the narrow tavern are the other ends of deer. "That's my grandfather's sense of humor—deer asses over the bathrooms." The collection is so

vast that the local Shakespeare theatre once borrowed a bunch of the Nardelli's stuffed birds for a production of *King Lear*.

Lots of well-known politicos and other Capitol Hill heavies have been drinking and eating at the Tune Inn for the last five decades. One of the most famous couples in American politics, James Carville and Mary Matalin, had their first date here (they left abruptly because it was too crowded). Janet Reno was a regular (for the burgers) and JFK the senator had his favorite booth (second one on the left). The bar also hosts regulars who have been coming in for decades. "It's like a big family, which is unusual in a big city, so close to the Capitol," Lisa pointed out. It's also home to countless numbers of students looking for cheap beer and good burgers, yours truly being one of them a few decades back.

The menu is mostly modest comfort food. The burger takes center stage and starts as a six-ounce ball of 80/20 ground chuck. Chef Mike Tate told me, "We use a measured scoop, then form a patty." The meat is delivered fresh every morning from a local butcher that also supplies the well-known upscale Old Ebbitt Grill, a Washington landmark near the White House. "It's the same exact meat," Lisa told me.

The patty is cooked to perfection on a flattop griddle and served on a buttered, toasted bun. The result is a loose, moist burger that melts in your mouth. It really is the perfect bar burger—not so big that you can't finish your beer and not so small that you go hungry. Following an appearance on the television show *Diners, Drive-Ins, and Dives*, a burger that was formerly a specialty item went to the daily menu—the "Beer Batter Burger." "After the show, everyone who came in wanted one," bartender Michelle told me. They basically take a griddled burger, dunk it in beer batter, then drop it into the deep fryer.

The Tune Inn was the fifth bar in the District to receive its liquor license after Prohibition was repealed, and today is the oldest drinking establishment on Capitol Hill. During Prohibition the bar served as a speakeasy and regulars have told stories about that time for decades. One day recently, Lisa was wondering about a certain out-of-place wall in the basement. She tapped on it, found it hollow, and proceeded to smash the wall with a sledgehammer. What she uncovered was an indelible piece of American history. "There was a trap door that led to right here," and she pointed to a spot behind the bar. "Apparently they used to pass the booze through here to the bartender."

You can visit the Tune Inn for a burger, for a few drinks, or as longtime bartender Susan Mathers believes, for love. "You think I'm kidding. Many people find their own true love at the Tune Inn," Susan told me with a straight face. "I have observed many people meet and fall in love here." She looked over at the third-generation Nardelli. "Lisa met her husband here."

7

FLORIDA

EL MAGO DE LAS FRITAS

5828 SW 8TH ST | WEST MIAMI, FL 33144

305-266-8486 | WWW.ELMAGODELASFRITAS.COM

MON–SAT 8 AM–7:30 PM | CLOSED SUNDAY

Erase any pre-conceived notions you have about the traditional American hamburger. If you find yourself in Miami, get away from the glitz of South Beach, brush up on your Spanish, and prepare for the taste explosion that is the "Frita." Also known as a "Cuban Hamburger," the Frita offers one of the most unique hamburger experiences in America. It is unquestionably the most genuine gastronomic expression of the Cuban-American experience.

In the middle of the twentieth century, the Frita was a ubiquitous street food of Havana. By 1959, when the smoke from the Cuban Revolution had cleared, many fled to set up shop in America. As entrepreneurism was squashed in the new Cuba, it flourished in Miami. Today the best examples of the Frita are found not at its birthplace but in its adopted home of South Florida.

In a bright and tidy lunch counter, tucked into a strip mall with only three parking spaces out front, you'll find, arguably, one of the best Fritas in Miami. The man behind this tasty Cuban treat is the affable septuagenarian Ortelio "El Mago" Cardenas. El Mago opened his lunch counter in 1984 after splitting from his brother-in-law's successful Miami chain El Rey De Las Fritas. Both restaurants are on 8th Street, aka *Calle Ocho*, which is the main artery through Little Havana in South Miami. Many lunch counters on Calle Ocho serve Fritas but El Mago is in a league of its own.

El Mago's Frita is made with fresh ground beef and what seemed to be chorizo and several spices mixed into the patty. I sat at the counter one day with friend, guide, and translator, the Florida burger blogger Burger Beast, Sef Gonzalez, and asked El Mago what else was in the patty besides chorizo. He turned from the

and gives the patty a generous squirt of a thin, deep red liquid. A handful of chopped onion is sprinkled on as the patty cooks in the red bubbling sauce.

What makes a Frita a Frita is the generous heap of super-thin fried potatoes that virtually obscure the patty on the bun. It's presented on a soft, warmed Cuban roll with more chopped onion, a squirt of ketchup, and a bird's nest of the wiry potatoes. The extraordinary flavor profile made me nearly fall off my stool. When I told El Mago how happy I was he just looked at me and smiled. After inhaling that first Frita I did the only sensible thing I could think of. I ordered another.

Burger Beast told me, "There are Frita places that use those canned potato sticks instead of fresh and that's just wrong." El Mago makes a batch of his ethereal fried potatoes every morning.

El Mago De Las Fritas has refreshing watermelon juice and the old Cuban standby soda, Materva, on the menu. But don't leave El Mago without trying one of his *batidos,* or Cuban milkshakes. You won't find American classics like the chocolate malt here. Instead, indulge in tropical fruit flavors like guanabana, papaya, or the amazing mamey fruit. Or get the incredible flan de leche. I swear I've never had a better flan.

Directly translated El Mago means "The Magician" and this one hails from a long line of Cuban Frita purveyors. Like a good magician, El Mago harbors trade secrets that only his son seems to know. Let's hope he plans to pass along those secrets so that this Frita endures.

griddle and shouted with a smile, "No chorizo!" Burger Beast was confused and I was in disbelief. The presence of another red, spiced meat was undeniable, but what was it?

When you place your order, El Mago disappears into the back and returns clutching a wad of refrigerated ground meat. The multihued chunk is tossed onto a hot griddle and pressed flat. He reaches for an unmarked plastic bottle

LE TUB

1100 NORTH OCEAN DR | HOLLYWOOD, FL 33019

954-921-9425 | OPEN DAILY NOON–4 AM

After Le Tub was chosen by *GQ* magazine for having the #1 burger in America, the *Oprah* show did its own report backing up the claim. The only problem is, the most crowded no-frills burger shack in Florida just got more crowded.

Located on a stretch of A1A just a half hour north of Miami, Le Tub is a former Sunoco gas station converted into a strange pile of flotsam collected over three decades. Most of Le Tub's seating is outside on a meandering multilevel porch surrounded by lush foliage, worn wood, chirping birds, and hot breezes. Its proximity to the Intracoastal Waterway offers a constant boat show. I once sat at a table on the water and watched an entire bachelorette party in bikinis float by, the bride opening gifts of lingerie and giggling.

The restaurant got its name from owner Russell Kohuth's collection of discarded commodes, tubs, and sinks, which basically hold the place together. In addition to the porcelain collection are parts of boats, buoys, and other planks that actually make up the basic structure of the restaurant. Russell started collecting stuff on early morning jogs along Hollywood beach and opened the restaurant in 1975. "This place wouldn't hold up in a hurricane," the guy at the next table told his wife.

The Sirloinburger at Le Tub is a beast—13 ounces of fresh-ground, hand-pattied, char-grilled sirloin served on a soft kaiser roll. When I prodded the waitress for the actual size of the burger, she told me, "They are big and messy!"

The grill cook works at a small three-foot-square grill on a level just below the bar in basically an enclosed un-air conditioned space. There is smoke everywhere and the smell of searing beef permeates your clothes if you spend any time at the bar. Why the grillman does not pass out from the heat three times a day is beyond me.

The crowd at Le Tub is a mixed bag—confused tourists, beachgoers, and boaters fill the tables. A dock on the patio allows you to arrive by water if so inclined. Order your burgers THE MINUTE YOU WALK IN THE DOOR. I'm not kidding when I say that mine took one hour and twenty minutes to arrive. When I asked our waitress upon ordering if their famous burgers really took that long, she warned, with a straight face, "Could take up to an hour and a half." I placed an order for myself and a friend who had just landed at Miami International Airport. By the time she got off the plane, got her luggage, rented her car, and drove to Le Tub, she still had to wait 45 more minutes for her burger.

The good news is that the burger is worth the wait. Also, don't forget, you are in a bar, on the water, in Florida—the beers will go down easy, especially because you'll be sitting there for a while.

IS THERE REALLY A "CHEESEBURGER IN PARADISE"?

Imagine that you are sitting in a beachside bar somewhere in the Caribbean or south Florida eating what you consider to be, at that moment, the best-tasting burger you have ever had. You tell the waitress or bartender, and they say, "Well it should be the best. This is the burger Jimmy Buffett wrote the song about!" This hypothetical conversation plays out every day somewhere in the warm climes of vacationland, in claims that stretch from the Bahamas to New Orleans and back to the Florida Keys. Places like the Cabbage Key Inn on Captiva Island, Florida, where the wait for the fabled burger can be up to two hours because up to 500 people a day are there just for the burger "Jimmy sang about." Or Le Select, a comfortable beach dive on St. Barths where the claim has some merit because Buffett has been known to swoop in on his Cessna seaplane, go straight to the bar, and put on an impromptu concert.

One claim that seems to make the least sense but is worthy of inspection comes from Rotier's in Nashville, Tennessee. The burger at Rotier's has been on the top of every poll in Music City for decades. It's a worn-in, dark, friendly place that has served excellent burgers since 1945. Pointing at the bar, Margaret Crouse, the giggly owner and second-genera-tion Rotier, told me, "He used to sit right here and write songs," referring of course to Buffett, who lived and tried to make a go of his music career in Nashville in the late '60s. It's easy to see how over the years a connection could be made between the best cheeseburger in town and a starving artist-cum-star's early low-income diet. Alas, there is no connection.

Where is the famed cheeseburger then? Turns out Buffett came clean a few years back and told the truth. The "cheeseburger in para-dise" stemmed from a hallucination. As the story goes, he was sailing near Puerto Rico in the mid-'70s and ran into weather and equip-ment trouble. He and his crew floated at sea for over five days eating nothing but canned food and peanut butter, and naturally fanta-sized about juicy cheeseburgers. Eventually the ship limped in to the Village Cay Marina on Tortola, BVI, and the hungry sailors headed for the dock bar. There they feasted on what he recalls as overcooked American-style burgers on burnt buns that tasted "like manna from heaven." The song that followed was not about that burger, but about the fantasy. Buffett made his dream burger a reality in 2002 when he opened the first of his 32 Cheeseburger in Paradise restaurants.

GEORGIA

ANN'S SNACK BAR

1615 MEMORIAL DRIVE SE | ATLANTA, GA 30317

404-687-9207 | MON–SAT 11 AM–9 PM

CLOSED SUNDAY

A visit to Ann's Snack Bar is not for the faint of heart. I warn you now, the list of rules posted on the wall covers only a fraction of how you should behave in Miss Ann's small outpost on the southeast side of Atlanta. I'll do my best here to prepare you for the onslaught that will lead to one of the best hamburgers in America.

"When I die, I want them to say, 'She was a mean bitch but she made a great hamburger!'" While she works alone in the burger and hot dog shack she has owned and tended to since 1972, she keeps the waiting patrons amused with a running comedy routine that covers everything from new condos going up and down the street to her retirement and Social Security woes. The guy sitting next to me explained, "It's like a barbershop in here." The routine is real, though, no acting here. I found out the hard way when she threw me out of the restaurant for wanting to interview her. "I threw *Southern Living* out just last week! I don't give a damn . . . Get out!" I stuck it out and was rewarded with the only thing that seems to get ordered from her short menu—the "Ghetto Burger."

In 1994 a Checkers drive-in hamburger stand opened up just two doors down from Ann's. Realizing that she had to offer something different to maintain her business, Miss Ann (as she is affectionately called by regulars) ditched the frozen patties she was serving for fresh ground beef, and lots of it. The gimmick worked. "If I had known that's all it took to be world famous I would have done this years ago," she told the crowd at the eight-stool counter. But fresh beef was only the beginning. The Ghetto is an enormous burger, a glorious heap of sin, a pile of just about every ingredient in the restaurant. Two hand-formed patties that are unmeasured but look close to a half pound each

are slow cooked on a flattop griddle and sprinkled often with seasoned salt as they cook. The construction of the Ghetto Burger includes the two patties, toasted bun, onion, ketchup, mustard, chili, lettuce, tomato, cheese, and bacon. If that were not enough, the bacon is deep-fried. The finished product resembles a food accident and tastes as it should—amazing.

"One lady came in here and watched everything I did and said 'Miss Ann, how come I can't make a burger at home like yours?' and I told her 'because you ain't Ann, and you ain't BLACK!'" She punctuates her delivery by repeatedly slapping the counter hard. The mostly black crowd laughs at all of it and waits patiently for their burgers, which can take up to 45 minutes.

Ann wants to retire, though she keeps pushing the date back. Preventing her retirement has been the search to find the right buyer. "I don't want some developer coming in here and tearing the place down," but she smiles, "though the money would be nice."

IDAHO

HUDSON'S HAMBURGERS

207 EAST SHERMAN AVE I COEUR D'ALENE, ID 83814

208-664-5444 I MON-FRI 9:30 AM–6 PM

SAT 9:30 AM–5:30 PM I CLOSED SUNDAY

If you had found yourself in Coeur d'Alene at the turn of the century, chances are you would have paid a visit to Harley Hudson's tiny canvas burger tent for some greasy nourishment. The great news is that over a hundred years later you can still visit this landmark burger counter for the same greasy nourishment. The tent may have gone brick-and-mortar and has moved four times (only a few blocks each move), but the burgers are still made with pride by the fourth generation of the Hudson family.

This classic burger counter is just what you'd expect to find in picturesque downtown Coeur d'Alene, Idaho. From the front window of the restaurant you can see a piece of the enormous Lake Coeur d'Alene and imagine the hydroplane speedboat races that took place there in the 1950s and 1960s. Find a spot at the long counter and order a burger, the only thing on the menu.

"We also have drinks and pie," grillman Eli told me, "but that's it. No fries, no chips, no nothing." By design, the menu focuses on the hamburger, as it should, because this one was worth the drive.

The choices are single or double, cheese or no cheese. Condiment options are pickle and a slice of raw onion. If you request pickle, watch closely what happens. You'll witness something

you'd be hard-pressed to find anywhere else in America. The grillman takes a whole dill pickle and hand slices five or six pieces and neatly arrays them on a waiting steamed bun. The same happens for a slice of onion, sliced in a worn groove on the butcher block in front of the griddle. Nothing is presliced.

A pan of high-quality, fresh ground round sits to the left of the small flattop griddle. The grillman takes a guesstimated quarter-pound wad of the fresh beef and swiftly forms it into a patty, and it hits the griddle with an audible splat. The griddle only holds 18 burgers at a time, so expect to wait for a stool during peak times. Eli told me that during the summer, the line can go out the door and down the street. "When it's busy, we are behind all the time."

Hudson's serves what could be considered a nearly perfect burger. Relish the moment and plot your return because you'll be forever changed. The simplicity of the elements and the burger's ideal proportions will win your heart (and stomach).

One unique feature of the burger experience at Hudson's is a proprietary "spicy ketchup" that locals and regulars put on their burgers. Fair warning: this stuff is HOT and looks like regular ketchup in its traditional squirt bottle. Todd explained that the ketchup was invented not for culinary reasons but for economic ones. "During the Depression, some people would come in and load up their burgers with ketchup to stretch the meal." Todd's grandfather added fiery spice to

discourage the practice. Over 70 years later, Hudson's still does not offer the classic red stuff.

Today, brothers Todd and Steve Hudson run the historic burger counter. They each take a three-day shift and do their share of burger flipping. Burgers have not been the sole passion of the Hudson family, though. Their proximity to the lake has led to a lifetime on the water. Great-grandfather Harley flipped burgers in the early part of the century, but also owned a steamboat that he rented for excursions on the lake. During the decade that speedboat racing was allowed on the lake, it was the Hudson family's unofficial job to set up the racecourse markers. When you have finished your burger at Hudson's, wander into the back of the restaurant, where you'll find one of the most impressive collections of hydroplane racing ephemera and memorabilia anywhere.

A few years ago, a McDonald's Express opened four doors down from Hudson's and it lasted only two years. Seems as though the fast-food empire was no match for a 100-year-old burger institution. Todd told me that people would ask if they could go buy McDonald's fries and eat them with their burger at Hudson's. He repeatedly told them, "Sure, as long as you bring enough for everybody."

"The secret is our longevity," Todd explained as he smiled and shrugged. In 2007, that longevity was recognized when the state of Idaho issued a proclamation to honor the Hudson family for a hundred years of business. 100 years of great burger making is definitely cause for celebration.

ILLINOIS

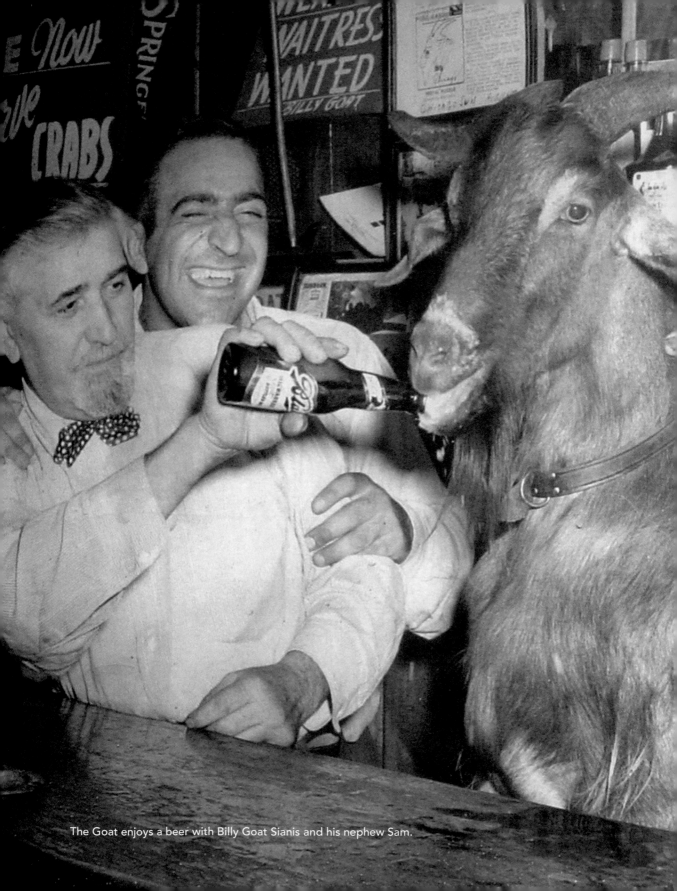

The Goat enjoys a beer with Billy Goat Sianis and his nephew Sam.

BILLY GOAT TAVERN & GRILL

430 N. MICHIGAN (LOWER LEVEL) | CHICAGO, IL 60611

312-222-1525 | WWW.BILLYGOATTAVERN.COM

OPEN DAILY 6 AM–2 AM

The Billy Goat is responsible for one of the most famous lines in hamburger history, delivered by John Belushi on *Saturday Night Live* on January 28, 1978. But the Goat is more than just "Cheezborger! cheezborger! No Pepsi, Coke! No fries, cheeps." The Goat is steeped in history, so much that it makes you wish you were a Chicagoan, and probably makes many Chicagoans proud. All this from a tavern opened in 1934 by Greek immigrant William "Billy Goat" Sianis.

No one is really sure if the Billy Goat got its name from the far-fetched story of how a goat wandered into the bar one day and became a mascot/pet, or if the name came from the gray goatee Sianis sported, but the nature of its origins is part and parcel of all stories emanating from the Goat. The famous "Curse of the Billy Goat" was also dreamed up by Sianis, a curse that has endured and still exists today: a curse that has spiritually kept the beloved Chicago Cubs out of the World Series for over 65 years despite Sianis's nephew Sam's attempts to "remove" it. And it's all because the media-friendly tavern owner and his smelly goat were denied entry to the 1945 World Series.

The history of the Goat, carried on today by Sam Sianis and his son, Bill (Billy Goat Jr.), along with the 8x10 glossies of past newspapermen who drank and debated there and the bizarre subterranean location, actually add a different type of flavor to the burger. The Goat has what I like to call the "whole burger experience"—it's not just about the burger. It includes the place you are eating it, and who you are eating with.

The "cheezborgers" at the Billy Goat start as fresh beef that is machine pattied into quarter pound slivers. "Triple much better!!" is the call you are likely to hear as the countermen take your order. Just try and order a single cheeseburger. A "Sosa" is four patties, named after the home run king of the Cubs. There really are no fries so don't even ask. You remember the call "No fries, cheeps, no Coke, Pepsi!" They actually do have Coke, no Pepsi; Belushi flipped that in the skit. You dress your own burger with onions and specially made pickle slices, then take a seat at the bar, one of the longest I've ever seen.

There are so many things to look at that it would take days to read all of the clippings and photo captions. Not a problem here, since the Goat is open every day, 20 hours a day.

Probably every old hamburger joint has its share of stories and lore, but none wears it on its sleeve like the Billy Goat. There are so many stories to hear that you'll have to go there and ask Sam or Bill yourself. I'm sure they'd be glad to tell a few—ask about the butter on the ceiling, or the goat that ate the $20 bill.

CHARLIE BEINLICH'S FOOD & TAP

290 SKOKIE BLVD | NORTHBROOK, IL 60062

NO PHONE | WWW.CHARLIEBEINLICHS.COM

TUE–SAT 11:30 AM–10:45 PM

CLOSED SUN & MON

There's a sign behind the bar at Charlie Beinlich's that says, "Business hours subject to change during fishing season," and I believe them. This 60-year-old bar in the suburbs north of Chicago is filled with an impressive collection of mounted fish, most of them caught by Charlie himself. "Grandma caught that one," third generation owner Linda Rainey told me, pointing to what looked like the largest in the collection. Her father, John Barnes, who retired after running Beinlich's for over 30 years, is also a fisherman and can claim two of

the large fish on the walls as well. John told me, "Charlie used to say, 'The time you spend fishing doesn't count against your lifespan.'" In his retirement, John spends a fair amount of time in Florida . . . fishing.

Linda recently assumed ownership of the bar with her husband, Tom. "He [Tom] got this place the same way I did," John joked loudly sitting at the bar, "the old fashioned way: he married the boss's daughter!" The bigger-than-life former owner married Charlie's daughter, Karen, and helped run the business side-by side with him. Over the decades virtually nothing has changed at Charlie Beinlich's. "We added an

ATM and switched to a soda gun from canned soda," John told me. "That's about it."

The interior of Charlie Beinlich's looks more Northwoods tavern than suburban hangout. The long bar sports 13 very comfortable stools and the dining area is a sea of no-nonsense black tables. The place is spotless and attracts a slightly older crowd that come for Bleinlich's famous shrimp cocktail and of course, the burgers. Families and kids are welcome but Beinlich's offers no booster seats. "We have phone books and duct tape for the kids," Tom pointed out. The servers all wear white oxford shirts and crisp maroon aprons that have their names embroidered on them. They can be seen rushing through the packed dining room with up to five burger plates up their arms.

Burgers were introduced to Beinlich's customers a few years after Charlie opened the place. "He used to give food away," John told me. "He'd have big platters of cold cuts out." Tom told me there used to be a sign near the bar that stated simply, "Food is served for the convenience of our customers drinking alcoholic beverages." Eventually, a kitchen was constructed off the back of the bar and a booming burger business was born.

There's only one burger to order and your choices are with or without cheese, Swiss, American, or cheddar. Lettuce and onion are available but you'll have to forgo the tomato. In the half-century that Beinlich's has been serving burgers not one has ever seen a tomato and probably never will. If you ask for a "deluxe" burger you'll get coleslaw and fries on the side, and longtime customer Jeff Goldman told me, "I put the coleslaw on the burger." Slow-cooked and very tasty sautéed onions are also available.

The beef for the burgers is, as John described it, "a sirloin and chuck combo, supposedly," and is amazing. It comes to them daily, ground in bulk from a supplier that they have worked with for decades called Lakeside Foods in Winnetka, Illinois. There's a huge sign behind the bar proudly declaring this. As John explained, "It's just a local grocery store and sometimes they deliver twice a day." In the early seventies John switched from hand-pattying to pressing the patty and purchased a patty maker. "I wanted a third-pound burger but the guy cut the mold too big," John explained, leaving Beinlich's with a burger that still today is something closer to a half pound.

As you've probably guessed at this point, there are a lot of great signs to read at Beinlich's. One of my favorites hangs just inside the front vestibule and says, "No tank tops, muddy boots." The suburban setting and mall across the street are hardly the place to find hungry burger-seekers wearing muddy boots so there had to be a story. As construction began nearby on what was the first expressway out of Chicago in 1950, workers would naturally find their way to Beinlich's. "They were building the Edens when this place opened," Linda told me. "My grandmother wanted to have none of that." Although the Edens Expressway has been finished for over half a century the rule is still enforced.

Charlie is long gone but one of his more curious legacies remains. On the bar you'll find little wooden red birdhouses with HADLEY SCHOOL FOR THE BLIND printed on their sides. You can make a donation to a charity that has been the been the recipient of loose change dropped into these boxes for well over 50 years. "Charlie was deathly afraid of going blind," John explained.

Charlie Beinlich's future looks strong even though John joked, "When I die, Linda's selling the place!" Linda and Tom have two girls and no intention to sell. Linda told me, "We hope they'll want to take over the business." Their future husbands may get to own Beinlich's too, the old fashioned way.

GRANT'S WONDERBURGER

11045 SOUTH KEDZIE AVE | CHICAGO, IL 60655

773-238-7200 | MON–SAT 10:30 AM–8 PM

CLOSED SUNDAY

When the first version of this book came out I started getting e-mails from fans that were driving around the country trying to visit all the burger joints in the book. One of those fans was Larry Hodek from just outside of Chicago who was eating his way across America. In a long, handwritten letter to me he voiced his concern that I didn't include his hometown favorite. I have to admit, the burger joint he was talking about was not even on my radar. It was so far south of downtown Chicago that everyone I had asked had never heard of the place. But it doesn't take much for me to try a new burger so thank you, Larry, for leading me to this classic gem.

First you'll see the sign. The absurdly oversized sign dwarfs the façade of the building and can be seen from blocks away. Across the street is a Burger King and owner Karen McCormick told me, "It has been there for 30 years and has not affected our business."

The interior is a mix of 50 years of decorating style with faux-Tiffany stained glass pendant lamps overhead, bent wood café chairs, and green checked floor tile. Green topped swivel stools line a green Formica counter and the walls are wood paneled trimmed with, you guessed it, green.

Karen, wearing peace symbol earrings, is a feisty piece of work. She has a few employees that make change and such but Karen is a powerhouse and seems to fill all of the orders that come in. "I do it all, baby," she told me as she jumped from fryer to griddle. She bought Grant's Wonderburger in 1988 from her father-in-law, Bill Grant, who was looking to retire. Bill opened the restaurant in 1958 after working at the long-gone Superburger on Stoney Island Avenue, another Southside favorite. Bill wanted to emulate the burger that he knew so well and with Superburger's blessing opened his own burger joint and changed the name slightly. (The owner, Moose Bowen, even came over to flip the first Wonderburger and Bill was on his way.) The restaurant moved three times, all within a block or two, with the last move in 1969 to a location directly across the street. Karen told me that Bill and a few employees even dragged the counter across the street late one night.

Grant's burgers come to the restaurant as fresh, pre-formed patties five to the pound. They are thin and wide and cook very fast on the seasoned flattop griddle. The burger to get is the "Double Wonderburger Basket," which comes with American cheese, grilled or sliced onion, shredded lettuce, and the super-secret Wonder Sauce. The burger is presented on a toasted white squishy, wrapped in waxed paper, and served in a green basket full of their famous curly-q fries. I asked Karen what was in the

Wonder Sauce and she replied quickly, "It's a secret." I can tell you, though, that it was great, and was basically a tangy, sweet, red relish.

The fries are a big draw at Grant's Wonderburger. On some days Karen can go through a few hundred pounds of potatoes to make the curly-q fries. When an order comes in, she grabs a handful of fresh-cut ribbons of potatoes from a bin and tosses them into the deep fryer. I swear I pulled a curled fry out of my basket that when stretched out was no less than a foot long. I also noticed (too late) that the curly-q fries can be ordered with melted cheddar. Could there be a better side dish?

As you scarf down your Wonderburger, take a look at the walls around you. Then take a look at the full name of the restaurant. The menu and enormous sign out front bill the place as GRANT'S GRILL & GALLERY. The gallery that covers the walls features local artists and their Chicago-centric subjects. The art is for sale and ranges from rudimentary to the bizarre. One strange phantasmagorical painting depicts a woodland scene with fully uniformed hockey players (Chicago Blackhawks?) hitting the puck around a frozen creek. In the distance is a Native American standing on the ice in traditional feathered garb watching, possibly looking to join in. "I think Bill did it just to cover the walls for free," Karen told me. "Some of it is good, some weird."

Make your way down to the far south side neighborhood of Mt. Greenwood and look for the oversized Wonderburger sign. Get a classic burger with a "secret" sauce and bite into a piece of Chicago history that few in Chicago have actually heard about. You will come away with a better appreciation of old Chicago, and maybe some art too.

HACKNEY'S ON HARMS

1241 HARMS RD | GLENVIEW, IL 60025

847-724-5577 | WWW.HACKNEYS.NET

SUN–THU 11 AM–10 PM | FRI & SAT 11 AM–11 PM

Before there were suburbs, there was Hackney's. "There was nothing out here in the beginning," third generation owner Mary Welch told me. Hackney's sits way back from Harms Road on a lush, tree-filled piece of property. Across the street is a large for-est preserve. It still sort of feels like the middle of nowhere, but drive a few hundred feet in either direction and you'll find yourself in the center of Chicago's suburban sprawl.

The history of Hackney's is so complicated that Mary actually drew a chart for me on the back of a paper placemat. Here is the abridged version. In the '20s, Helen and Jack Hackney converted the back patio of their home into an illegal prohibition-era bar that served burgers. "It was so deserted out here that they thought they'd make money on booze," Mary explained. Eventually, the Hackneys moved the business from their backyard to a barn-like structure opposite the house. "We're not really sure what it was," Mary told me. "Maybe a chicken coop or a barn." In 1939, Mary's father, Jim Masterson, who was Helen's nephew, and her mother, Kitz, purchased Hackney's for $1 and endured the slow war years with business being fueled by sol-diers from a World War II POW camp in the for-est preserve across the street. When the war ended, the suburbs exploded and Hackney's was suddenly surrounded by hungry families. "There were mostly German bars here then," Mary explained, "and this was the first real family place." It was a mixed blessing, however. Thanks to new residential zoning after the war Hackney's was not able to expand the restaurant on the property. In 1955, Jim and Kitz were turning away 100 people a day. Their solution? They opened a second Hackney's just down the street.

When the Mastersons assumed ownership of

The Hackneyburger

Hackney's they introduced a burger to the menu that remains today—the "Hackneyburger." This North Suburbs classic is unique to the burger world because, since day one, it has been served on dark rye. And not just any dark rye, homemade dark rye prepared daily in Hackney's own bakery. "Originally, my parents made the bread at home," Mary told me, in the house that sits just opposite the restaurant. The bread is soft and sweet, not what you'd expect from dark bread. In fact, it's so soft that it has a tendency to disintegrate quickly thanks to the juicy eight-ounce burger that it cradles.

The Hackneyburger comes unadorned, with lettuce and tomato on the side. Onions are available, and if you ask for them grilled, you'll get an entire onion's-worth on the side. Cheese choices are American, Swiss, and cheddar. The half-pound burger, kept thick, is cooked on a flattop griddle and can be prepared to the temperature of your choice. Hackney's used to buy ground beef from a local butcher and Mary's parents would hand-patty the burgers daily using a coffee cup as a mold. They eventually purchased a patty machine, and one day gave the patty machine to their butcher. That butcher, who has been supplying Hackney's since the beginning, is now the sole provider of hamburger patties to the six Hackney's locations in the Chicago area. "That's all he does for a living, makes burgers for all the Hackney's," Mary told me.

No visit to Hackney's would be complete without trying one of their signature sides, the french fried onions. It arrives as a deep-fried brick of thin-sliced onions fused with fried batter standing tall at about 7 inches. It's an impressive presentation and was invented by a cook at Hackney's in 1962. In an effort to placate a customer who had missed out on the perch one fish fry Friday, a cook named Carmen tossed a handful of battered onions into the deep fryer and invented a new side dish. The concoction emerged whole, in the shape of the fryer basket, and to this day is still served as a block of deep-fried goodness on a plate.

Not surprisingly, Hackney's has a great selection of German beers on tap and a solid bar lined with substantial leather-topped stools. The bar is carpeted, quiet and dark, even on bright, sunny days. I could see myself passing many hours there. The small dining room is also clean, dark, and cozy and a young, cute server told me, "It kind of reminds me of a cozy Wisconsin bar." Me too, but Hackney's is even cozier than what I've seen in Wisconsin. Across the parking lot, behind the original house, Hackney's also operates a patio that seats 200 in the warm months.

"It hasn't really changed since my parents were here," Mary told me, which is a good thing because everything seems to work just fine. Mary is one of seven children, all of whom are partners in the business and separately manage the six Hackney's in the area. Mary has the shortest commute though, a short walk across the parking lot from the family home she grew up in. "I'm not complaining," she told me with a smile.

MOONSHINE STORE

6017 EAST 300TH RD

MOONSHINE (MARTINSVILLE), IL 62442

618-569-9200

MON–SAT 6 AM–1 PM, GRILL CLOSES AT 12:30

CLOSED SUNDAY & MAJOR HOLIDAYS

The Moonshine Store is one of those places you hope no one finds out about. I never would have known about the Moonburger if I had not seen a clip on *CBS Sunday Morning* calling it the "Best Burger in America." A claim like that makes me a skeptic from the start but naturally my interest was piqued. I had all but written the place off when I just happened to be in the neighborhood. Believe me, this is not an easy thing to do.

Thanks to Ryan Claypool, a resident of nearby Marshall, Illinois, I was coaxed into giving the Moonburger a shot.

The Moonshine Store is at a crossroads in east central Illinois surrounded by cornfields. The drive to Moonshine (population two) is a blur of cornstalks and soybean fields for hours on two-lane roads and the nearest city is Terre Haute, Indiana. There's a reason the lines are not out the door with city people—it's too damn far away. But it's true; the Moonshine does make one of the best burgers in America.

The large country-store-turned-burger-spot does a brisk business regardless of its remote locale. There are no tables inside, just recycled church pews and chairs that line the counters and cases. You place an order at the back of the

store and when your burger is ready, you take it to the bountiful condiment table in the center of the room. If you can't find a spot on a pew, there is ample seating out back at the picnic tables.

The staff is a sight to behold—a bevy of chatty country women all taking turns at the grill and register. "I don't work here, I'm just helping today," laughed one behind the counter. Helen Tuttle, owner and grillmaster, explained, "Friends and family all come down for the lunch hour to help out. When we're busy we'll even ask someone in the store to do dishes—we're not bashful."

The Moonburger is a beauty: pure and simple, 80/20-ground chuck cooked on a hot gas griddle until moist inside with a delicately crunchy exterior. I asked what the size of the burger was and Helen told me, "All sizes. Depends on what my hand grabs." They look to be around a third of a pound and served on an untoasted, white squishy bun. Cheese is treated like a condiment and tossed on cold. Trust me—this burger needs no cheese.

The three new gas griddles can hold up to 150 burgers, which is an improvement over the previous electric griddle that only held fifteen. "We can sell 50 to 600 burgers a day depending, and at least 400 on a Saturday," Helen told me. Many motorcycle tours make the Moonshine a destination for burgers every year, and one visit on April 8, 2010 resulted in a new record. "We made 1908 that day." Helen once told me, "We do no advertising. I believe the Lord has a hand in this business." Believe it. These burgers are touched by something.

TOP NOTCH
BEEFBURGER SHOP

2116 WEST 95TH STREET | CHICAGO, IL

773-445-7218 | MON–FRI 8 AM–8 PM

SAT 7:30 AM–8:30 PM | CLOSED SUNDAY

I was tipped off to Top Notch by a friend in Chicago who is a key grip in the film business, the same friend, incidentally, who told me about Mr. Beef on North Orleans (for which I am eternally grateful). This is definitely the kind of spot you need to be tipped off to because it is very far from downtown Chicago. In fact it's about 25 minutes by car south of the Loop in a neighborhood called Beverly. The journey to Top Notch is worth it because they make, without a doubt, one of the best burgers in Chicago.

Top Notch has the standard-issue brown Naugahyde booths, fluorescent lighting, and wood paneling from the '40s but takes it a step further to include Bob Ross–inspired oil paintings of soothing waterfalls and mountain scenes. The staff is extremely friendly and the menu lists true diner fare. The shakes, fries, and tuna sandwiches are all good, but the reason to visit Top Notch is of course for the "beefburgers." They come in three sizes—the quarter pounder, the half-pound "King Size," and the three-quarter-pound "Super King Size." A deal breaker for me is the absence of fresh ground beef in a burger restaurant, so I always ask the question "fresh or frozen?" I was directed to the manager of 19 years, Sam Gomez, who, without asking for cre-

dentials, dragged me into the kitchen and into their small meat locker. There I was surrounded by the real thing—about five sides of beef and various cuts waiting for their turn in the grinder. Sam told me "our burgers are very fresh." I had a hard time doubting him.

The burgers are cooked on a large vintage cast-iron griddle in plain view of the counter patrons. They are griddled wide and flat, allowing more of the beef to have contact with the griddle surface. A favorite condiment is the grilled onions, so much so that burgers requested without onions still gather an onion essence. The bun is my favorite kind—white and squishy with sesame seeds, probably six inches across, toasted in the same upright conveyor toaster that Louis' Lunch in New Haven uses. Sam describes the fries as "pre-WWII," which I took to mean from a time before fries were frozen. Sure enough, there in the kitchen one employee had the task of gathering up fresh-cut fries that soak in cold water and bringing them to the fryer. The fries are excellent.

I want to have a party there someday—the place is huge and can hold over a hundred hungry burger lovers. Bring your appetite and order at least the half pounder with cheese.

Top Notch
BEEFBURGERS
BURGES FRIES
SHAKES
THE BEST
SI CE 1942.

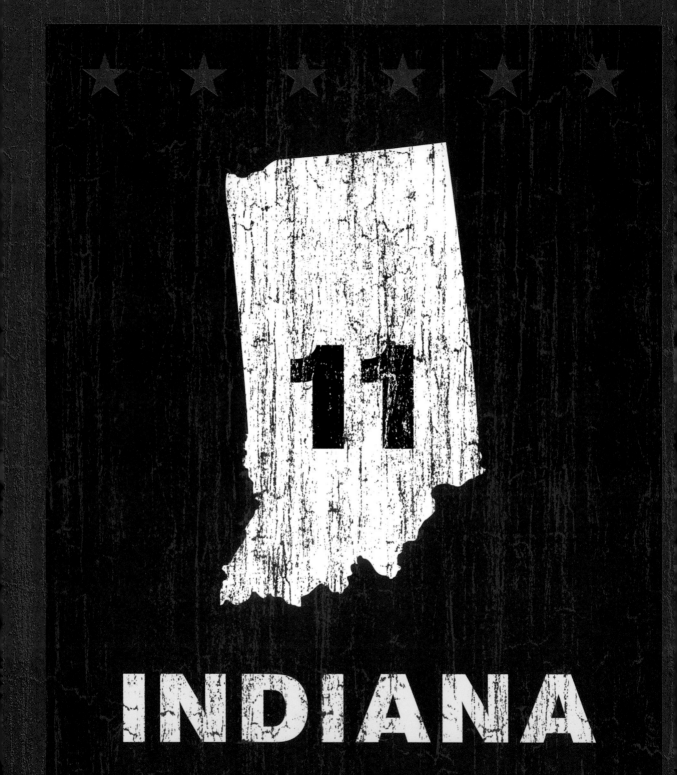

11

INDIANA

HEINNIES

1743 WEST LUSHER AVE | ELKHART, IN 46517

574-522-9101 | WWW.HEINNIESRESTAURANT.COM

MON–THU 10 AM–10 PM | FRI 10 AM–11 PM

SAT 4:30 PM–11 PM | CLOSED SUNDAY

Friend and food columnist Marshall King led me to this hamburger. He told me about a decades-old bar down by the train tracks in an industrial part of town that had been serving burgers forever—I was sold.

When I first visited Heinnies, Bill DeShone, third-generation owner, was doing what his grandfather and father did for decades before him—he was walking around the dining room, greeting people, and checking on their food. "There's always a family member here," Bill told me, "whether it's me or my brother." It's that kind of pride of place that keeps people loyal. That, and of course, a world-class hamburger.

In the early 1950s, Henry "Heinnie" DeShone chose a spot for his tavern that was a bit remote for the residents of Elkhart. His new venture would be located across the street from one of the busiest railroad hubs in North America. "There was nothing else out here," Bill explained, and told me that most of the clientele were railroad men. "It has always been a place where the working man could come get a burger, though back then it was a beer and a burger." True to its roots, the area is still very industrial, though today the local industry is focused on motor home repair and manufacturing.

When Heinnies opened in 1951, the low-ceiled bar had a sign on the door prohibiting women (but by 1956 the sign was removed). A small dining room was added to the bar in 1983, and in 1996 a full renovation was completed. Bill's younger brother, Troy, did the decorating and his obsession with NASCAR is apparent—the walls are lined with an impressive collection of American racing memorabilia.

The menu is loaded with burgers, but the ones to focus on are the classic "Heinniecheeseburger" and the "Claybaugh." The latter is a larger version of the classic that includes two one-third-pound patties and a wild pile of ingredients including, but not limited to, bacon, mushrooms, and four types of cheese. This one should be reserved for the truly starved. The burger is named after a local policeman and regular named Scott Claybaugh who, Bill explained, just like the burger, "is big and full of shit." But it's the Heinniecheeseburger that they come back for, a moderately priced, well-seasoned, great-tasting burger.

Made from fresh-ground prime beef, the Heinniecheeseburger in its simplest form (no condiments, on a bun) is a taste explosion. That's because of a not-so-secret ingredient included in the DeShone family burger recipe—chopped onions mixed into the beef. "We used to mix in bread crumbs and egg too," Bill told me, "It was sort of like a meat loaf." But because the meat turned bad quickly, the DeShone family decided to stick with the basics—chopped onion, salt, and pepper.

The meat for the Heinniecheeseburger comes from a local butcher, the same butcher Heinnies has been using forever. The butcher uses scraps from sirloin, filet, and strip steaks and grinds them for the restaurant. After the ground prime arrives, it is blended with chopped onion and pattied on an ancient family heirloom. The tool is a unique patty maker that presses the burgers one at a time to the proper thickness without forming the traditional cylindrically "squared" sides. The result is a patty with craggy edges that looks hand formed.

Bill is slightly befuddled by a newfound group of fans who have discovered the decades-old tavern—the Amish. On Friday nights the back room is full of people from the nearby Amish communities of Nappanee and Shipshewana. Bill assumes that they are drawn to the restaurant by the huge, horse stable–themed dining room that was added in 1985 to the back of the restaurant called "Heinnies Back Barn." Knotty pine frames each booth like a horse stall and vintage farm equipment lines the walls. "They come in by the vanload," Bill told me. "Strawberry daiquiris and steak for two!"

The Heinniecheeseburger

POWERS
HAMBURGER SHOP

1402 SOUTH HARRISON ST | FORT WAYNE, IN 46802

260-422-6620 | MON–WED 5 AM–10 PM

THU–SAT 5 AM–12 AM | CLOSED SUNDAY

Powers is the real deal. Not unlike White Manna in New Jersey or The Cozy Inn of Kansas, Powers is a complete time-warp hamburger joint. You'll be sent straight back to 1940 and a simpler time when the all-American slider was made with fresh-ground beef and your only option was with or without onions.

I could smell Powers a block away as I approached old downtown Fort Wayne. Across the street from the beautiful, well-preserved Art Deco burger joint are two stately federal buildings. If you snapped a photo of the corner in black and white it may look identical to one that could have been taken in the '40s—virtually nothing on this corner has changed.

Onions are the name of the game at Powers. There'll be no hiding the fact that you grabbed a few sliders here because the deep essence of steam-grilled onions will stick with your clothes for hours after. The bouquet of sweet onion wafts throughout the parking lot the minute you step out of your car.

I was clearly the only non-local regular in the place the first time I visited. Two women ran the place—one named Sarah took orders and served pop and made change while the other managed the tiny, crowded flattop griddle. Country music played and both women sang along and knew every word. Sarah greeted each person that walked in the door by their first name and said, "Bye honey," as they left.

The classic sliders at Powers are the primary source for the American hamburger. Tiny two-ounce balls of ground beef are grabbed from a pile in a fridge behind a sliding door adjacent to the griddle. The balls are tossed on the griddle and covered with a thick layer of thinly sliced sweet onion. The griddleperson gives the onions a gentle press until the balls of beef are flattened. When the patties are flipped, a potato roll is placed on the burger to steam until soft. A burger with everything comes with cheese and onions. Pickles

are available, but as Sarah curtly pointed out, "Only if you ask." If you require a double, two balls are pressed together to make a larger patty. Several doubles with everything is the way to go.

There is no mistaking the presence of onions on a Powers slider. Even with the double meat, the soft, limp onions made up 50 percent of the burger and ruled the flavor profile. The cheese acts as a sort of glue for the whole glorious mess and the locally made soft potato roll completes the package. As I was thinking about this, a customer walked in an, ordered a bunch with extra onion, which was hard to imagine. As I popped the last bite in my mouth, I placed an order for two more. The fear of walking out of a place like Powers unsated was too much to bear.

All types of folks dine at Powers. Next to me was a tattooed dude with a mohawk and next to him a clean-cut man and his daughter. Harley types and old-timers also occupied stools and nary a word was spoken, just quiet consumption and the dull thwack of onions being pressed into beef.

In the beginning, Powers, like many other burger stands of the day, was open around the clock. Today, Powers has fairly normal hours, opening at 5 a.m. Six days a week. Sarah told me, "We'll make burgers at 5 a.m. if you want 'em."

TRIPLE XXX FAMILY RESTAURANT

2 NORTH SALISBURY ST | WEST LAFAYETTE, IN 47906

765-743-5373

WWW.TRIPLEXXXFAMILYRESTAURANT.COM

OPEN 24 HOURS | CLOSED SUN 8 PM–MON 6 AM

"**T**his place was on the brink of folding," owner Greg Ehresman told me as I sat at the twisting short-order counter for the first time. Greg would know, because he flipped burgers at the Triple XXX decades before he was an owner. He obviously saw the value in this burger counter at an early age and told me, "I wanted to buy this place when I was seventeen."

The Triple XXX opened in 1929 as a seasonal root beer stand, or "Thirst Station," only a few blocks from Purdue University. At one point there were 100 Triple XXX Thirst Stations around the country selling root beer by the mug to a population in the midst of Prohibition. Over the decades the stand morphed into a full-scale diner with carhop service but slipped into decline in the 1970s. Greg's father Jack Ehresman, who grew up only a block from the restaurant, swept in and saved the iconic hamburger stand in 1980 even though, as Greg put it, "He was not a restaurant guy." Jack, his wife, Ruth, and son, Greg, decided that the key to their success would be to go back to the old way of making everything by hand—a failsafe measure that has proved to be an enormous success.

The burgers at Triple XXX start as sirloin steaks from a local butcher that are ground daily upstairs in the restaurant and formed into tall "pucks," not thin patties. The puck is smashed thin with great force by the hand of the grill person just before it hits the hot griddle. As I watched Greg make a burger for me he did something that caught my eye, something I had never seen before in my endless hamburger research: the patty was nonchalantly tossed into a bin of flour before it hit the griddle. Perplexed, I asked him why. Like all great stewards of tradition his only response was, "Because that's the way we've always done it." The result was predictable and amazing. The flour mixes with the sizzling fat to create an even more pronounced griddle char and flavor.

If you are looking for a hamburger on the extensive menu, you'll need to search for the "Chop Steak." A cheeseburger is a Chop Steak with cheese. Skip those, however, and head straight for their signature burgers, all named after All-American football stars from Purdue. One of the most popular is the "Boilermaker Pete," a triple with cheese and grilled onions served on a toasted, white squishy bun. A triple sounds unmanageable but the proportions are perfect on this beauty, a pure expression of the classic American burger. Wash your burger down with the restaurant's namesake root beer, still made on premises as it has been for over 75 years.

The Triple XXX is a 24-hour restaurant. That's right, you can show up at any hour of the day to eat amazing burgers. Students make great use of this feature by filling the place well past 4 a.m. on weekends. "On a football weekend," Greg told me, "we'll go through 700 pounds of beef easily."

Today Greg and his wife, Carrie, run The Triple XXX and stay very busy thanks to a visit by Guy Fieri in 2007. "We saw a 40 percent uptick in business since that show aired," Greg told me. For a collegetown watering hole surrounded by soulless chains that is music to my ears. Even though the McDonald's only 100 feet away from the Triple XXX is open 24 hours, Greg confidently told me, "It does not affect business here at all."

WORKINGMAN'S FRIEND

234 NORTH BELMONT | INDIANAPOLIS, IN 46222
317-636-2067 | WWW.WORKINGMANSFRIEND.US
MON–FRI 11 AM–8 PM | SAT 11 AM–3 PM
CLOSED SUNDAY

You'll know you are close to Workingman's Friend when the sweet smell of crude oil fills your car. This unpretentious bar sits across the street from a Marathon oil refinery on the edge of a working-class neighborhood only a few miles from the famous Indianapolis Motor Speedway. Look for the bar with the large vintage Pepsi sign and a façade made almost entirely of glass block.

Expert burger taster from Dallas, Wayne Geyer, alerted me to Workingman's. He had asked me for a recommendation for a burger in Indianapolis and I told him I didn't have anything. Put to the challenge, he discovered the double cheeseburger at Workingman's and scored big. Add to this burger discovery a bar that serves thirty-two-ounce goblets of tap beer in a bare-bones tavern setting and you have a homerun.

Opened in 1918 by Macedonian immigrant Louie Stamatkin as Belmont Lunch, the place mostly served sandwiches and burgers to workers at the nearby B&O Railroad maintenance facility. Louie would run tabs for the workers knowing that they had little money to spend. The workers dubbed Louie the "workingman's friend" and a name was born. In the late '40s, Louie passed away and his two sons Carl and Earl assumed ownership of the bar. They changed the name out of respect for their father. They began construction on a new, larger building to replace the converted house that Louie called Belmont Lunch. To avoid shutting down for months, the brothers instead built around the existing structure. During construction, pieces of the old structure were carted out the side door and they were never once closed for business. "They did it to stay open," Becky Stamatkin told me. Becky is Louie's granddaughter and the third generation of the Stamatkin family at Workingman's Friend. She has run the bar and smashed burgers to perfection for over 30 years.

Today, the large, open tavern is a sea of utili-tarian red chairs and tables. Sixty feet in length, it boasts one of the longest bars in Indy. The bar sits atop a wall of glass block that is backlit by two tubes of pink neon. Decoration is minimal, and sections of the linoleum flooring have worn through to the concrete. Two non-functioning vintage cigarette machines sit by both doors to the bar as a vestige of the Workingman's past, not some purchased history for the sake of kitchy decor.

"99.9 percent order the double cheese-burger," Becky told me. And there's a good

reason for that—it's amazing. Becky takes two balls of fresh ground 80/20 chuck and smashes them super-thin on the nearly half-century-old flattop griddle. The burger cooks through but stays moist and the edges become lacey and crisp. The double is served on a toasted, white squishy bun with a third bun inserted to separate the two patties. If you ask for everything, your double will come with shredded lettuce, sliced tomato, raw onion, and mayonnaise with pickle slices on the side. The grease, cheese, and mayo worked well with the beef, and I asked Becky if there was more than just mayo between the buns. She told me with a wink, "It's only mayo, but I tell people it's a special sauce."

The double cheeseburger is a sight to behold. The floppy edges of the smashed-thin burger hang far outside the bun, making this beast seem unmanageable. Fortunately the entire package is quite manageable. The patties each weigh in at around a quarter pound but Becky could not confirm this. "Ah, I don't know how big they are," she confessed. "I've been doing this for so long that I don't know anymore. I make balls of beef, then I smash them." Whatever the size, it's perfect.

One thing at the bar that is almost unmanageable is the beer. If you like your tap beer large, then don't miss the thirty-two-ounce "Frosty Fish Bowl." Bartender Terry, Becky's half-brother, pulls a heavy goblet out of a freezer behind the bar and fills it with ice cold Budweiser or Bud Light. That's a lot of beer and it's almost hard to heft when the glass is full. If you don't want to look like a Medieval king at a banquet with this ridiculously large goblet, go for the smaller sixteen- or ten-ounce sizes.

On a diet? Workingman's Friend offers a burger called the "Diet Special" that sounds

crazy but good. Becky cooks a large hand-pattied burger on the flattop (not smashed) and serves it on a plate with lettuce, grilled onions, pickles, cottage cheese, and no bun. "We sell maybe two a week," Becky told me. But hey, you didn't come in here because you are on a diet.

I was across the street snapping a few photos after leaving Workingman's Friend for the first time when an old-timer on mobility scooter rolled by and offered his own review. "It's the best burger in Indy!" he shouted and kept rolling. And he's absolutely right.

ZAHARAKOS ICE CREAM PARLOR AND MUSEUM

329 WASHINGTON ST | COLUMBUS, IN 47201

812-378-1900 | WWW.ZAHARAKOS.COM

MON–FRI 8 AM–8 PM | SAT & SUN 9 AM–8 PM

When I first stepped into Zaharakos, my jaw dropped. What you'll find at this 110-year-old ice cream parlor will astound you. In 2009, after being purchased (and saved) by local businessman Tony Moravec, Zaharakos reopened completely renovated to its original décor from opening day in 1900. During the century that the Greek-owned restaurant was in business the place saw many renovations (and a car through the front window) but when Tony purchased the parlor his goal was

clear—to restore Zaharakos to its original grandeur, complete with period marble soda dispensers, stamped tin ceilings, wire-back café chairs, and an enormous vintage Welte player organ. I have never seen anything like this in my life.

Tony Moravec is extraordinarily passionate about ice cream parlor memorabilia, ephemera, and history. His passion is fueled in part by his very successful pharmaceutical company located nearby in Columbus. The renovation cost Tony $3.5 million and took 2 years to complete, but as he explained to me, it was his pleasure. "It was a fascinating trip," he told me. The last Zaharakos family member running the parlor passed away in 2006 as the restaurant was in decline. Tony saw his purchase of the aging relic as a chance to give back to the community.

"In the renovation we kept the original bones of the place and renovated around that," Tony explained. But this wasn't just any renovation. Tony had specialists come in from all over the country to manage things like restoring and cleaning the original marble, repairing the vintage soda dispensers, and most notably to bring the Welte organ back to its former glory. "I wanted to make it first-class and make Zaharakos a destination." He most certainly has, with stunning detail and unfaltering commitment.

The menu was also restored and updated but still reflects some of the early offerings from the Zaharakos family, like the dizzying selection of fountain soda favorites and the famous "Gom Cheese-Brr-Grr." The Gom is not really a burger but, like the Maid-Rite "loosemeats" sandwich of Iowa, it is an intriguing take on the marriage of beef and bread. There is a regular burger on the menu at Zaharakos but trust me, go for the tasty Gom.

The Gom Cheese Brr-Grr is basically a Sloppy Joe fused with a grilled cheese sandwich, although this one has far less tomato sauce than a typical Joe. Its history is mostly unknown but it is believed that over 75 years ago the Zaharakos Brothers may have actually invented the original Sloppy Joe. The general profile of the slop is kind of sticky, or "gommy" (from the German slang for "sloppy") and is loaded with tasty spices and a little bit of brown sugar. The buttered, toasted white bread and gooey cheese make this one savory sandwich.

I glanced around the restaurant and noticed that most people were enjoying Gom sandwiches, with and without cheese. The cheese is great on this concoction because it acts like glue to keep the loose contents together. Tony told me, "It still outsells everything we do."

You'll need a drink with your Gom and good luck trying to choose just one. The original soda dispensers behind the long marble counter are still functional for the most part and operated by an actual soda jerk with experience, the sassy Wilma. She suggested the "Jerk's Special," a cinnamon Coke, "Because that's what the jerk likes!" The cinnamon Coke, hand-mixed from Coke syrup, cinnamon syrup, and soda water, is intoxicating. "The cinnamon enhances the flavor of the Coke, right?" Wilma asked. You can also

get a number of other fountain sodas, like chocolate Coke, red Raspberry Coke, and the old Prohibition-era favorite, the neon-green "Green River" (lemon-lime flavored). The shakes and floats are amazing too. I asked Wilma for a chocolate malt and she asked me, "Do you want a real one or one made with Hershey's?" Piqued by my options naturally I chose the real one. Instead of mixing in Hershey's chocolate syrup she used the chocolate syrup for their sodas. The flavor was unlike anything I've ever tasted, a sort of refined chocolate milkshake experience.

At some point during your meal, you may hear the towering Welte player organ come to life. This perfectly restored centerpiece of the dining room was originally installed in 1908 and remained in place until the Zaharakos family, in need of cash, sold it to a California collector. Tony, hell-bent on a perfect restoration, tracked down the original and spared no expense to bring it back. He found an automatic musical instrument restorer in Baltimore who admitted that his love of player organs came from a visit to Zaharakos in his teens. The restored organ sounds like an entire orchestra in a box and is probably just as loud. If you want to be transported back to the glory days of ice cream parlors just ask manager Gary to crank it up for you. You'll probably hear the Zaharakos theme song, Scott Joplin's "The Entertainer," though Tony personally changes the reels every few days from his collection of over 200.

The Smithsonian Institution should honor Tony Moravec for his role in preserving this piece of long-gone history. His commitment to the culture of ice cream parlors makes him a true American hero. "I don't think he'll get rich from it," manager Gary mused and he's probably right. But we are all richer for Tony's service to America.

12

IOWA

HAMBURG INN NO. 2

214 NORTH LINN ST I IOWA CITY, IA 52245

319-337-5512 I WWW.HAMBURGINN.COM

OPEN DAILY 6:30 AM–11 PM

Chances are that if you've been to Iowa City you've been to the Hamburg Inn. Since 1948 this hamburger destination has been serving fresh-ground burgers to University of Iowa students and professors and faithful regulars, and more recently has become a sort of base camp for politicos rambling through town on the campaign trail. Everyone from local politicians to presidential hopefuls has made press stops at the Hamburg Inn. They are there to talk to the people and, naturally, be photographed enjoying America's favorite food. But the burger at Hamburg is not just a photo-op prop, it's the real deal and, thanks to second-generation owner Dave Panther, a high-quality one at that.

Dave inherited the Hamburg Inn No. 2 from his father, Fritz Panther. Fritz's older brother Joe opened Hamburg Inn No. 1 in the mid-1930s, a small, classic ten-stool hamburger stand featuring burgers for a nickel. In 1948, Fritz and another brother, Adrian, bought a defunct restaurant (the current location) and called it Hamburg Inn No. 2. At one point there was a No. 3 in Cedar Rapids but today both No.1 and No. 3 are long gone. Only No. 2 remains.

Dave, who moonlights as a professional clown, started working for his parents at the restaurant at age thirteen, peeling potatoes. After a stint in the U.S. Air Force, Dave started working full time at the Hamburg Inn and in 1979 assumed ownership.

Since the beginning, chuck steaks have been ground daily on premises. A six-ounce ice cream scoop is used to measure the balls of ground beef. The balls of meat are pressed on the griddle and assume a somewhat uneven beauty. Fritz bought a patty maker back in the 1950s but returned it after three days, fully dissatisfied with the results. "He said the patty maker changed the complexion and nature of the whole product," Dave remembered. Five decades later not a single preformed patty has ever graced the griddle at the Hamburg Inn.

The burgers are served on large, toasted, cornmeal-dusted kaiser rolls. Five different types of cheese are available, as are an abundance of toppings ranging from the standard tomato and lettuce to the slightly bizarre pineapple. Honestly, don't be blinded by the options—this burger, made from choice beef, is so fresh it'd be a shame to cover it with anything other than a bun.

The menu at the Hamburg Inn is enormous, offering every type of comfort food imaginable. Dave gradually expanded the menu over the decades and was responsible for adding a favorite breakfast item, the omelet. The burger takes center stage for lunch and dinner but it's the omelet, served in unlimited combinations, that captivates the morning crowd. "We have a guy that comes in and orders a cream cheese, black olive, and raisin omelet," Dave told me. "That's about the weirdest combination we've made." One of the restaurant's most popular omelets contains, not surprisingly, a healthy dose of the Hamburg Inn's ground beef. It's called the "Zadar" and is named after a local movie that was filmed at the restaurant. With ground beef and American cheese, it's basically a hamburger omelet. A great idea and probably the only one of its kind in America.

While campaigning for the presidency, Obama stopped in but got an omelet to go (apparently it was early in the morning). The walls of the Hamburg Inn are covered with vintage photos and one wall is dedicated to American politics. There's even a plaque over table #6 that trumpets a visit by former president Ronald Reagan. President Clinton visited as well, but has not been honored with a plaque (yet). I asked Dave where Clinton sat on his visit to the Hamburg Inn and he told me, "Just to the left of Reagan's table." The political humor was not lost on me.

THE IRISH SHANTI

17455 GUNDER RD I ELGIN, IA 52141

563-864-9289 I WWW.THEGUNDERBURGER.COM

MON–SAT 10 AM–10 PM I SUN 10 AM–7 PM

If you find yourself eating a burger at the Irish Shanti, deep in the rolling farmland of northeast Iowa, it's because you made a point of being there. "People come here to eat the burger," son of the Shanti's owner Hans Walsh told me, "or they are lost." The town of Gunder, Iowa is barely on the map and the Irish Shanti, across from a defunct gas station, is the only business in town. Though remote, this destination restaurant manages to fill the dining room on most nights and suggests reservations on weekends. "People will drive for several hours to come here to eat," Hans told me. Many of them are in search of a menu item that has made this corner of Iowa famous—the "Gunderburger."

The Irish Shanti has only been around in name since the mid-seventies but the building itself dates to 1929 when it opened as a grocery store. The restaurant has changed hands many times over the years and at one point the tiny town of Gunder was in danger of being literally wiped off the map. The unincorporated town, with a population barely in the double digits, was rescued by a grill cook at the Irish Shanti named LaVonne Christianson. In 1985, she had an idea to concoct a colossal burger for all to see and name it after the town. The plan worked and today Gunder remains on the map, and the enormous Gunderburger remains on the menu.

Hans, the chef at the Irish Shanti, explained, "We weigh out a 20-ounce ball of fresh ground beef that cooks down to around 16 ounces." A very large wad of beef is slapped on the flattop and pressed into a patty by hand. Hans sprinkles a bit of a "secret fairy dust" on the patty then drops a bacon weight on it. The burger cooks slowly over low heat on a griddle that has an excellent, dark patina. "We don't aggressively clean it," Hans said of the griddle.

If you order a Loaded Gunderburger get ready to flex those jaw muscles. To the one-pound cheeseburger Hans adds lettuce, tomato, bacon, sautéed onions, and grilled mushrooms and he is not stingy. After construction, this burger weighs in at around one-and-a-half pounds.

The appearance of the Loaded Gunderburger is part of its shock value. To say that the bun is disproportionate to the patty is an understatement. Hans purposely uses a standard-sized bun that does not stand a chance in holding back the burger's contents. The patty and piles of condiments protrude cartoonishly from under the bun leaving the uninitiated with a challenge. I actu-

ally tried to heft the beast to my face only to find that the bottom half of the bun had virtually vanished into the copious juices. I ate the burger gripping the patty but eventually had to use a fork because stuff was falling everywhere. "The strategy I tell people is to go around the outside of the bun with a fork first," Hans told me. The Gunderburger was a mess but well worth it. You'll need a hose-down after this one.

Kevin moved from his native Boston and left his job as a registered nurse to buy the restaurant in 2005 with his wife, Elsie. One of the first major changes he made was to add a sizeable kitchen. "It used to be here," Kevin explained with his arms outstretched at the end of the bar.

Kevin is Irish and this probably explains the proudly displayed Irish flag in the center of the dining room and the Guinness on tap.

Start your meal with a retro appetizer, the relish tray. It's a sort of midwestern version of the antipasto plate featuring ham salad, diced cheese, olives, carrots, and crackers. The Irish Shanti also serves fried cheese curds, one of my absolute favorite guilty pleasures available in this part of the country. Everything at the Shanti is made fresh in-house and most of the produce during the warmer months comes from their garden.

So if you are rambling around northeast Iowa in search of nourishment seek out the Irish Shanti. Indulge in a few pints of Guinness, meet some great people, and eat the burger that saved a town.

PAUL'S TAVERN

176 LOCUST ST | DUBUQUE, IA 52001

563-556-9944 | MON–SAT 8 AM–2 AM

SUN 9 AM–2 AM

There was a time in American tavern culture when the drink reigned supreme. Certain bartenders probably noticed the need to serve a modicum of edible nourishment to keep their customers from leaving for meals and the bartop grill was born. The foodservice at Paul's is a vestige of this tavern past that holds a tiny footprint behind the bar. Although small, the bar kitchen at Paul's still cranks out amazing burgers to comfortably buzzed patrons.

I've heard people refer to Paul's as a "dive," and after my first visit I have to say that Paul's is the cleanest dive I've ever set foot in. Somehow, this broken-in bar shows its age but maintains its gritty character without coming off as a dump. The place is filled with perfectly preserved vintage beer signs and the most amazing collection of taxidermy you'll ever see while sipping a Miller High Life. The bears, bighorn sheep, deer, and alligators that line the walls were all hunted by former owner Paul Schollmeyer. The displays go beyond the traditional random, dusty deer head over the bar. The work that went into these displays is astounding and the taxidermist was clearly a master at the craft. Think Museum of Natural History in a bar setting. There are large, well-lit glass cases on either side of the bar and one that is actually mounted on the ceiling for effect. That case contains a massive polar bear, shot in 1966. Paul, who is now 83 and still visits the bar frequently, told me he bagged the polar bear years before restrictions were placed on hunting them. As I surveyed the impressive collection of mounted big game overhead Paul leaned and whispered to me, "I don't mean to brag, but I can shoot."

The centerpiece of the tiny kitchen area at the end of the long bar is an ancient Norge Broilator. The thick, black stove is one of the more unique cooking apparatuses I've seen for burger making and clearly the precursor to the salamander broiler found in many professional kitchens. The

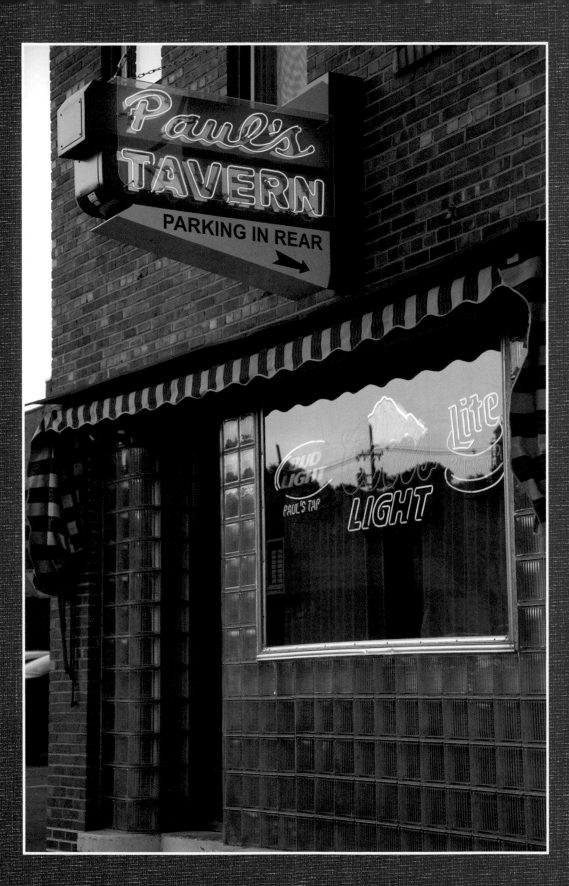

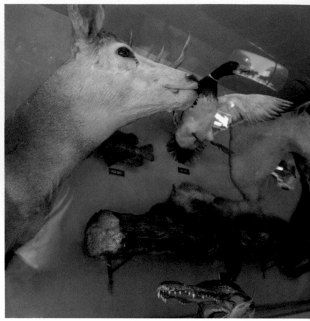

most obvious difference in the Broilator is that the burgers cook on a small, well-seasoned flattop that can't be more than 2 feet wide and only 1 foot deep. Burgers are slapped onto the tiny flattop and the operator pulls on a bar that simultaneously closes the door and sends the burgers up and into the center of the stove. The burgers then cook from above by indirect flame as they sizzle on the griddle. Totally unique.

Though the cooking area inside the Broilator is limited, bar manager Dave explained, "It can cook eight at a time." The burgers start as quarter-pound scooped balls of 90/10 fresh ground beef that are placed in a single patty press. "We use lean beef because anything too fatty and it'll flare up and burn," Dave told me. Soft white buns are warmed in a nearby toaster-oven and the burgers are served on tiny paper plates with pickles and a slice of raw onion. When I inquired about additional condiments Dave

responded gruffly, "No lettuce, tomato, or any of that stuff." The burger at Paul's is simplicity personified.

Today the tavern is owned by a former manager from McDonald's, Tom Koch, a friend of Paul's who purchased the place in 1991. Paul actually approached Tom and asked him to take the reins, probably so that his big game collection would remain intact. "Everybody loves this place," Tom told me. "I told Paul I'd try it for a year and [20 years later] I'm still here." Tom's brother, Dave, helps manage the tavern and his daughter, Amber, bartends and makes burgers. I believe the future of Paul's is secure.

As we polished off our fourth or fifth beers and finished our burgers, my wife, Casey, (the former vegetarian), surrounded by the taxidermy said, "Every bar in New York City wishes they were this cool." It's true. Paul's Tavern is the real deal. Everything else is just trying to be Paul's.

TAYLOR'S MAID-RITE

106 SOUTH 3RD AVE | MARSHALLTOWN, IA 50158

641-753-9684 | WWW.MAIDRITE.COM

MON–SAT 8 AM–10 PM | SUN 10 AM–10 PM

Taylor's does not serve hamburgers. Taylor's serves a "loosemeats sandwich." For those not familiar with the popular Iowa hamburger-influenced sandwich, a loosemeats, or Maid-Rite (and sometimes referred to as a "tavern"), is basically a deconstructed hamburger, or a Sloppy Joe without the slop. The recipe is simple: fresh ground-on-premises beef is steamed and crumbled in a cast-iron cooker. Nothing is added but salt. Upon getting an order, a member of the extended Taylor family or longtime employee grabs a bun that has been "doped" with pickle and mustard, and with the other hand scoops up an impossible amount of the pebbly, moist meat. That's it, and there's nothing else on the menu but shakes, ice cream, pie, and soft drinks, and they have been doing it this way since 1928. The order is wrapped up even if you are eating at the counter. "Wrapping makes the bun soft," Zac told me. Zac is a fifth-generation Taylor proving that Taylor's is clearly a family-run business.

Cliff Taylor purchased the franchise for the third Maid-Rite in Iowa for $300 and called it Taylor's. His son, Don Taylor, took over the business in 1944. In 1958, Taylor's moved across the street into a new modern building, its current location. Cliff Taylor's granddaughter, Sandy, remembers the move well. "We moved the entire contents of the restaurant overnight making trips back and forth across the street. I remember helping to carry the plates." One element of the move that didn't work out so well was the new steam cooker. "My dad thought the meat just didn't taste right so he brought the cooker over from the old place," Sandy told me. "This could be the same cooker from 1928," Sandy said, pointing to the strange stainless cabinet with the deep, cast-iron trough.

Taylor's is a bright, clean, friendly place with floor-to-ceiling windows in the front of the restaurant. A large horseshoe counter surrounds a short-order kitchen that offers amazing views of your food being prepared. One wall of the restaurant is covered with enormous world and U.S. maps with the phrase above, "Go 'round the world, but come back again."

Unlike other Maid-Rites in the well-known Midwestern franchise, Taylor's has kept things simple. The other Maid-Rites offer everything from roasted chicken and corn dogs to tacos. At Taylor's, a loosemeats sandwich has always been the solitary sandwich on the short menu.

The loosemeats sandwich may be some of the fastest food you'll ever come across because the meat is already cooked and warm. An order can arrive at your spot at the counter in under a minute. Unwrap and sink your teeth into one of the softest, tastiest sandwiches around and you'll start wondering why the rest of the country has not caught on yet.

One time when I visited the Central Iowa eatery there was a debate going on about the proposed introduction of ketchup, not to the sandwich, but to the counter. The sign out front announced STOP IN VOTE YES OR NO FOR KETCHUP. The votes were tallied, and in August 2006, ketchup was introduced to the counter, 77 years after opening day.

Sandy retired from a job as a schoolteacher in North Dakota only to return home and find herself drawn to Taylor's. Her son, Don Taylor Short, was looking to move on after 20 years managing the popular loosemeats institution and Sandy agreed to jump in. "This is my retirement!" she told me laughing. She's there every day and makes a point to warn customers about the pitfalls of the metal cup that holds your "extra" milkshake. "You need to stir it before you pour it," she reminds me. "Someone dumps their shake on the counter everyday."

RECIPE FROM

THE HAMBURGER AMERICA TEST KITCHEN

THE BEER MAID-RITE SANDWICH

This is an interpretation of the Iowa classic loosemeats sandwich. At Taylor's Maid-Rite in Marshalltown, there are no secrets and their recipe is simple. They grind meat at the restaurant, add salt, and use a cast-iron steam cooker that has been in use for almost 80 years.

MAKES 5 OR 6 SANDWICHES

1 pound fresh ground 80/20 chuck

5 pinches salt (to taste)

1 cup beer

3 squirts (teaspoons) yellow mustard

6 white squishy buns

Pickle slices

Chopped onion

More yellow mustard

Place a heavy cast-iron skillet over medium heat to warm for five minutes. Turn heat to medium high and crumble the beef into the skillet. Add salt. Using the blade end of the spatula, chop the beef as it cooks until it is pebbly. When the beef loses most of its pink, add the beer and turn the heat up to high. Add the mustard as the beer begins to bubble and stir to mix contents. Cook over high heat, stirring constantly, until most of the liquid has evaporated. Scoop onto buns that have been "doped" with onion, pickle, and more mustard. Enjoy with the remaining beer.

13

KANSAS

BOBO'S DRIVE IN

2300 SW 10TH AVE | TOPEKA, KS 66604

785-234-4511 | MON–SAT 11 AM–8 PM

CLOSED SUNDAY

Bobo's is one of only a handful of original drive-ins in America still using carhops. That's right, the ones who come to your car, take your order, then come back with food and clip a tray onto your car door. Sonic may have capitalized on the modern version of the drive-in, but there's still nothing like an original one-of-a-kind like Bobo's.

At one point there were two Bobo's Drive Ins in Topeka. The one remaining opened in 1953. The first location was opened just a few blocks away in 1948 by Orville and Louise Bobo. "Mrs. Bobo still comes in and buys pies two to three times a week," Kim, a former carhop told me. Bobo's is now owned by Richard Marsh who recently purchased the drive in from Bob Humes. He is only the third owner in the restaurant's more than six decades in operation. Richard bought Bobo's and all of the secret recipes in 2007 and kept everything pretty much the same.

Bobo's plays the part of the mid-century American road icon with a neon tower shooting out of its roof and a large arrow pointing the way. There are twelve stalls for cars and two carhops during the day running orders and food back and forth from the kitchen to waiting drivers. You can see why so many fast-food restaurants moved to the economical drive-thru; the drive-in is without question a lot more work.

The burgers at Bobo's are excellent. They start as fresh ground 85 percent lean one-eighth-ounce patties and are cooked on a superhot flat-top griddle, pressed flat. "You don't always get a perfect circle," grill cook Robert admitted. The thin patty is sprinkled with salt and pepper, then griddled until crunchy on the outside but perfectly moist inside.

A strange burger creation proprietary to Bobo's competes equally with their flavorful double cheeseburger—the "Spanish Burger." What's on the Spanish? "Spanish sauce," Jonette told me bluntly. Turns out, the Spanish sauce is a tangy, sweet tomato sauce. Just then, someone sat down and ordered one. "You see? We sell as many of them as cheeseburgers."

Not to be missed are the onion rings. I mean it when I say that these were probably the best I've ever eaten. I still think about that inviting pile of not-too-greasy gnarled, deep-fried onions. I couldn't stop eating them. Homemade root beer is also a draw.

Jonette knows just about everyone who drives up or walks in the door. "For a lot of people who pull in here," Jonette said, "we can have their order on the grill before they even tell us." Now there's a perk that could lure you to Topeka.

COZY INN HAMBURGERS

108 NORTH 7TH ST | SALINA, KS 67401
785-825-2699 | WWW.COZYBURGER.COM
SUN 11 AM–8 PM | MON–SAT 10 AM–9 PM

The Cozy Inn is a classic well-preserved hamburger stand built in 1922 in Salina, Kansas. Not surprisingly, the Cozy, with its six white-painted steel stools and short counter, was modeled after the successful White Castle hamburger chain. In 1921, only one year earlier in nearby Wichita, a man named Walt Anderson had opened the first White Castle: it was to become the first hamburger chain in America. In the next few years the White Castle model, a clean, small stand serving wholesome burgers, would be copied by entrepreneurs all over the country. The secret ingredient to White Castle's success was chopped onions that, when cooked with the burger, created an intoxicating smell that drew customers from near and far. Bob Kinkel, an amateur baseball player from Salina, liked what he saw (and smelled) and immediately opened the Cozy Inn.

On one of my visits to Cozy, a woman sitting at the counter named Phyllis told me, "My father built this place for Bob—$500 turnkey." This would have been a bargain even by 1922 standards, with the possible exception that the place is incredibly small. It takes only a few people to fill up the low-ceilinged burger joint, so understandably, a line builds quickly outside at lunchtime.

To sit and watch the grillman at work is a treat. He stands in front of a smallish recessed griddle that has room for 60 of the aromatic sliders for which the Cozy has become famous. A steam cloud envelops his head as he flips row after row of the small onion-covered burgers. The cloud fills the tiny restaurant with an aroma so thick your eyes will tear and make your clothing smell for days. It's an oniony goodness that once saturated thousands of burger stands just like the Cozy Inn from the 1920s to the 1950s. Today Cozy is one of only a handful of its kind still in operation.

So now you're thinking, can I get a slider without onions? No. For over 80 years the same sliders have been sold at Cozy. If you don't like onions, you won't like their burgers. But if you do, you'll be in heaven. A burger "all the way" comes with ketchup, mustard, pickle, and a pile of steam-cooked onions. Today you can choose any combination of these condiments, but in the old days you had no choice—a burger at the Cozy came "all the way" and that was that. And for all of these decades, cheese has never graced a burger at Cozy, so don't even ask. "It's amazing how many people come in here and ask for a cheeseburger," former manager Nancy Durant once told me, "even though we have 'no cheese' signs everywhere." No fries either. Grab a bag of chips at the counter.

The burgers are small, so order a bunch. A familiar call from a customer might be, "A sack and a pop, please," which is local vernacular for,

"six sliders and a soda to go."

"We roll our own meat here," Nancy said, referring to the one-ounce wads of fresh bull beef that make up a Cozy slider. The tiny stand will go through 500 pounds of onions and an incredible 1,000 pounds of meat a week. "On our 80th anniversary we sold 8,800 burgers in three days," Nancy boasted. The buns, soft and pillowy, are made especially for the Cozy Inn and come all the way from Missouri.

For the first time in almost 90 years a second Cozy Inn location is opening. The lucky college town of Manhattan, Kansas will soon be able to indulge in a sack and and a pop.

On my first visit to the Cozy Inn, I was walking out, reeking of onions, and an older woman on her way in stopped me and excitedly asked, "Was it as good as you remembered?" Now that's the kind of sentiment the Cozy deserves.

JACK'S NORTH HI CARRYOUT

603 WEST 13TH ST | WICHITA, KS 67203

316-264-2644 | MON–SAT 10 AM–7 PM

When I learned that Jack's had sold I panicked. During research for this book I had visited the vintage 1950s Wichita burger joint, ate their double cheeseburger, and was thoroughly satisfied. I called to speak to Jack's new owner Austin

Herron just to find out how things were going and if he had planned to keep things the same. "Well, we opened today and just served my first customer," he told me. I almost dropped the phone and said, "So why are you talking to me!" Austin had much more important things to do.

Austin, who is only 25, somehow possesses

the notion that some old things are good things, a trait that few twentysomethings have. With the help of his grandmother he was able to buy Jack's at auction. "She knows I'm a hard-working person and she liked my business plan." Fortunately, the only changes he made were for the better.

Jack Robards opened the tiny burger stand in 1951 in an absolutely brilliant location—directly across the street from the enormous North Senior High School. For decades, students have made the short walk and lunched at Jack's. After Jack, the burger joint was passed to Nola Behan, who ran Jack's for over 30 years. In 2007 the restaurant had a catastrophic fire and closed its doors. A year later a man named Joe Moore, whose dream it was to own a vintage burger joint, bought the burned-out restaurant and put everything he had into its rebirth. When it opened in 2009 regulars were happy to see that Jack's was back, but 7 months later Joe suffered a massive heart attack at the restaurant and died. Joe's wife ran Jack's in her husband's absence but her heart was not in it. She put the restaurant up for sale and eventually, at auction, the young Austin became the owner.

Austin has actually made Jack's better. He switched from using one-sixth-pound patties to quarter-pounders and got rid of the frozen fries. "We now have fresh-cut fries, no frozen," he told me. The burgers are still made the way Jack did it 60 years ago. A flat patty of fresh ground chuck is slapped on the flattop and sprinkled with a handful of diced onion. The onion is pressed into the patty and cooks into the burger. Soft white buns are toasted on the griddle with butter and the burger is served with lettuce, pickle, ketchup, and mustard. Cheese, jalapeños, bacon, and chili are also available.

North High lets out for lunch around noon on weekdays and the Jack's is instantly mobbed with students. "The people that live around here know not to come then," Austin told me. "The old timers and regulars know to come after one o'clock."

Seating at Jack's is mostly limited to counters along the big picture windows that look out onto 13th Street and North High. In warmer months, take a seat at a picnic table outside. Also, check out the beautiful hand-painted menu board over the grill. Don't get your hopes up, though. Twenty-five cent hamburgers are a thing of the past. The sign hails from the early days of the burger stand and depicts a mountain scene with teepees (North High's teams are the Redskins).

I asked Austin why he bought an old burger joint and he told me, "It was something I had been looking for. I wanted to buy the burger place near my old high school but it was long gone." Owning a Wichita tradition near a rival high school will have to do.

We owe thanks to Austin for having the foresight to own and operate a place with strong ties to the past. This is not an easy venture, but I'm glad he's young and willing to take Jack's into the future.

NUWAY CAFE

1416 WEST DOUGLAS AVE | WICHITA, KS 67203
316-267-1131 (4 OTHER LOCATIONS IN WICHITA)
WWW.NUWAYCAFE.COM
OPEN DAILY 10:30 AM–9 PM

When we rolled into Wichita looking for burgers I was shocked when we came across the NuWay Cafe. I know a lot about regional burgers in America and where these microcosms exist. I'm also pretty familiar at this point with how far certain burger trends have traveled, but most crazy ideas usually remain within the city limits. The Jucy Lucy has not gone much further than a handful of burger joints in Minneapolis, the steamed cheeseburg only exists in the geographic center of Connecticut, and as far as I know you can only find a Cuban Frita on Calle Ocho in Miami. So when expert burger taster Kris Brearton and I plopped down at the counter at NuWay, we found that the loosemeat phenomenon of Iowa may have found its way to Kansas.

Of course, the loosemeat sandwich is not really a hamburger. I put Taylor's Maid-Rite in this book as a fine example of where to find the sandwich, a sort of deconstructed burger. All of the elements for a great burger are there—the soft white bun, fresh ground beef, pickles, mustard, and onion. But the beef, instead of being a patty, is crumbly and moist. It's a sort of Sloppy Joe without the sloppy part and it's heavenly.

At NuWay, they call them "Crumblies," or

the "Crumbly Sandwich." The menu lists them as the "Original," and I've also heard them referred to as simply "NuWays." Whatever you decide to call them they come in various sizes and configurations at NuWay. The traditional size is the large, which is around a third of a pound of super-moist, crumbled meat that has been scooped by a spatula into a soft white bun and served with pickle, onion, and mustard. The amount of meat you'll find in a NuWay varies but usually in your favor. "It's a very unscientific method," owner Neal Stong said of the amount that gets scooped into a NuWay. "We try to overserve rather than underserve."

Neal did not open the first NuWay in Wichita but he is certainly the protector of this Wichita tradition. In 1930, Tom McEvoy opened the first NuWay on Douglas Avenue after leaving a partnership behind in Iowa of (you guessed it) a new concept called the Maid-Rite sandwich. In search of warmer weather he headed south and settled on Wichita. He found a potato patch to lease just east of downtown for 25 dollars a month and built the location that still exists today. McEvoy brought with him his patented cooker for making the crumbly beef sandwich and guarded the process. People would try to get a glimpse of the cooker in action and

according to local legend McEvoy would chase them out of the restaurant.

The cooker is still out of view and the process of making the NuWay sandwich kept a secret. "We only use high quality USDA ground beef but we have a secret grind," Neal told me. And unlike the chain of Maid-Rites in Iowa and beyond (with the exception of Taylor's in Marshalltown) the meat is not spiced. As Neal put it, "Tender love and care is the only thing we add. People think we put something in there but we don't."

The NuWay is similar to the Maid-Rite sandwich but actually beefier and definitely moister. "The fat is where the flavor is," Neal told me. Some call it sauce, some call it grease, but in reality, the NuWay is so good because some of the fat is not drained off when you get your sandwich. "You can ask for it 'light,'" said Neal, but the sauce, soaked into the soft bun, is where the flavor is.

In the beginning, NuWay only served NuWays, malts, and root beer. Today the menu has expanded greatly, but the core menu is still available. A regular at the counter named Vicki told me, "I've been coming here for 40 years and back then there was only NuWays on the menu." Everything is made fresh in the restaurant, including the popular garlic salad (which is basically coleslaw spiked with garlic) and the homemade root beer.

Neal became a partner in the business in 1981 with Gene Friedman after buying out McEvoy's widow, and Neal has owned NuWay on his own since the late 1990s. Under their leadership four new locations have been opened around Wichita and the original location has been kept intact. "It's an icon," Neal told me. "I see it as a museum. Other than a coat of paint we're not going to change a thing."

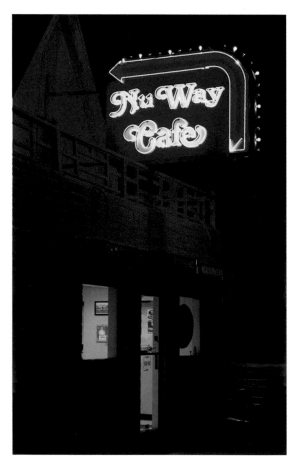

14

LOUISIANA

BOZO'S

3117 21ᵀᴴ ST | METAIRIE, LA 70002

504-831-8666 | WWW.BOZOSRESTAURANT.COM

TUES–THU 11 AM–3 PM, 5 PM–9 PM

FRI–SAT 11 AM–3 PM, 5 PM–9:30 PM

CLOSED SUN & MON

Bozo's is not the kind of place you'd expect to find a great burger. The restaurant is a destination for fresh oysters and excellent fried seafood and the burger is listed at the bottom of the menu. Southern food writer and friend, John T. Edge, led me to Bozo's, calling their burger a "sleeper." Nevertheless, Bozo's has sold the same amazing hamburger po'boy (Louisiana vernacular for submarine or hero sandwich) for over 80 years.

Bozo's sits in a fairly nondescript industrial neighborhood in Metairie, a half block from the Lake Pontchartrain Causeway. The low wooden building is set back from the street with a large parking lot in front. If you didn't know what you were looking, for you'd drive right past. No ostentatious signage or loud neon here—just a small stained-glass window with the name Bozo's subtly printed on it. The dining room is pure function, clean and well lit with wood-grain Formica tables and sturdy industrial seating. The only real decoration is a floor-to-ceiling mural of two fishing boats near a dock. "Those were two of my dad's boats," former second-generation owner and septuagenarian chef Chris Vodanovich pointed out to me.

Yugoslavian immigrant Chris "Bozo" Vodanovich Sr. opened Bozo's Oyster House on St. Ann Street in New Orleans in 1928. At one point, Bozo had a fleet of eight boats to service the needs of his restaurant. Fresh oysters, shrimp, and catfish were the reasons most locals patronized the tiny restaurant, but from the beginning, Bozo offered a hamburger po'boy as an alternative to seafood.

The burger at Bozo's is a combination of over 80 years of experience, a proprietary mixture of meat and onions, and a twist on a regional specialty—the po'boy sandwich. Among those for whom the perfect po'boy is a passion, it is understood that the bread used is as important as what goes on it. Because of this Chris uses only the best—French bread from Leidenheimer Bakery, an institution in New Orleans for over 100 years.

I asked Chris how big the burger was and he didn't know. "We just make them to fit the bread," he told me, smiling. The bread is not small, making this hamburger po'boy a filling meal. The fresh ground beef has onions and "other spices" mixed in before being hand pattied and cooked on a flattop griddle. The combination of the perfectly cooked burger and the pillowy bread makes for a great regional hamburger experience.

Chris inherited Bozo's and moved his father's business out of downtown New Orleans to Metairie in 1979 because, as he put it, "the

neighborhood was gettin' rough." The Metairie location was expanded to accommodate 120 diners in two dining rooms separated by a large bar.

Today, Bozo's is owned and run by Mark and Susan Fayard, but Chris still comes in to visit. "He's here at least three times a week," Susan told me, and added with a laugh. "We can't get rid of him!"

While I talked to Chris, every patron said "Thanks, Mr. Chris" as they paid their tabs and left. He speaks with a gentle Louisiana twang and has piercing blue eyes and wavy grey hair. I asked him "Why Bozo?" "In the old country, Bozo was the word for Christ," he told me, "and my name is Chris."

PORT OF CALL

838 ESPLANADE AVE | NEW ORLEANS, LA 70116

504-523-0120

WWW.PORTOFCALLNEWORLEANS.COM

SUN–THU 11 AM–MIDNIGHT | FRI & SAT 11 AM–1 AM

Port of Call is a bar and restaurant that sits on the far northeast end of the French Quarter in New Orleans. I say this because when people tell you this place is in the Quarter your thoughts first go to drunken tourists with their souvenir hurricane glasses, lame strip clubs, and big-ass beers. Not so here. Port of Call is on the other end of the quarter, in a quiet, beautiful neighborhood.

The building Port of Call calls home dates back to the turn of the century, where it started as a sailor bar. Over the years it went from grocery store to tavern and then opened as a steakhouse in 1962. Burger sales one day eclipsed the steak, and today Port of Call is the most popular (and best) burger destination in New Orleans.

The decor is comfortably nautical and has dark wood floors, wood walls, wood tables, and a wood bar. The entire ceiling is a web of sisal rope and the whole place feels like it might start rocking with the tide.

There are four burger choices—Hamburger, Cheeseburger, Mushroom Burger, and Mushroom Cheeseburger. It's the Mushroom cheeseburger that keeps them coming back.

Port of Call grinds its own sirloin and forms burgers into eight-ounce patties. The burgers are char-grilled and served on a bun that seems too small for the amount of meat provided. In order to make the patty fit, the burger is a tall, inch-and-a-half-thick, perfectly cooked fist of meat. The cheese is shredded cheddar and the mushrooms are sautéed in wine, butter, and garlic and melt in your mouth. It looks like a mess when it arrives at your spot at the bar (or at one of the many tables in two dining rooms) but is actually easy to handle once you get going.

Port of Call was spared major damage during the devastating Hurricane Katrina in 2005. "The flooding stopped two blocks that way," general manager of over thirty years Mike Mollere told me, pointing north. "We were extremely fortunate and had little damage. After the neighborhood opened back up, I just turned the key and we were open for business." Mike followed his post-hurricane opening by serving first responders and the press.

I arrived at Port of Call just before opening, hoping to beat the crowds. No such luck. By the time the ancient, windowless wood doors were unlatched there were over 20 people waiting on the sidewalk to get their mushroom burger fix. "It's like that every morning," Mike said, shaking his head. I took a spot at the bar and watched as the restaurant filled almost to capacity with an additional 50 hungry tourists, locals, and construction workers. Within ten minutes the Port of Call was transformed from an empty, dark bar into a bustling, lively hot spot. Mike pointed out that they have the best jukebox in town. "Hey, where else can you hear Zappa on a jukebox?"

15

MAINE

HARMON'S LUNCH

144 GRAY RD | FALMOUTH, ME 04105

207-797-9857 | MON–FRI 10:30 AM–3 PM

SAT 11 AM–7 PM | CLOSED SUNDAY

My first question for owner Pete Wormell was a dumb one—I asked, "Why Harmon's Lunch?" Through a thick monotone Maine accent he told me, "We're only open for lunch." Even though this tiny burger spot in Maine is open for only four and a half hours a day, they still manage to sell over 80,000 burgers a year.

Amazingly, Pete knows exactly how many burgers he sells every year because he jots down the day's total on a calendar. When I asked him why, he said, "I'm weird, I guess." You can ask him how many he sold on any day in the last decade and he'll be able to tell you. "Look," he said, pointing to the calendar, "We only sold 144 that day because of snow."

Pete and friend Cliff bought Harmon's in 1995 from Marvin Harmon, who was looking for the right people to buy the place. "I blame him," Pete said, pointing at Cliff, who was working the grill. Cliff had seen an ad in the paper that the restaurant was for sale. He has since sold his portion to Pete, who joked, "We're still friends part-time."

Marvin built the small wood-frame burger joint in 1960. Today, not much has changed, but Pete started an impressive collection of vintage Maine dairy bottles that line the walls. It's a collection that is rooted in his family's dairy past.

Both Pete and Cliff share time at the busy seasoned griddle cranking out excellent burgers. The menu is limited to burgers, hot dogs, and grilled cheese, but fresh-cut fries are also available. If you ask for milk, specify either "white" or "chocolate" or be pegged a tourist.

The burger at Harmon's is small but tasty. Pete buys fresh ground beef and uses a patty former at the restaurant to make two-ounce patties. "We made them by hand for the first six months," Cliff told me. "That was enough."

A fully loaded burger comes with mustard, fried onions, and a signature sweet red relish. "Most people think it's going to be hot because of its color," Pete told me. A local bakery provides preservative-free buns that are steamed to limp. The bun creates an impossibly soft, warm pillow that cradles the perfectly cooked thin patty.

The wait at Harmon's, especially on a Saturday, can be up to 45 minutes. "We get backed up," Pete said, "but to have the quality you can't do more."

When Pete and Cliff first took the helm at Harmon's, they decided to slightly alter the menu and offer a traditional Maine favorite—the lobster roll. The attempt backfired and the roll was pulled from the menu after only a few weeks. "This is a hamburger place," Pete explained, and attributed the failure to the old adage "If it ain't broke, don't fix it."

16

MASSACHUSETTS

MR. BARTLEY'S BURGER COTTAGE

1246 MASS AVE | CAMBRIDGE, MA 02138

617-354-6559 | WWW.MRBARTLEY.COM

MON–SAT 11 AM–9 PM | CLOSED SUNDAY

Bill Bartley is an original. He stands at the griddle at his family's Harvard Square eatery shouting things at me like "We're the BEST!" and "This is the greatest burger ANYWHERE!" He's smiling and extremely energetic and has the kind of cocksure confidence and running dialogue usually reserved for someone like Muhammed Ali in his prime. Fortunately, all of it is true—the burgers at Mr. Bartley's are unbelievable.

"I've probably made over five million burgers in the last 30 years," Bill told me as he shifted some thick patties on the 600-degree griddle, "All good ones too, all cooked to temp." If you ask for medium-rare, that's what you'll get. Every burger goes out exactly the way Bill wants them to, which means perfect. If you ask for cheese it's cooked *separately* from the burger. Where most chcfs melt the cheese atop the burger as it nears completion, Bill cooks the perfect burger, tosses a thick slice of cheese directly on the griddle for a minute, then gently transfers it to the burger as it is dispatched to a table. As Bill eloquently explained, "The cheese is ambivalent to the temperature of the burger."

Mr. Bartley's is a busy place. Just across the street is Harvard University, so you can imagine the crowd. The restaurant feels like a big broken-in bar, yet no booze is served and the walls are covered with Red Sox stuff, political ephemera, and the types of posters a student might have in their dorm room. Many tables, including a long communal one, and green plastic chairs complete the scene.

The first time I visited, there was a line out the door at 2:30 p.m. on a Thursday. The man who started it all, Joe Bartley, was taking names outside, his wife, Joan, was managing the tables inside, and their son, Bill, was at the grill cranking out perfect burgers. "You don't have a line outside because you're slow," Bill explained, "you have a line because you're GOOD." The turnover is quick and the service lightning fast.

The burger selection is enormous. With the same seven-ounce patty, Bill and his team can add any one of the over forty dressing concoctions on the menu. Everything you can imagine on a burger is available here, from feta cheese to baked beans, but the big seller is the Viagra Burger. The Viagra is topped with creamy blue cheese and bacon, and the menu asks you to "rise to the occasion." The reality is that these burgers need no condiments. They are that good and don't even need a bun. Of course Bill put it best when he explained, "The bun is just the envelope for the good news that's coming."

Mr. Bartley's burger starts as fresh-ground chuck that comes from a local butcher daily. A special patty former in the restaurant is designed not to compress the meat too much as it creates the fist-sized burgers. "We use an Acu-Pat," Bill told me. "It's made of stainless steel so it doesn't use heat during patty forming like most. Heat is the worst thing for an uncooked burger." On the intensely hot griddle the burgers are seared to almost a burn to seal in the juices.

Even though the burger selection is daunting, your toughest choice will be deciding what to drink. Mr. Bartley's serves up some of the city's greatest frappes (milkshakes) and an amazing raspberry lime rickey. My advice? Get both.

Joe Bartley ran a lunch counter seven days a week in the back of a pharmacy in Garden City, New York in the 1950s. "I was going to be a cop on Long Island, can you believe that?" He decided to move back to his native Boston one day and opened a grocery store in 1960 in Harvard Square. By 1962 he was making burgers because, as he told me, "When I started there wasn't a good burger around."

As I stood and watched Bill's genius at work, I tried to figure out what made these burgers so special. Without missing a beat Bill offered this insight: "The person who has this skill level thinks they should be doing something better. Not me. I make the best burgers anywhere."

WHITE HUT

280 MEMORIAL AVE I WEST SPRINGFIELD, MA 01089

413-736-9390 I WWW.WHITEHUT.COM

MON–WED 6:30 AM–6:30 PM

THU & FRI 6:30 AM–8:30 PM I SAT & SUN 8 AM–6 PM

White Hut is one of the few remaining "White" restaurants in America. During the 1920s and 1930s America was blanketed with ten-stool hamburger joints with names like: White Tower, White Diamond, White Clock, and the one that started it all—White Castle. Placing the word *white* in your name conveyed a sense of cleanliness, an important tenet in a time when hamburgers were considered dirty food for wage earners. By the 1930s in America, thanks to the tremendous success of White Castle, the word white also became synonymous with quality fast food.

And then along came White Hut. In the late 1930s, Hy Roberts opened a small three-stool hot dog shack on a busy corner in West Springfield, Massachusetts. A year after opening, Edward Barkett was asked by Roberts to run the stand for a few weeks. Barkett liked what he saw and negotiated the purchase of the business for $300. He bought a plot of land across the street soon after and built a tiny 600-square-foot burger counter. That same burger counter, over 60 years later, serves a thousand burgers a day and is still run by the third generation of the Barkett family.

The interior of White Hut is a classic burger counter with 12 vintage stools facing a large flat-top griddle, bare white walls, and a long counter supported by a wall of glass block. The floors are sprinkled with a generous amount of sawdust, giving the place an old-time meat market feel. "That's so people don't slip—this floor can get slippery," manager Kathy told me. The place was built during the Depression, at a time when most building materials were scarce. "The White Hut was built with black-market lumber," current owner and grandson EJ Barkett pointed out. "Nothing else was available during the war." His grandfather was also forced to use the only flooring available, a slick beige terrazzo. Booths lined the back wall of the restaurant for the first few months, but were removed when Barkett noticed that people tended to hang around in them too long. "My grandfather needed the turnover and replaced the booths with a large table to stand around."

Don't look for a menu—there is none. White Hut offers only three things: hamburgers, cheeseburgers, and hot dogs. And, as of only a few years ago, fries. If you love onions, you'll love the burgers at White Hut. Every morning a large pile of chopped Spanish onions is placed on the griddle. The onions cook slowly until they are translucent and limp, then hearty amounts are spooned onto the burgers. "We go through about 250 pounds of onions a day," counterperson Roberta told me. Roberta is actually owner EJ Barkett's mother and a fount of White Hut lore. White Hut receives an order of fresh, thin, two-ounce patties every morning made of a special blend they have been using for years. "There's less fat so there is less shrinkage," Roberta pointed out.

The daily lunch crowd is large and the method for ordering a burger at peak times requires well-tuned survival instincts. Order your burgers when a counterperson *makes eye contact with you.* Roberta told me, "People will stand four and five deep at the counter at lunchtime." Nothing is written down and somehow every-

one's order is produced perfectly. Regardless of the hungry mob and apparent lack of order, the average dining experience at White Hut lasts only 15 minutes. A unique rule, imposed at the counter, may help. "No newspapers between 12 and 2," Kathy told me, "because they are not paying attention."

White Hut is a family place, run by family and visited by families. A regular named Michael, in a suit, standing and eating a quick lunch told me, "I bring my kids here just like my dad brought me here years ago." "We've had four generations sitting at the counter at the same time," EJ told me, "I love to see that." For many in this part of Western Massachusetts, White Hut is an enduring tradition that shows no sign of fading any time soon.

MICHIGAN

HUNTER HOUSE HAMBURGERS

35075 WOODWARD AVE

BIRMINGHAM, MI, 48009 I 248-568-9911

WWW.HUNTERHOUSEHAMBURGERS.COM

MON-WED 8 AM–10 PM I THU 8 AM–12 AM

FRI & SAT 8 AM–3 AM I SUN 11 AM–9 PM

Hunter House is not a roadside burger joint or a fading relic of the past. It is a thriving 60-year-old diner in a Detroit suburb that probably looks the same as it did on opening day in 1952. What's more, in keeping with its status as a surviving, historically accurate mid-century burger joint, Hunter House is located on Woodward Avenue, the first paved road in America. In 1904, when Detroit became the center of automobile production in America (thanks to the Ford Motor Company), it was inevitable that paved roads would follow.

The interior of Hunter House looks impossibly clean for a diner this old. It's clear from first glance that the stools, the long counter, the basket weave tile floor, and the enamel steel walls that this diner is no imitation. "Everything in here is original," charming owner Susan Cobb told me with a smile. The line of refrigerators and vintage appliances behind the counter are eye candy for the lucky ones that grab a stool, though apparently repairs to these beauties is not easy. Susan told me, "Servicemen come in here [for repairs] and always start by saying 'I'm not going to have parts for these.'" It's not uncommon for Susan to have parts fabricated for ailing appliances in order to keep Hunter House original.

The hamburger is the main attraction on the limited menu at Hunter House. "When you come here you need to order the burger the way we've always made it," Susan told me with a smile. The way they've always made the burgers is with paper-thin sliced Spanish onion cooked with the burger. If you don't want onion, you have to ask for no onion, but the flavor profile of this burger is equally about the onions as it is the beef. Just about everyone orders theirs with onions and as the server's T-shirts aptly explain, ONION BREATH IS BETTER THAN NO BREATH.

A flattop griddle sits at one end of the counter adjacent to a functioning carry-out walk-up window. The burgers start as 80/20 chuck that comes to the restaurant as fresh-ground beef formed into "pucks," or tall patties. The puck is pressed thin into a patty on the griddle and covered with sliced onions. When the burger is flipped, the grillperson places both halves of the bun atop the patty (or patties if you are getting more than one) and

with a squeeze bottle full of water sends a thin stream that encircles the patty. Not surprisingly this sends up an explosive vapor cloud. As grillman Bret explained to me, "We do that to steam the buns." It looks like they also do it for fun. Who wouldn't want to spray cold water on a hot griddle and see what happens? "It's amazing," Susan told me, "The buns poof right up." The result is a bun-and-burger combo that arrives impossibly soft and tasty.

The double is the way to go because the single patty, weighing in at 3 ounces, is just a snack. There are crazy eating records on the wall that go beyond the standard notion of the number of burgers consumed. One note gives props to a guy that ate 6 quadruple burgers in 8 minutes, 10 seconds, and another exclaims that "The Blue Burke" once ate "7 hamburger patties in one bite!!!" Other accolades go to kids, one only 5 years old who polished off 4 cheeseburgers, fries, and an Orange Crush with his parents watching. "The people that compete are not what you'd think," Susan told me. "They are smaller than me!"

On the third Saturday in August every year, Woodward Avenue is transformed into the world's longest, largest classic auto show in the form of the Woodward Dream Cruise. Over 35,000 vintage cars and one million visitors descend to "cruise" a section of Woodward that extends from Detroit out to the suburbs. The event is crushing to the tiny hamburger icon so Susan shuts down the restaurant and sets up flattops outside in the parking lot to feed the masses. "We use the restaurant for the crew to take breaks," Susan explained. During the Cruise, Hunter House has served up to 40,000 burgers to hungry car enthusiasts.

Susan's parents, Al and Martha Cobb, bought the vintage burger joint when it came up for sale in 1982. They were the third owners and ran the place until 2005 when Al sold Hunter House to his daughter. Fortunately she hasn't really changed a thing, with the exception of adding a catering trailer for parties. "It's booked every weekend spring to fall," Susan explained. I guess the trailer was a good idea.

Hunter House is a comfortable, pleasant place that serves high quality burgers. Go there to meet the ridiculously friendly staff and if you are lucky you'll get the impossibly extroverted server Chelsea. The future of Hunter House is secure too. "We just had a family meeting and discussed the future," Susan told me. "The kids never want to sell."

KRAZY JIM'S BLIMPY BURGER

551 SOUTH DIVISION ST | ANN ARBOR, MI 48104

734-663-4590 | MON–SAT 11 AM–10 PM

SUN NOON–8 PM

A visit to Blimpy Burger can be a daunting but rewarding experience. Theatrically, the cooks behind the counter engage in a sort of Soup Nazi berating of customers who do not follow the cafeteria-style rules of ordering. "Just answer the questions I'm asking you," grill cook Brian told a group of newcomers the first time I visited. In reality, the rules are there to help you, not scare you. They are there to allow the cooks to get your food to you fast, which is a good thing because you'll need this burger in your mouth as soon as possible.

Blimpy Burger is on the edge of the University of Michigan campus, surrounded by student rental houses with mud lawns. For students, the positioning of this decades-old greasy spoon could not be better. The interior of Blimpy Burger is wholly utilitarian and the opposite of a comfy dive. A low drop ceiling and greenish fluorescent lighting give the place a construction trailer feel. A collection of vintage cast-iron swivel stools bolted to the floor serve most tables. The original owner, Krazy Jim Shafer, purchased the stools from a department store that had gone out of business in the 1950s for $1.75 apiece.

In 1953 Jim Shafer turned a corner grocery into a burger stand to sell cheap burgers to University of Michigan students. At his previous burger venture, shoehorned into an alley in downtown Ann Arbor, a friend at a neighboring business called Jim "crazy" for selling food for so cheap. The moniker stuck, as did the famous phrase that greets customers at Blimpy Burger: "Cheaper Than Food." Current owner Richard Manger told me, "Back then it was cheaper to buy a 20-cent burger than to eat at home."

Richard bought the restaurant in 1992 from Krazy Jim, who was already in retirement. Jim and Rich had a past together at that point—Rich had worked as a cook flipping burgers in the late '60s for Jim at Blimpy, had met his wife, Chris, there (also a student), and had designed the Blimpy logo that is still used today. It's a drawing of a seated, chubby bear smiling and hoisting a burger. "Jim wanted me to draw a cow. I told him 'I don't draw cows. I draw bears.'"

Richard's menu design is an elaborate piece of R. Crumb-inspired line art that is suitable for framing. It lists a dizzying assortment of comfort foods and toppings for the burgers. Rich told me, "When Jim opened he only had burgers, American cheese, pie, and coffee." Not so today.

The selection of toppings and burger sizing is so vast it prompted a math student to deduce that there are more than 2,147,483,648 possible burger combinations.

The fresh chuck that is used for Blimpy burgers is ground daily in the back. When you ask for a burger, you tell the grill cook how many you'd like (up to five, a "quint") and he'll grab that number of one-and-a-half-ounce balls of beef. The balls are tossed onto the hot griddle and smashed together, creating a sloppy, misshaped, flat patty. The burgers are pressed and pressed until they can get no thinner, flipped, pressed some more, then tossed on a bun. You'd think these guys had pressed the life out of your burger, but relax; you are in good hands. The result is a glorious grease

bomb—a pile of loose, griddled meat that is crunchy in parts and soft in others. The meat is so loose it's practically pebbly. A grill cook once told me, "These things are held together by hope."

The choice of roll for your burger, toasted on the griddle, includes pumpernickel, onion, or kaiser, the latter offered with or without sesame seeds because, as Rich explained matter-of-factly, "Some people have diverticulitis." The onion roll is hands-down one of the best I have ever eaten, soft and tasty and able to soak up the copious amounts of grease a Blimpy burger produces. "Onion rolls most places suck," Rich told me bluntly. "These really are great rolls."

Following the rules for ordering is important. Start by grabbing a tray and getting in line. Everyone gets a tray because, as Rich pointed out, "It keeps the tables clean when we're busy." Then grab a drink and order your fried food of choice first. French fries and onion rings are offered, but skip the usual for excellent deep-fried vegetables like mushrooms and cauliflower. Next, order your burger, but hold your cheese selection until the end of the process. Follow the rules and be rewarded with one of the best burgers in America.

A group of healthy-looking sixty somethings were enjoying their burgers the last time I visited and told me, "This is where we celebrate our birthdays. We've been coming here for over 50 years." When one of the grill guys, Skinny, heard that, he blurted out, "And they STILL don't know how to order their burgers."

MILLER'S BAR

23700 MICHIGAN AVE | DEARBORN, MI 48124

313-565-2577 | WWW.MILLERSBAR.COM

MON–SAT 11 AM–12:30 AM | CLOSED SUNDAY

The first time I visited Miller's it was in the middle of a torrential springtime downpour. It was 11:15 a.m. on a Wednesday, the bar was packed and everyone was eating hamburgers. Doesn't that pretty much say it all?

Miller's is on a commercial stretch, six lanes wide, in Dearborn, Michigan. Across the street from a large Ford dealership, the windowless bar is painted with a fresh coat of red paint and emblazoned with enormous white letters spelling out the name of this nearly 70-year-old institution. Despite the cool functionality of the exterior, the interior, with its original 1940s Brunswick bar of undulating high-gloss wood and booths made of supple deep-red leather, feels more like a long-lost private men's club than the bunker that the outside evokes. The immaculate well-preserved dining room is dark and cozy and, according to part-owner Mark Miller, has not needed renovation since 1964.

There is no menu at Miller's but the options are simple—burgers, fries, and onion rings are available, as are tuna, ham, and corned beef sandwiches and of course, drinks from the bar. The clientele is mostly local devotees and regulars from the nearby world headquarters of the Ford Motor Company. They come for the

burgers and have been since 1941, when Mark's uncle, George Miller, opened the bar. Today, thanks to topping many "Best-of" lists in America, Miller's Bar sells over 1,200 burgers a day. Every one of those burgers is cooked on a griddle next to the bar that is no more than three feet square.

"Our butcher starts grinding beef for us at 4 a.m. everyday," Mark told me. Mark owns the bar with his brother, Dennis, and the two are second-generation owners. The Miller's father Russell bought the bar from his brother George in 1947.

The sprightly grill cook, Kim, who has been flipping burgers at Miller's for over 20 years, is responsible for griddling the hundreds of perfect, award-winning burgers during the lunch rush. I overheard her take an order for a few burgers "well-done." Well-done? "Oh gosh yes," she sighed, "People don't know how to order their burgers here." Mark told me he won't eat anything over a medium, and rightly so, because Miller's meat is some of the freshest I've ever tasted.

The Millers have been using the same butcher for over 40 years. The bar used to get a 400-pound delivery daily of fresh ground beef that would have to be hand pattied by the kitchen staff. "It got to be too much," Kim told me, so the butcher offered to start delivering preformed patties. Knowing that the Millers wouldn't accept just any patty, he employs a special patty maker

that injects a blast of air back into the beef. "It makes the patty looser," Mark explained, "and it has an almost hand-pattied feel."

The seven-ounce burger is served on a steamed white bun and delivered to you on a square of wax paper. Lettuce and tomato are not offered. Swiss or Velveeta are available, as are the standard condiments like ketchup, mustard, pickle, and sliced onion. But this burger needs no embellishment—so forgo the condiments. The meat is so good you could eat it plain. I asked what it was that made the burger taste so great and Mark told me, "It's the meat. The meat is great. There are no seasonings and we have no secrets."

The secret may be in longevity. The staff is great and many have been with Miller's forever. The day-shift bartender, Jeff, has been pouring drinks for almost 30 years and a waitress named Linda has been delivering burgers at Miller's

since Nixon was in office. The secret may also be in the Miller brothers commitment to the family business. Every Sunday, when the bar is closed, Mark and Dennis take apart the entire kitchen and grill area for a thorough cleansing. Mark told me, "We completely disassemble the griddle, dishwasher . . . everything." What did *you* do last Sunday?

MOTZ'S HAMBURGERS

7208 WEST FORT ST | DETROIT, MI 48209

313-843-9186 | MON–FRI 9 AM–6 PM

SAT 10 AM–5 PM

f I told you that when I first arrived at Motz's Burgers I ran into the place with unbridled enthusiasm I'd be lying. On my first visit to the vintage burger joint that shared my name, needless to say, I was very nervous. What if the burgers were crap? What if this tiny ex-White Castle, nestled in an industrial wasteland on the outskirts of downtown Detroit, was a washed-up version of its former self? How would I explain that this perfect little burger joint was a bust?

The first five minutes inside Motz's Burgers was a complete blur. I quickly spotted the griddle and a cook smashing balls of fresh meat, and noted the glorious smell of onions that filled the little diner. There were a few stools and a counter and people walking off with paper bags full of steaming sliders. The scene was right out of a Depression-era FSA black-and-white photo. I had stumbled into hamburger nirvana and I was beyond relieved.

Even though we share a name, the pronunciation differs. Originally, the restaurant was called "Motts Burgers," named after the man that scooped up a handful of Detroit-area White Castles that were being sold to offset the financial strain of the Great Depression. Motts purchased a few in the '30s and put family members

in charge of each one. Robert Motts, the son of the original owner, decided to sell the West Fort Street location in 1996 to current owners Bob and Mary Milosavljeveski. Bob had just left his father's 36-year-old local bakery and was searching for something new. Motts asked Bob to change the name since there was another Motts Burger still in operation down the street. Bob chose to replace the *t*'s with a *z*, thus making my visit to the place destiny.

Bob's wife, Mary, makes change and takes orders at the counter while grill cook of 20 years Tammy (from the Motts days) flips burgers. At one point during my conversation with Bob, Tammy leaned over and audibly whispered to him, "Did you tell him the secret ingredient?" A pregnant pause followed and I was compelled to blurt out, "What is it?" "Love," Tammy told me with a straight face. "Love is the secret ingredient. If you don't love what you are doing, it ain't gonna taste good."

The burgers basically come in three sizes—a

single, a double, and a "King Motz," which is a triple. "Motts said 'keep the burgers the same' and he was right," Bob told me at the counter during the busy lunch rush. The burgers at Motz's are really oversized sliders but cooked the exact same way a place like White Castle would have done it over 80 years earlier. Bob picks up fresh ground beef for the restaurant every morning. A rolled ball of 88/12 chuck and rump round mixture is tossed on the flattop behind the counter and pressed flat with a spatula. A handful of thinly sliced Spanish onion is sprinkled on top that softens and intermingles with the patty once it's flipped. The result is, well, the burger that I make at home—the purest form of the American hamburger that I know of. An original Motz Slider is served on white squishy bun with mustard, ketchup, and pickles and is very tasty. Although I prefer my burgers without ketchup, I gave in to tradition and was pleasantly surprised.

When Bob and Mary bought the place in 1996, it was a dilapidated relic. "The place was a dump," Bob said with conviction and explained how he gave the interior a major facelift without destroying the integrity of the place. "We moved the griddle but kept it in sight." Bob explained, "Places like this will never die out because you can see the cook, see the meat."

The neighborhood surrounding Motz's Burgers ain't pretty. The only other visible sign of life is the enormous Detroit Produce Terminal directly across the street. Truckers and employees from the Terminal make up the bulk of business.

"That's the only reason we are surviving," Bob told me. At one time in this neighborhood's history, West Fort Street was lined with factories and bars and this burger joint probably fit in perfectly. The fact that this national treasure is still standing and serving great burgers is an absolute miracle. I wondered why Bob and Mary would take a chance in a neighborhood like this but I got my answer. "If it has survived 80 years, it'll be around for a while."

REDAMAK'S

616 EAST BUFFALO ST | NEW BUFFALO, MI 49117

269-469-4522 | WWW.REDAMAKS.COM

MON–SAT NOON–10:30 PM | SUN NOON–10 PM

CLOSED IN WINTER

Redamak's is a burger destination. Vacationers come from miles around for a weekend at Lake Michigan and most visit Redamak's for nourishment. George and Gladys Redamak opened a tiny mom-and-pop burger restaurant in the late 1940s. In 1975 the Maroney family bought the restaurant from Gladys, with the stipulation that they keep it the same. It didn't really turn out that way, though—they actually made it better.

Redamak's is enormous. Years of expansion and updating to the structure have created a profoundly successful restaurant that can comfortably seat 400. Crowd control is aided by two sets of double doors at the front—one marked ENTER, the other EXIT. If you have kids, you won't be alone here—kids and families populate the place. There are two separate video arcades and a sizable kids' menu. If you need a drink, there's a bar right in the center of it all. And of course, if you need a burger, Redamak's makes one of the best in the country.

The menu is round, the size of a large pizza, and has more text on it than the front page of the *Chicago Tribune.* You won't believe the options you'll have. Everything from corn dogs to clam strips is offered, along with seven different types of French fries. There's even lake perch on Fridays. The endless selection of lakefront comfort food can't disguise the fact that the burgers are the star attraction here. The menu proudly proclaims the Redamak's burger is "The Burger That Made New Buffalo Famous."

Fresh Iowa beef chuck steaks are ground in the kitchen for the six-ounce burgers at Redamak's. Manager Matt told me, "They are grinding all of the time back there." They have to keep grinding because the kitchen cranks out over 2,500 fresh patties a day. "We are going to break our record again this year," Charles Maroney pointed out. In 2010 Redamak's ground over 135,000 pounds of chuck steaks for burgers, which is amazing for a restaurant that's only open eight months of the year. What's even more baffling is the method by which this astounding number of burgers is cooked every day—each one is cooked in a pan by itself. This sounds impossible, but I saw it with my own eyes. There must have been five stovetops lined up, 30 burners in all. On each burner, a single skillet. In each pan, only a few burgers. "We do it that way to keep the juices with the burger," Charles told me, "On a griddle, those juices dissipate." Charles also pointed out that, along with their use of Velveeta cheese, the Maroney family is committed to doing things the way the Redamaks did for so many successful years.

Tomato and lettuce are not offered with a Redamak's burger. "Redamak's started as a tavern and there was no place for lettuce and tomato in bar food," Charles told me. Again, a tradition the restaurant holds dear. A burger with everything comes with ketchup, mustard, pickles, a slice of raw onion, and melted Velveeta. Don't panic. The oldest and most venerable burger destination in America, Louis' Lunch of New Haven, also indulges in the yellow stuff. Besides, it tastes good.

Bring the family, bring your friends, bring everyone you know—Redamak's can handle the crowds with ease. You'll probably have to wait, so go to the video arcade or browse the merchandise at the front. It might be the only place in America where you can buy a souvenir yo-yo in the shape of a hamburger.

MINNESOTA

CONVENTION GRILL

3912 SUNNYSIDE RD | EDINA, MN 55424

952-920-6881 | MON–THU, SUN 11 AM–10 PM

FRI & SAT 11 AM–11 PM

There are times when a diner looks vintage inside and out but the menu and ownership fail to live up to its historical roots. The Convention Grill, a Twin Cities institution, looks the part as you first step in off the street, almost too much so. The original tiled floor, the red leather swivel stools, the off-white patina to the walls, and the griddle behind the counter all look too good to be true. The waitstaff, scurrying around in pressed white uniforms with white shoes, makes you feel like you've just stepped into a period film from the '30s. The good news is it's not all show. The Convention Grill is a perfectly preserved time capsule from diner culture of the early twentieth century. The burgers at Convention Grill stand up to the image, and the whole package makes for a

genuine, throwback hamburger experience.

The Convention Grill opened in 1934, built by a diner fabrication company that had planned to start a chain. When the company struggled, a Greek immigrant named Peter Santrizos took the Edina location off the company's hands for paltry $75. Peter ran Convention Grill until Twin Cities restaurateur John Rimarcik came along in 1974 and bought the iconic burger counter from Peter. John, at the age of 34, already the owner of several area restaurants, saw amazing potential in the Convention. He also knew that by changing any-

thing he would destroy the ethos of the place. John has worked in the restaurant business since he was 12 years old, loves hamburgers, and clearly also has a soft spot for the classic American diner.

The only major change visible at the 76-year-old diner is the expansion to the dining room. In the late '80s, and again in the early '90s, John purchased the neighboring beauty salon and barbershop, greatly increasing his seating capacity. The additions lack the genuine feel of the original section of the diner but most regulars don't seem to care.

The burgers are cooked on a flattop in plain view of anyone seated at the curved counter. The Convention Grill uses fresh ground 80/20 Angus beef that is hand-pattied daily to around a quarter-pound. The burgers are basic because John believes that when you stray from the simplicity of an all-American burger you end up with, as he put it, "Something else." Stick with the cheeseburger and you can't go wrong. The Convention offers Swiss, American, Muenster, and an amazing smoky cheddar cheese and standard condiments like tomato, lettuce, and bacon.

There's a very curious burger on the menu at the Convention that I had been warned about—the "Plazaburger," served on a dark bun with a dollop of sour cream, chives, and chopped onions. In all my travels I had indeed come across the actual Plazaburger at the Plaza Tavern in Madison, Wisconsin, and right there on the menu, the Convention was giving credit to this University of Wisconsin staple. "It was suggested to me years ago by a regular named Dudley Riggs," John explained. Dudley told John that he ought to have the burger on the menu. "It sounded despicable," John told me, "but I put it on there out of respect for him and it became our biggest seller." Years later, John went to the actual Plaza Tavern to try the burger that made it to his menu. "Theirs was the furthest thing from what had been described to me, and ours was better." Thanks to a healthy dose of the telephone game the two burgers have very little in common. I know how tight-lipped Plaza Tavern owner Dean Hetue is about the recipe for his secret sauce and was actually happy to find that the code had not been cracked.

A large chunk of the menu at the Convention Grill is dedicated to ice cream and drinks. Indulge in a malted milk, the Convention's vernacular for a milkshake. They come ridiculously thick and with the steel cup it was mixed in. Or get a phosphate, the old-time terminology for soda water with flavors mixed in. The Convention offers cherry and lime phosphates, and they are pleasantly refreshing.

We should all be glad a guy like John Rimarcik owns the Convention Grill. He told me, in complete seriousness, "I love hamburgers and we take pride in serving them here." John explained that the name of the restaurant came from a "meeting place" or "a place for people to get together and have fun." Considering the Convention Grill's legacy its meaning is probably even deeper today.

★ ★ ★ ★ ★

GORDY'S HI-HAT

411 SUNNYSIDE DR I CLOQUET, MN 55720

218-879-6125 I WWW.GORDYS-HIHAT.COM

OPEN MID-MARCH TO MID-SEPTEMBER

OPEN DAILY 10 AM–8:30 PM

"We are the real deal drive-in," Gordy's owner Dan Lunquist said with confidence. "You won't find burgers with fancy stuff on them here." And you won't, because nothing has

Gordy and Marilyn

changed since what Dan's father Gordy refers to as the "good old days"—fifty-some years ago when the drive-in first opened. "Consistency is the key," Dan told me, and he was serious. Pretty much, the burger you ate there years ago will be no different than the one you'll get today.

Gordy's is a destination burger stand. "Forty percent of our business comes from people from Minneapolis stopping on the way to their lake cabins," Dan explained. Gordy's is just off I-35, the main artery connecting the Twin Cities to Duluth. "They get in a pattern of stopping here." And they do. During the six warm months that Gordy's is open, the restaurant will serve up to 2,000 burgers a day. That's pretty

impressive for a place that's not in or near a major metropolis.

The most popular burger at Gordy's is the double cheeseburger. Ask for everything, and you'll get a burger with pickles, ketchup, mustard, and raw or grilled onion. Other condiments are available like tomato, bacon, and lettuce but you really need to follow history and appreciate the simplicity of this amazing burger. My wife, Casey, pointed out that she had never seen a better-constructed hamburger. Somehow this burger, even though it was soft, tasty, and loaded with cheese and more managed to not drip or fall apart before you finished. A perfect package of beefy goodness.

The fresh ground beef comes from a supplier

in Minneapolis and is hand-pattied daily using an ice cream scoop for sizing. Dan told me that they wear out the flattop griddle every 7 years.

Today, Gordy's is owned by Dan but his parents, both in their eighties, still come up from Florida to spend the summer working at the drive-in. When I was there (during a busy early dinner rush), Gordy was sweeping up with a broom and dustpan and Marilyn was at her post in the kitchen warming and prepping buns at a griddle. "I've been doing this 58 years," Marilyn said with a smile as she gave multiple buns a squirt of ketchup without looking. "58 years!"

The kitchen is alive with energy and dozens of employees (a lot of them Lundquists). During a rush, the kitchen kicks into high gear, working like a well-oiled machine. Everyone has a task and repeats that task over and over again as the orders come pouring in. Marilyn is the point person, calling out orders from tickets as they are handed to her, all the while toasting and prepping buns. It's truly mesmerizing.

Before there was the Hi-Hat, Gordy and Marilyn Lundquist opened the first A&W Root Beer stand in Minnesota in 1950, and after that the wildly popular London Inn of Duluth in 1955. In the '40s Gordy did some research out in California and came across a little-known burger stand called McDonald's Famous Hamburgers. He liked what he saw and immediately hatched a plan to replicate the stand in his home state of Minnesota. The London Inn became the spot to go in Duluth in the mid-fifties and Gordy told

me, "It was a riot. I think we had every student from University of Minnesota–Duluth, every day!" Dan added, "My father used to always say, 'If I had a nickel for every time someone burned rubber in the parking lot, I'd be a rich man.'" Gordy and Marilyn sold the London Inn in 1960 because, as Gordy put it, "Someone offered us too much money to stay." They decided to move 20 miles west to the village of Cloquet to raise a family and set down permanent roots. Soon thereafter, Gordy's was born.

Gordy's has expanded many times over the years and started as a tiny box with a walk-up window to order from. Today, the kitchen area is still where it was half a century ago, but many rooms have been added, bringing the seating capacity to over 100 inside and out. The efficient ordering system and enormous staff is all geared toward getting you a hot hamburger as fast as possible. This is the unwavering, 50-year-old mission at Gordy's. Dan left me with these words: "We don't do anything magical. We just keep it simple and don't screw it up."

MATT'S BAR

3500 CEDAR AVE SOUTH | MINNEAPOLIS, MN 55407

612-722-7072 | WWW.MATTSBAR.COM

MON–WED 11 AM–MIDNIGHT

THU–SAT 11AM–1 AM | SUN NOON–MIDNIGHT

"We had a bad Sunday," waitress Devon told me on my first visit. Before I realized what she was talking about, I assumed that things were slow at this South Minneapolis bar. Devon pointed out that the bad Sunday was attributed to the large number of "Jucy Lucys" that had exploded on the griddle that day. If one explodes, the grill cook starts over. There's no way to mend a broken Lucy.

If you have no connection to or have never visited the Twin Cities then there's a good chance you have never met the beloved Jucy Lucy. The famed burger concoction can be found all over Minneapolis, but the epicenter of the Jucy Lucy legacy is a small, friendly, stuck-in-a-time-warp bar on the south side of town. In 1954, then owner Matt cooked up the first Jucy Lucy for a customer sitting at the bar who asked for "something special." The result was two fresh quarter-pound patties crimped together with a folded slice of American cheese hiding inside. What happened next was pure science.

Over 50 years have passed and the burger recipe remains unchanged. The burger is griddled and closely monitored (much like a science project), delicately flipped, then pinpricked to prevent it from exploding. As it nears doneness, it resembles a large clam wobbling on the griddle.

The delivery of the burger to your table always comes with a warning. Bartender of 18 years Margaret Lidstone said to me sternly, "You will burn your mouth off if you bite into it too soon. Let it sit." The phrase FEAR THE CHEESE printed on the waitstaff's shirts was warning enough. I tried to wait, but became a victim instantly. The molten goo was HOT, really hot, and kept the burger moist all the way through. Everyone who ordered the Jucy Lucy got the same stern speech. "I know," a regular responded, "not my first time." A woman sitting at the next table had no problem saying to me, "You're doing it all wrong. Just nibble at it, take small bites while it cools down."

The Jucy Lucy comes on waxed paper—

no plate, no utensils. Onions, fried or raw, are optional and pickles are standard. No tomato, no lettuce. Coke? Sure, no ice. Diet Coke? No lemon. Matt's is bare-bones dining at its very best.

The griddle is positioned behind the bar in full view. The grill cook told me, "We can sell up to 500 on a good day." The staff, and whoever is available, spend hours a day pinching and stuffing Jucy Lucys. "It's endless," said Margaret, and opened a low bar fridge to reveal hundreds of prebuilt Jucys ready for their turn on the grill that day.

The only menu is the one on the wall behind the bar and it has not changed in over five decades (with the exception of the prices, of course). It's on this menu that the "Jucy Lucy" is misspelled. "I think it was a mistake that just stuck," Margaret told me.

Matt Bristol worked at the bar, then named Mr. Nibb's, before purchasing the quiet corner tavern in 1954 and changing the name to his own. Scott Nelson bought the bar from Matt's daughter in 1998 and changed nothing. Even the crazy '50s wallpaper (which can be viewed on the tavern's website) remains. "It's quite tacky, actually," Scott explained, "but people don't want change." In a time when so many restaurants, and even bars, all look the same from city to city because of franchising, Scott believes that there is a place for Matt's. "Everything looks like a chain. We don't."

Matt's commitment to hamburgers starts with a concept that has its roots in the 1950s,

and the simple menu is a testament to the fact that great burgers are immune to fads. Scott said it best when he pointed out, "Burgers and fries don't go out of style, and neither do we."

★　★　★　★　★

THE 5-8 CLUB

5800 CEDAR AVE SOUTH
MINNEAPOLIS, MN 55417
612-823-5858 | WWW.5-8CLUB.COM
MON–WED 11AM–11 PM
THU–SUN 11 AM–12 AM

"5-8" was the address for this former speakeasy in south Minneapolis on the corner of 58th and Cedar Avenue. In 1928 when it opened illegally, it was a small stucco house out in the country where the owners had constructed a secret underground garage to make smuggling booze easier.

Today the 5-8 is a crossroads restaurant that is no longer rural. The dirt road that ran beside the building is now a highway, and the end of the runway for the Twin Cities airport is only half a mile away. It is not uncommon to get a close-up view of the belly of a Northwest jumbo jet as you walk from your car to the restaurant.

The 5-8 is home to the "Juicy Lucy," the same cheese-stuffed burger concoction made famous by Matt's just up Cedar Avenue, though Matt's spells theirs "Jucy Lucy." Regulars and waitstaff were reluctant to talk about the origins of south Minneapolis' favorite burger. "Oh, I don't know," said one regular, "they both make pretty good Lucys." The only person willing to talk was the kitchen manager at the time, coincidentally named Matt. He was still pretty vague saying, "It's always been a thing between here and Matt's on who invented it."

Regardless, the 5-8 makes a great "upscale" Juicy Lucy, because there's a twist to the recipe—you can order one stuffed with classic American cheese, Swiss, pepper Jack, or blue cheese. Matt told me, "People love them—we sell tons." As a burger hits the grill, it is marked with a colored fuzzy-tipped sandwich toothpick to identify its corresponding molten cheese core. Yellow for Swiss, blue for blue cheese . . . you get the idea. Has Matt ever gotten them mixed up? "Never." That's pretty impressive for cranking out over 300 Juicy Lucys a day for the large sit-down lunch and dinner crowd. All of the Juicy Lucys are made from fresh-ground Angus chuck. Two large patties are pinched together and stuffed in-house daily. The buns seem too large to fit in your mouth but are superlight, locally made, and fresh.

In a nod to Matt's Bar's T-shirts (which ask you to "Fear the Cheese") the 5-8 sells tees that ask you to "Free the Cheese." It's recommended that you wait to eat your burger after it shows up in the basket at your table. The hot cheese interior will burn your mouth if you are impatient. I made the mistake of cutting mine in half to let it cool; I was left with a cheese-goo mess.

Don't do what I did and enter the 5-8 through the welcoming front door, complete with a lawn, low hedges, and a flag. True to its speakeasy heritage, the back door is the way to enter. And don't be put off by its clinical looking rear entrance—behind the door is a comfortable dining room with a large outdoor patio.

The 5-8 may be known for its burgers but don't miss out on its long list of comfort food like jojo potatoes, pork tenderloin sandwiches, and the Midwest's own fried cheese curds. And if you order a drink with that, the 5-8 guarantees "free refills 'till you float." I don't think this applies to beer, though.

19

MISSISSIPPI

BILL'S HAMBURGERS

310 NORTH MAIN ST I AMORY, MS 38821

662-256-2085 I SUN–FRI 7:30 AM–5:30 PM

SAT 7 AM–5 PM I BAR OPEN TILL MIDNIGHT

The drive to Amory is quintessential backcountry Deep South—miles of two-lane roads lined with cotton fields, cotton gins, and, when I visited, lots of loose cotton all over the road. Amory is a small town and Bill's is a small restaurant at a spot where Main Street bends. Locals affectionately refer to this spot as "Vinegar Bend."

Bill's has twenty-three stools and about two tables, so chances are you'll probably be sitting at the counter. Nothing fancy here—in keeping with tradition, burgers are still served at your spot at the counter on waxed paper.

Before it was Bill's, it was Bob's. In 1929 Bob Hill borrowed $48 from a local baker named James Toney to open a hamburger restaurant. A stipulation of the deal was that Bob had to buy all of his hamburger buns from Toney's bakery.

One year after opening, Bob hired Bill Tubb to help slice and prep buns with the only two condiments available in the '20s at Bob's—mustard and onion. World War II meat rationing forced Bob's to close, but after the war Bob reopened and later sold the business to Bill in 1955. Naturally, Bill changed the name to his own, then turned around and sold it in 1957 to another Bill, who then rehired Bill to work there. After a string of Bill's relatives owned and operated the small burger stand, Bill's was sold to the current owners, Reid and Janice Wilkerson.

"I grew up eating here. It was such a big part of my childhood. When it came up for sale, I had to buy it," Reid told me as he emerged from the back room of the restaurant. He grinds fresh beef there every day for the burgers as it has been done since 1929. Another tradition Reid and Janice adhere to—mustard and onion only— also dates back to the beginning. "Not much has changed here, except that the burgers got bigger," grill girl Amy told me. Toney's bakery closed in 1970, which led Bill's to start using standard four-inch buns. The new burger size was determined by the size of the buns.

The burgers start as quarter-pound balls of beef that are pressed onto a well-seasoned flattop griddle. The burgers at Bill's are unbelievably tasty, beefy, and rich with grease flavor. The mustard, onion, beef, and bun combination is

heaven. Cheese is unnecessary, though available, but tomato and lettuce are nowhere to be found. If you really need ketchup or mayo, Amy hides packets behind the counter. "They're really only for takeout orders."

Ever had a burger for breakfast? Bill's opens at 7:30 most mornings and does not serve eggs or bacon. "We serve burgers all day. People do come in here first thing and order burgers, especially the third shift at the local factories," Amy told me as I polished off my double.

On the front of the restaurant is a large painted portrait of the beloved former employee Junior Manasco, a gently disabled fixture at Bill's for over 20 years starting in 1977. On a wall opposite the counter is a framed resolution from the State of Mississippi presented to Junior "for his service to his community." Reid recalled, "He knew and greeted everyone that came in the door."

As I was leaving an old-timer at the counter told me, "The first time I came here the burgers were 25 cents." When I pressed for just how long ago that was he said, "A long time ago."

PHILLIPS GROCERY

541 EAST VAN DORN AVE

HOLLY SPRINGS, MS 38634

662-252-4671 | MON–FRI 10 AM–4 PM

SAT 10 AM–6 PM | CLOSED SUNDAY

Downtown Holly Springs, Mississippi, looks like it may have looked 70 years ago. American flags and freshly painted turn-of-the-century storefronts line the streets. Phillip's Grocery is not here though.

Phillip's is down the road by the train tracks across from a semi-restored 150-year-old ornate train depot, and the area looks a lot like William Eggleston's photography of the South—gritty and real. I got lost trying to find this burger destination, and you will too.

Phillips serves one of the best burgers in America. Not just because I said so; their burgers have been the subject of many journalistic accolades, including being awarded, "Best Burger In America" twice by *USA Today*.

The restaurant was first established as Phillips Grocery in 1948 when the Phillips family bought an existing grocery that sold hamburgers. Current owner Larry Davis told me, "The burger's been made here since the '30s." Mrs. Phillips had planned to do away with the burger when they bought the store, but changed her tune when she saw how many they were selling. "She put her kids through college with burger money."

Their success is no accident. The secret lies in the mixture of ground beef and other "secret" ingredients. Adding breading to ground beef was popular in the South during the Depression, and I suspect the burger at Phillips may be a vestige of this lost art. I arrived at Phillips before it opened and interrupted Larry's morning ritual of making the ground beef mixture for the day's burgers. He actually disappeared behind a closed door and reappeared a few minutes later with rubber gloves and large stainless mixing bowls filled with ground beef. "It's the same recipe since the '30s," Larry said of the secret recipe he purchased with the store in 1989. "I do this every day, sometimes 40 to 50 pounds on Saturdays."

A burger at Phillips can be ordered as a single one-third pound patty, a double with two quarter-pound patties, or a deluxe half-pound patty. That sounds confusing, but not to the kitchen staff who electronically weigh and portion each ball of ground beef. The balls are pressed on a well-seasoned flattop griddle and served on white buns with only mustard, pickle, and onion. Mayo, ketchup, cheese, and bacon are offered (but unnecessary). The burger is so tasty as is you could eat it with only a bun and emerge contented.

Phillips no longer sells groceries. The business shifted in the '50s when supermarkets killed the corner store. The décor is pure country store kitsch today—Coke advertising from every decade is represented, as well as old grocer's scales, saws, and a vintage John Deere bicycle dangling from the ceiling.

You can sit at one of the random tables offered or find an old school desk to enjoy your burger and one of Larry's homemade fried pies. Look out the window of this 120-year-old building toward the train crossing and savor the sounds of locomotive whistles and the clanking of the active Mississippi Central Railroad rumbling by.

MISSOURI

TOWN TOPIC

2021 BROADWAY ST | KANSAS CITY, MO 64108

816-842-2298 | OPEN DAILY, 24/7

Most people might drive by Town Topic and see a cute old hamburger stand, an icon of the past, or a relic in a rundown neighborhood. Not me. The people who know better see a vibrant keeper of the flame, a lesson to learn from, and a restaurant that knows its place in history. I couldn't drive by anyhow. Every time I try, I need to stop for a burger.

There are three Town Topics left in Kansas City where there once were seven. Today, only the Broadway location, also known as #3, is open 24 hours. At one point all of the Town Topics were open 24/7, as were many other ten-stool mid-century hamburger joints across America.

When I approached the Town Topic for an interview for this book, I had already been there a few times. The night I chose to visit I hit the jackpot—Bonnie Gooch was at the grill. Bonnie should be defined as a hard-boiled sweetheart. She's just what you'd want from a short-order lifer—a woman who takes no crap but takes care of the regulars. "See that guy down there?" she said to me, pointing down the counter to an older man. "He's been like a daddy to me. I've known him since the day I started so I try to take care of him." With that she slid an unordered slice of lettuce onto his burger and sent it off.

Bonnie started working at the little burger counter in 1965 when she was 13. For the next 23 years she worked the night shift alongside her husband Richard. When he passed away, she switched to the early evening shift. To date she has put in 40 years at the Town Topic. Needless to say, she knows how to make a great hamburger.

The burger at Town Topic is a classic thin patty. Small one-eighth-pound wads of fresh ground 80/20 beef are delivered to the restaurant daily. Bonnie presses the meat thin on the hot, well-seasoned griddle and drops a small handful of shredded onions on the patty. Not unlike the fried onion burgers of El Reno, Oklahoma, these onions are then pressed into the patty as it sizzles on the grill. The result is a tasty combination of griddled beef and caramelized onions.

"Ninety-nine percent order their burgers with onions," Bonnie told me as she built my double cheeseburger, the most popular burger on the menu. It comes with pickles on a white squishy bun and resembles a burger Popeye's Wimpy might have eaten—a classic American burger. Bonnie imparts to each burger a sort of nonchalant perfection that is reserved for those who have made short order burgers for decades.

Fortunately, those of us who understand the significance of a counter like Town Topic need not worry about its future. "The city tried to turn this place into a parking lot," Bonnie's counter partner Keisha told me, but a grandfather clause spared the restaurant based on its age. "Some people have been coming in here since they were kids," Bonnie reflected during a lull at the grill. "They just love the place."

WHEEL INN DRIVE-IN

2103 SOUTH LIMIT AVE | SEDALIA, MO 65301

660-826-5177 | OPEN DAILY 10 AM–10 PM

Just before the first edition of this book came out I received some really bad news. A friend had called to say that the 60-year-old burger icon Wheel In Drive-In was closing. The drive-in was featured in my film *Hamburger America* and seemed, at the time, to be invincible.

The vintage diner sat on the busiest corner in Sedalia, Missouri and expansion of the road was going to cut the parking lot in half. "They are putting in a turning lane that will come right up to the window," former owner John Brandkamp told me. And as you can imagine, it'd be kinda hard to run a drive-in with no parking lot. John had the option to move and start over, but he opted to throw in the towel. With the closing of the restaurant, we all said good-bye to the famous peanut-butter-covered "Guberburger."

But at the last moment someone stepped in to save the Wheel Inn. Longtime employee Judy Clark offered to move the business down the street and reopen in a defunct video store, and the plan worked. It took 2 months, but moving items piece by piece, Judy and her sisters managed to resurrect the Wheel Inn. The horseshoe counter and the stools made the trip, and even the big wooden wagon wheel that used to sit in the center of the drive-in made it. Judy literally saved the Wheel.

Judy started at the Wheel Inn when she was 14 years old. "I've worked here on and off all my life," she told me. The Keuper family opened and ran the drive-in from 1947 until they leased the business to John Brandkamp in the 1980s. John had worked his way up from washing dishes and was at the Wheel Inn for an astounding 47 years. I guess we can't really blame him for wanting to retire.

The key to the success of the Wheel Inn may be a burger that they've had on the menu forever. The Guberburger starts as a portioned wad of fresh-ground chuck that is scooped into balls daily. The beef balls are pressed thin on the flat-top and when the patty is flipped a spoonful of warmed, creamy peanut butter is ladled on top. In theory it sounds disgusting but in reality the burger is perfect. The Wheel Inn offers lettuce, tomato, and mayo on a Guberburger but I like mine plain with extra "guber." The peanut butter works so well with the burger grease that it actually adds to the complexity of the beefy profile.

Think beef satay and you get the picture. Southeast Asian countries have been putting peanut butter on beef since the 1800s.

Carhop service is long gone at the new Wheel Inn but the place is a lot larger. "We have booths and tables now," Judy told me. And the original rotating neon Wheel Inn sign is still showing people the way to Guberburgers, but at a location just down the road from where the old one was demolished. The new location is directly across the street from the Missouri State Fairgrounds, and the Wheel Inn stays busy all summer long. Judy was afraid that with the move they'd lose customers. "It's actually better than we expected," she says. "People have found us."

Most of Judy's sisters work with her at the Wheel Inn as they did at the old location. And the Guberburger is back and safe in the hands of a woman that cared enough to save this drive-in. You could say that it's business as usual, except that Judy told me quietly, "They say ours are better."

WINSTEAD'S

101 EMANUEL CLEAVER II BLVD

KANSAS CITY, MO 64112

816-753-2244 I WWW.WINSTEADSKC.COM

MON–SAT 11 AM–8:30 PM I CLOSED SUNDAY

In the hearts of many Kansas City natives Winstead's is the only place in the world that serves great hamburgers. Even Kansas City's own Calvin Trillin, food writer and journalist, once said jokingly about Winstead's, "Anyone who doesn't think his hometown has the best hamburger place in the world is a sissy." More than three decades have passed since Trillin made that statement and almost nothing has changed—Winstead's still serves one of the best burgers in America.

Gone are the carhops, replaced by a drive-thru in 1989. On my first visit to the vintage time-warp diner I was led to longtime employee Judy Eddingfield. Judy started working at Winstead's when she was only 16 years old, over 45 years ago. "When I was just a kid my father would take me here for a strawberry shake and a single burger," she told me. Over the decades her mother, brothers, sisters, and aunts would all work at Winstead's in some capacity.

I asked Judy how she was on skates as a carhop and she quickly pointed out, "No, no. There were no skates back then. Winstead's opened in 1940, which predates skates." True, carhops on skates were a fad and gimmick for some drive-ins of the 1950s. Winstead's main-tained carhops for 50 years until the popular drive-thru was installed.

Today there are ten Winstead's restaurants in the Kansas City area but the mini-chain was actually started in Springfield, Illinois by sisters Katherine and Nellie Winstead. Their first location in Kansas City, located adjacent to the Midwest shopping mecca Country Club Plaza, remains the flagship restaurant in the chain.

The physical structure of Winstead's is a stunning, well-preserved example of mid-century restaurant architecture. The entire building is sheathed in pastel pink, and yellow, glazed enamel brick. The dining room is large and seats 280 comfortably. The wide, clean, open space is a sea of well-laid-out booths sitting beneath enormous hot pink neon-rimmed ceiling light fixtures. On one of my visits, an entire elementary school (close to 75 kids) had comfortably taken over the restaurant for an early lunch and there was still plenty of room for regulars.

The menu at Winstead's is split—one half lists food items, the other shakes, malts, and drinks, reminding one and all that ice cream is just as important as burgers to drive-in clientele. Winstead's has built its reputation on the "Steakburger," which served with "everything" includes a toasted white bun, a fresh-ground two-ounce patty, pickles, a very large slice of onion, and a "secret sauce" that is really just a mixture of mustard and ketchup. Make it a double and add cheese and you have a meal.

Bobby Chumley spends his entire morning at a patty maker in the restaurant's basement making hundreds of the day's burger patties. I met him as he emerged at noon one day to be greeted with a high five from the manager. The burgers are smashed thin and cooked on a flat-top griddle. The result is a moist, loose burger with a salty, crunchy exterior. Order a limeade and fries with your Steakburger to round out the perfect diner eating experience.

Winstead's today does a brisk business and employs over eighty people at the Country Club Plaza location. Judy told me as I took a sip from my ice-cold Mr. Pibb, "There are still a handful of us that have been working here for over 30 years." Now that's commitment to making and serving great burgers.

★ **21** ★

MONTANA

MATT'S PLACE DRIVE-IN

2339 PLACER ST | BUTTE, MT 59701

406-782-8049 | TUE–SAT 11:30 AM–6:50 PM

Matt's Place is a drive-in on the edge of the boom-bust Old West mining town of Butte, Montana. As you approach the hillside town on I-90, you'll notice first the abandoned copper mining equipment and the brick buildings of a somewhat underpopulated downtown. The streets of Butte are lined with vintage neon signage that reflects its colorful past—Irish pubs and Chinese restaurants among many others that existed to enter-

tain and feed the large number of immigrant mine workers.

Matt's Place opened in 1930 during the peak of copper mining in Butte. Through it all, Matt's has survived, so much so that it can proudly boast that it has a spot on the National Register of Historic Places. Recognized as historically important for its contribution to early American road culture, Matt's also serves amazing, fresh-beef burgers and milkshakes made from homemade ice cream. I visited Matt's for all of these reasons, but mostly to sample their fabled "Nutburger."

Of the thousands of burgers I have eaten across America, few piqued my interest like the

Nutburger. Maybe it was the remote, beautiful, Western locale, or the fact that Matt's has been in existence for over 70 years, but it was the description of the Nutburger that had me planning a trip almost immediately.

In 1930, after a visit to Southern California, Matt Korn returned home and opened a small drive-up burger stand only a few feet from a busy railroad right-of-way. After a few years of hanging trays on car doors, Matt built a structure 25 feet away that would serve as a drive-in, a counter with 16 stools, and living quarters upstairs for him and his new wife, Betty. That structure still stands today, a vestige of car culture stuck in time that was placed on the National Register in 2002.

Today, nonagenarian Mabel Laurence, only the second owner in the burger counter's long history, owns Matt's. Mabel started at Matt's in 1936 as a carhop, and in 1943 she and her husband bought the restaurant. Many people from "Mae's" family have worked at the vintage burger counter and for the last 25 years Matt's has been run by Laurence family member Brad Cockhill. Brad is proud of his family's heritage and committed to quality burgers.

Matt's is split in two; one half is a horseshoe counter, the other an efficient short-order kitchen. A server works the counter while Brad flips patties at the freestanding griddle in the kitchen. "This is the original cast-iron griddle from the 1930s," Brad told me. "There's nothing

The Nutburger

like cast-iron." He's right. Very few burger restaurants in America cook on vintage cast-iron because they are impossible to find.

Brad uses an ice cream scoop to make balls out of the fresh, lean ground round. When I asked Brad about the size of the burgers, he shrugged and showed me the scoop. "They're this big. We should probably have better portion control, but we don't." Brad believes the burgers are around a quarter pound each.

The most popular burger at Matt's is the double cheeseburger deluxe, which comes with mustard, pickle, onion, lettuce, and tomato. But do yourself a favor and indulge in a Nutburger.

"We don't really sell many Nutburgers anymore," former employee Paula told me. "Maybe six a day?" Just then the phone rang and in came an order for two Nutburgers.

The counterperson spoons chopped salted peanuts from the sundae bar into a coffee mug and adds Miracle Whip. It's that simple. The texture of the nuts and the creamy sweetness of the Miracle Whip synthesize perfectly with the salty, greasy meatiness of the burger. Standard condiments are available to dress up the Nutburger, but why mess with the simplicity? I understand if you are a little squeamish at the concept, but after your first bite, you'll be a convert.

The interior of Matt's is worth the price of admission alone. Grab a seat at the small horseshoe counter and take in the décor. You'll be hard pressed to find a single fixture not dating back to the 1950s. Everything, from the knotty pine walls to the Coke dispenser, is original. Even the cash register dates back to simpler times—it only goes up to $5, so they have to ring up big orders $5 at a time.

A carhop at Matt's will still take your order from your car if you drive up and toot your horn. "We'll still go out and hang a tray on a window," Brad told me as he dumped out a basket of fresh-cut fries. Imagine that. A functioning drive-in where you can pull up and order a fresh-beef Nutburger with a side of nostalgia. Can it get any better than that?

THE MISSOULA CLUB

139 WEST MAIN ST | MISSOULA, MT 59802

406-728-3740

OPEN DAILY 8 AM–2 AM (GRILL CLOSES AT 1AM)

The Missoula Club is not the only bar in town. In fact, there are more great bars and vintage neon signage in this western Montana town than I've ever seen in such close proximity to one another. Having 10,000 students at nearby University of Montana probably helps, but the Missoula Club is a local institution that has been serving beer and burgers to students and regulars, some believe, since 1903.

If you were expecting a cozy, dark pub, you'll be shocked by the Missoula Club's first impression. During the day, the "Mo Club" (as it's affectionately known) looks like any well-worn watering hole, but at night the daylight seems to linger. Thanks to super-bright bluish overhead fluorescent lighting, the place is lit up like an operating room in the midst of triple bypass surgery. There's no hiding at the Mo Club, and the lighting allows one to observe every detail of the bar. The lighting also seems to make patrons overly sociable, so expect to be involved in a random conversation with a stranger almost immediately. The first time I visited the famous burger and beer destination, I walked in with my friend Greg Ennis and we were greeted by a group of rugby players and a boisterous "Hello, LADIES!" It's a rowdy, drinker's bar that serves great burgers. You have been warned.

The burger at the Mo Club is legendary. "The hamburger is the best thing on the menu!" employee Jim Kelly told me. Of course the joke is that the hamburger is the only thing on the menu, aside from chips and milkshakes.

Tell the bartender what kind of burger you want. The choices are single, double, or the absurd triple known as the "Griz" (named after the

University of Montana's sports teams, the Grizzlies). American, Swiss, "white," horseradish, and hot pepper cheeses are available and the burger is served with a slice of raw onion and a pickle. The preferred burger at the Mo Club is the double with hot pepper cheese, a tasty pepper jack that doesn't really melt, but softens on the burger. Add some of the Mo Club's signature hot mustard and you'll be in burger heaven. As my friend Greg, a Montana native, squirted copious amounts of the fiery mustard onto his double cheeseburger, grillman Tyler warned, "Whoa, have you had this mustard before?" Greg just laughed and said, "Oh yeah, the hotter the better!"

Soft white buns are toasted on the tiny electric bar griddle alongside the burgers. I asked Tyler if the buns were buttered and he told me, "No, but the burger grease might work its way over there."

The burgers at the Mo Club are hand-pattied from unmeasured scoops of ground beef. The beef comes in fresh daily from the same butcher they have been using forever. One time while I was at the Mo Club, a man rushed in and dropped two enormous white paper-wrapped wads of fresh meat on the bar right next to me. They had run low and needed to augment the meat supply before the night crowd showed up hungry.

"Our burgers are over a third of a pound each," owner Mark Laslovich said of the large, juicy patties. Mark also revealed that the amazing tasting burger has chopped onions mixed into the raw meat before they are pattied. Mark has owned the century-old bar since 2000, but has worked there at some capacity for over 45 years. One of the recent changes Mark made at the Mo Club was installing a larger griddle. Well, not too much larger. "This one's a burger wider than the old one," Mark said of the tiny two-foot-wide griddle.

Expect to find all types enjoying burgers and beer at the Mo Club. "We get lawyers, doctors, bums, whatever," Mark pointed out. There is an old-school sports bar feel to the place, but not the kind that hangs gaudy memorabilia on every usable inch of wall space. The Mo Club's walls are blanketed with decades of UM team photos up to the high ceiling, as well as signed sports portraits of Missoula natives who went on to professional fame elsewhere in America.

As bars go, the Mo Club is a clean one. "It wasn't always this clean," Mark told me. "When I took over, this place was a mess." I asked Mark why the lighting was more conducive to a well-lit truck stop than a cozy Irish pub and he explained, "People come in here and look for themselves in these team photos." He and the other bartenders also believe it keeps people honest and the fights to a minimum. Mark told me that a group of women who frequent the bar once asked him to install a dimmer because they were getting older. His advice: "Have another beer."

22

NEBRASKA

STELLA'S HAMBURGERS

106 GALVIN RD SOUTH | BELLEVUE, NE 68005

402-291-6088 | MON–SAT 11 AM–9 PM

CLOSED SUNDAY

Stella's is not a fancy place. If you are looking for tablecloths and silverware— go elsewhere. If you are in search of a burger fix and don't mind eating off a napkin, you've come to the right place.

When I first found this burger outpost south of Omaha it was a ramshackle place on a hill surrounded by a dusty gravel parking lot. You could barely make out the name of the restaurant haphazardly spelled out in vinyl lettering on the front window. Today, the dirt lot is now paved and the entire restaurant has received a much needed facelift. In 2007 Stella's son, Al, and his wife, Mary, sold the decades-old restaurant to cousin Stephanie Francois. The restaurant is now run by Stephanie with the help of her parents Gene and Pam Francois. Stella's

Hamburgers remains a family business after all these years.

Tiny Stella Francois Sullivan Tobler opened the sunroom at the front of her home to burger lovers in 1936. Within a few years, her home had morphed into a restaurant with a gas station and a general store. She purchased the bar next door and in 1949 purchased a plot of land a mile away and moved both the house and bar. The bar became the restaurant, and the house and sunroom went back to being a home, and since then nothing much has changed. Look for the portrait of Stella hanging near the bar with the inscription OUR FOUNDER.

The burgers have increased in size since Stella's time from 5.2 to 6.5 ounces. Fresh ground beef is delivered to the restaurant, portioned, and made into patties daily. Frozen patties are not an option at Stella's and as Gene pointed out, "We go through so much that it would be impossible for it not to be fresh."

The burger at Stella's is an explosion of grease and flavor. Stella's granddaughter, Lisa, told me once, "You don't come to Stella's because you are watching what you are eating." It's served on an impossibly soft white pillow of a bun with lettuce, tomato, pickles, and a choice of either grilled or raw onion. Both top and bottom halves of the bun receive a generous layer of mayonnaise, and the burger is delivered no-nonsense on a paper napkin. Stella believed that good food didn't need to be fancy.

The menu has changed slightly under the new ownership and a new burger "challenge" has been added called the "Stellanator." If you can finish this 6-patty burger that stands over a foot tall, you'll get your name on the "Wall of Fame" and eat for free. If you can't finish, you'll have to pay for your meal. "Over 40 have tried," Gene told me, "but only 2 have finished it so far."

Stella's son, Al, took over the restaurant in 1974, and Stella continued to come in daily. "She worked up to three days prior to her death," Lisa told me. Al still comes into the restaurant just like Stella did in her retirement.

Stella's today may look very different but rest assured the same cast-iron griddle and practices are in place. Gene put it best when he told me, "Stella made it simple to follow in her footsteps."

23

NEW HAMPSHIRE

GILLEY'S PM LUNCH

175 FLEET ST I PORTSMOUTH, NH 03801

603-431-6343 I WWW.GILLEYSPMLUNCH.COM

TUE–SUN 11:30 AM–2:30 AM I MON 11:30 AM–6 PM

"You can always tell that it's someone's first time here when they pull the door like that," short-order chef Bambi told me. I had trouble getting in the front door of this six-decade-old diner because the door is not normal. It slides open like a pocket door, revealing one of the most beautiful hidden gems in all of New England.

Gilley's PM Lunch is an old Worcester diner. In the first half of the twentieth century, the Worcester Lunch Car Company of Worcester, Massachusetts, was the premier supplier of mobile lunch carts and prefabricated diners. Their distinct design set the precedent for all diners that followed in America.

Gilley's is now permanently situated on a lot donated by the City of Portsmouth, but prior to 1973 the cart was towed out to the center of town and served food to late-night workers and other hungry people until the wee hours of the morning. There was a time in America, especially in New England, when carts like this were everywhere at night. Many of them were Worcester diners and very few exist today. Gilley's is one of the last.

Though slightly modified, Gilley's retains its barrel-shaped roof and enamel steel paneled interior, and its kitchen still occupies one narrow end of the car. It's a true step back in time with its tiny griddle and eight stools lining the wood-framed windows. New owner (as of 1993) Stephen Kennedy told me, "I had to take two stools out because it gets pretty crowded in here from 11 p.m. to 2 a.m." He says sometimes over 40 people are crammed into the tiny diner waiting for their hamburgers and hot dogs. During the late shift Gilley's can move over 500 burgers.

"Isn't that beautiful?" a customer said as he tilted his plate showing off his double cheeseburger. Both hamburgers and hot dogs are served at Gilley's; the hot dogs preceded the burgers by more than sixty years. Starting in 1912, the first owners had a horse-drawn cart with wooden wheels that sold mostly hot dogs. Hamburgers were introduced in the 1970s, and share equal popularity today.

The burger to order at Gilley's is a bacon double cheeseburger. Gilley's uses only fresh-ground pattied chuck loin that is 85 to 88 percent lean. The patties are small, thin, and just under 3 ounces. Stephen pointed out that it was done that way traditionally for speed, adding, "A smaller burger cooks faster." The white squishy bun is toasted and no lettuce or tomato is offered. The tiny fridge next to the minuscule two-foot-square griddle is really only big enough for the day's hot dogs, hamburgers, and cheese.

In 1996 Stephen attached a construction trailer to the original lunch car to expand the kitchen. This allowed him to add a deep fryer and more refrigeration. Adding a barrel roof to one end of the trailer mimicked the original structure and preserved the integrity of the restaurant. The last truck to pull the mobile diner is still attached to one end of Gilley's, as are the diner's wheels, now covered by wood paneling.

"Portsmouth is the kind of place where things don't change much," cook Bambi mused as I ate my burger. That's a good thing, especially when it involves a historically significant slice of Americana like Gilley's. Thanks to people like Stephen Kennedy this tiny lunch cart may be around forever.

24

NEW JERSEY

HOLIDAY SNACK BAR

401 CENTRE ST | BEACH HAVEN, NJ 08008

609-492-4544 | WWW.HOLIDAYSNACKBAR.COM

OPEN MEMORIAL DAY WEEKEND TO LABOR DAY

DAILY 11:30 AM–9 PM

The ocean is only three blocks from the Holiday Snack Bar and you can smell it in the salty air. But once you step inside the tiny, seasonal beach diner the smell shifts to burgers. If you arrive at the peak of summer, there's a good chance that all of the stools at the counter will be taken. All of these customers, fresh from the beach, will be eating either burgers or one of the Holiday's signature cakes or pies. High school-aged server Hunter told me, "At lunchtime in the summer this place is packed. There are people up against the wall waiting for a spot." Most likely this is because the burgers are fresh and the bakery is on the premises.

A large, four-sided knotty pine counter takes up just about all of the real estate in the dining area of the Holiday. In the center, proudly displayed, are homemade pies and cakes that all counter patrons are forced to stare at, making a meal without a slice an impossibility. The kitchen adjacent to the dining area is where most of the menu is produced but in one corner of the dining room sits a tiny 2-foot-square flattop griddle. There's even a stool at the counter that can't be more than 3 feet from the griddle, a great front-row seat for the burger-obsessed. "In August the griddle is jammed," owner Glenn Warfield told me. Glenn and his wife are only the third owners of this Jersey Shore landmark that was opened in 1948 by the Whiting family. Glenn bought the restaurant in the '80s and with the purchase gained the Holiday's famous recipes.

Glenn is adamant about preserving the history of the Holiday Snack Bar and is hesitant to change a single thing about the place. One curious phenomenon I noticed at the Holiday was a dual menu system. If you ask for a menu you are handed one whose contents, for the most part, date to 1948. It includes classics like onion rings and burgers but also a strange old-time favorite, the Tomato Aspic Salad. Glenn has added items to the menu but did not want to add them to the original so he posts these items on a separate menu on the counter. I asked him why he hasn't merged the menus and he told me, "We don't want to stir it up too much."

The classic "Holiday Hamburger" is not the burger to order at the Holiday Snack Bar. Ask for that and you'll end up with an unadorned three-ounce patty on a toasted white bun. Ask for the double cheeseburger and you are getting somewhere. The ratio of meat-to-cheese-to-bun for this burger is perfect. Be sure to add some house-made sweet pepper relish that sits on the counter in plastic tubs.

One item on Glenn's separate menu sells as well as the burgers from the original menu—the "Slam Burger." Lettuce, tomato, and a large onion ring are piled high on a single-patty cheeseburger. A homemade Russian dressing is added and the entire creation is held together with a large toothpick. As you can probably imagine, the additional ingredients dwarf the three-ounce patty so I would suggest a double Slam Burger.

The burgers at the Holiday are made from fresh ground 90/10 lean chuck steaks that are ground in the kitchen daily. After grinding, a team of two use an ancient manual patty press to make the burgers. It's easy to assume that this contraption pre-dates the electric patty press. I've never seen anything quite like it. A large canister holds 15 pounds of ground beef that is extruded through a hole in the bottom. One person hand-cranks the press while the other slides a plate back and forth on the bottom that has a cutout the size of the patty, effectively "slicing" off a perfect patty every time. Glenn is clearly in the market for a new, fully automated patty, press but I don't think he'll be getting one anytime soon. He told me, "We've paid mechanics to fix it." Glenn does not want to change a thing about the Holiday Snack Bar.

The Holiday is run almost entirely by high school and college kids and this is their summer job. When I asked Hunter if she sees orders for the Tomato Aspic Salad, she winced and said,

"Never." Then after a moment said, "The people who do order it go crazy for it. But most people come here for the burgers."

ROSSI'S BAR & GRILL

501 MORRIS AVE | TRENTON, NJ 08611

609-394-9089 | WWW.ROSSIBURGER.COM

MON–SAT 11 AM–2:30 PM, 5 PM–10 PM

CLOSED SUNDAY

"Now we'll see if he knows how to eat a Rossiburger!" Sharon Jemison, part owner and Rossi family member, was heckling me and warned, "If you cut it in half, you're a wuss." As I stared at the enormous, inch-thick burger, I did the smart thing—I put the knife down.

Most great burger joints have their share of multi-generational family pride, but few are as proud as Rossi's. Throw in an Italian-American pedigree and you have a recipe for a burger born of unrelenting pride.

In the early 1930s, Michael Alfred Rossi bought a corner soda fountain in the Italian neighborhood of Chambersburg in Trenton, New Jersey, and lived upstairs. When prohibition was repealed in 1933, Rossi promptly turned the fountain into a bar. "Back then," Sharon told me, "they just had a meatball sandwich [on the menu]." Rossi eventually expanded the menu to include other Italian fare

and made a dining room out of the family's living space. But it was Michael's son, Alfred Michael Rossi, who would bring their now-famous burger to the menu in the early 1960s.

Al Rossi had a promising career in professional baseball and played for the Washington Senators farm team for 11 years. Just as he was offered a spot on the Philadelphia Athletics roster, his brother shipped off to fight in World War II. Al's dad told him to leave baseball, come home, and help run the restaurant. In this family, that's just what you did.

Maybe if Al Rossi had continued on his path to be a major league ballplayer there would be no Rossiburger, a thought most would probably not like to entertain.

There's only one burger to order at Rossi's and it is very large and only comes in one size. "That's the million-dollar question, 'Can we get a smaller burger?'" Sharon told me, "Nope."

Don't be put off by the enormous mound of meat in front of you though. Despite its size, the burger at Rossi's is moist and loosely packed, its center almost pebbly. It's actually a breeze to eat, especially if you are hungry.

Rossi's gets a delivery of fresh-ground 87/13 chuck daily and can go through 250 pounds over the weekend. The burgers are unmeasured but are around a half pound. They are loosely hand-pattied by Rossi family member and head chef Ted and cooked by indirect heat in a steak broiler. Nothing is added, no salt, no pepper, and it's served on a freshly baked kaiser roll with

nothing but a slice of raw onion.

Just about everyone involved at Rossi's is family. Sharon explained, "When we run out of family, we pull in other people." Today, Rossi's is run by Al's children, Sharon and Michael. They have both been at Rossi's for almost 40 years. The Chambersburg neighborhood is also like one big family. At one point during my interview with her in front of the restaurant, Sharon stopped a passing car for some fact-checking on the history of Rossi's.

Thanks to his involvement with professional baseball, Al Rossi had an impressive roster of buddies. Joe DiMaggio was a frequent visitor, as were Mickey Mantle and Ted Williams. Joe D

didn't go to Rossi's for the burger though, he went to see his good friend Al and have a bowl of his lentil soup. The restaurant is filled with authentic baseball memorabilia and the bar evokes a time when baseball greats might have mingled freely with their fans. For years, a pair of Mickey Mantle's cleats that were given to Al hung in a corner of the dining room.

Al worked at Rossi's right up until the day before he died in 2007. "He loved it," Sharon recalled of her father, "People came here just to talk to him." Al was involved with the business his entire life and, according to Sharon, "He'd see a pasta dish go out that wasn't right and he'd send it back."

WHITE MANNA HAMBURGERS

358 RIVER RD | HACKENSACK, NJ 07601

201-342-0914 | MON–SAT 8:30 AM–9 PM

SUNDAY 10 AM–6 PM

White Manna is, beyond a doubt, one of the most historically important burger joints in America. As the burger business began widespread franchising in the 1960s, most of the tiny burger counters across America were wiped out. Amazingly, White Manna survives and thrives, even with a McDonalds directly across the street.

There was a time in America when the burgers you ate were small and came from a tiny stainless steel or white porcelain paneled diner. Thanks to the success of White Castle in America, most burger counters used the word "white" in their names to convey cleanliness. In the case of this diner, the biblical word "manna" is used, as in *bread from heaven*.

White Manna is a vintage Paramount diner that still proudly serves the early-century American classic "slider" burger. The diner is the descendant of the 1939 Worlds Fair "Diner of the Future" that was built to represent the future of fast food. The original White Manna was purchased by Louis Bridges and brought to Jersey City, where it remains today. Louis built four

other White Mannas around northern New Jersey, but only the Hackensack and Jersey City locations survive. Inside and out, the tiny diner remains true to its original design. The structure is sheathed in stainless steel, has vertical white porcelain panels beneath the windows, and includes Paramount Diner Company's signature use of glass block throughout.

The interior cannot be more than 130 square feet. Behind a small horseshoe counter surrounded by stools, a short-order cook takes one order after the next, never putting pen to paper. You sit patiently, taking in the thick oniony aroma, until the cook makes eye contact with you. When you place your order, the cook reaches into a pan below the counter, grabs golf ball–sized balls of meat, presses them onto the tiny griddle, and places a wad of thinly sliced onion on top. If you ask for a double, two of the small balls of beef get pressed together. The cook uses a right-to-left system on the griddle to keep track and miraculously keeps all of the orders straight. Similar to the original White Castle system, buns are placed atop the cooking burgers to soften and soak up the onion essence.

The sliders are served on soft potato rolls on a paper plate with a pile of pickle chips. If you order cheese, expect not a picture-perfect burger, but a glorious pile of tangled beef, onions, and cheese that is barely contained by its bun. The burgers at White Manna may not look pretty, but they sure are delicious. You'll need more than a few sliders to fill you up. Order doubles

to accomplish a better beef-to-bun ratio. Esteemed food writer and blogger Jason Perlow prefers to make a meal out of four doubles.

Ronny and Ofer Cohen bought White Manna in 1986 as a business venture, but were also seduced by its charm. "You just fall in love with this place," Ronny told me. They have changed very little about the White Manna, but admitted an attempt to add potato salad and coleslaw to the menu early on in their ownership. "People walk into White Manna to buy burgers." Ronny feels the crush of commercial fast food all around him in Hackensack, New Jersey. "The only way I can survive is to do things the old-fashioned way."

Before walking into White Manna, strip down to the least amount of clothing. Not because it's hot in there, but because after you leave, your clothes will be infused with the unmistakable fragrance of grease and onions. There'll be no hiding the fact that you just dined at the famous White Manna.

WHITE ROSE SYSTEM

1301 EAST ELIZABETH AVE | LINDEN, NJ 07036
908-486-9651 | MON–SAT 5 AM–3:30 PM

At one time in north Jersey the slider reigned supreme. As the homogenization of burger culture in America swept over the tri-state area, the tiny slider emporiums started to disappear. Many of these gleaming, stainless-steel-and-porcelain diners had the word "white" in their names no doubt as a nod to the most famous slider joint of them all—White Castle. Places like White Diamond, White Manna, and White Tower were all trying to share the limelight with the more successful Wichita chain. What's incredible is that after all of these years, unlike White Castle, the places that survived have remained virtually unchanged and still serve the same classic slider that they always have. So if you really want to see what White Castle was like back in the day, you'll need to drop into a place like White Rose System in Linden, New Jersey.

The idea of a "system" in hamburgers was basically started by White Castle as a way to promote the uniformity of the product. Today, there are a few White Rose Systems in north Jersey but they are all owned separately. The Linden White Rose, according to the authority on Jersey sliders, Nick Solares, may be the best example. The first time I ate there with him I heard him quietly exclaim, "This is a great fucking hamburger," and he is absolutely right.

The White Rose sits on the edge of residential Linden on an industrial stretch that used to be dotted with automotive shops. "This used to be body shop row," Rich said. Rich has owned the White Rose since 1992 when he purchased

the diner from Jack and Bobby Hemmings, the family that started the mini-chain. The White Rose was moved to this location at some point in 1967, its origins unknown.

The menu has expanded slightly since Rich took over, but the original griddle still sees its share of sliders. Rich uses the same local butcher that he has for years, whose 75/25 ground beef comes from steak trimmings. They arrive in 2-ounce wads of beef that Rich presses thin on the flattop. You can order a "slider," which is one wad, or a "large," which is two wads pressed together. There is also a quarter-pound burger on the menu (three wads) that's served on a very soft Kaiser roll. Although it tastes amazing, I go to White Rose for the large slider, which has the best beef-to-bun ratio. The burger is served with a pile of pickle slices on the side on a small porcelain plate.

After the wads have been pressed, Rich tosses some thin-cut onion onto the patty. When the patty is flipped, the onions cook into the burger and both halves of a white squishy bun are placed on top to steam. The result is a soft, hot, simple burger that explodes with flavor.

The burgers at White Rose, with caramelized onions and gooey cheese, basically melt in your mouth. It really makes you concentrate on the simplicity of these elements and wonder why so many chefs overthink the hamburger. This slider, for me, is hamburger perfection.

Rich grew up in the restaurant business and you could say that owning a classic lunch counter was his destiny. "After college I was looking for something other than sitting in an accounting office," he told me with a smile. But his father, who had owned five luncheonettes in north Jersey, may have been a major influence. Rich told me that when he was a kid, "Every chance I got, I worked there. I loved it."

In 2010, White Rose became the subject of a *CBS Sunday Morning* episode with Bobby Flay. After the show aired, the tiny, out-of-the-way diner started to get visitors from near and far. Rich was so perplexed by the influx of new customers that he started keeping a log. "We have been getting people from all over." He then pointed to a regular at the counter named Teddy and continued, "But these are my friends. Teddy has been coming here for 18 years," and Teddy nodded quietly. "I think that's why I have been successful."

NEW MEXICO

BOBCAT BITE

420 OLD LAS VEGAS HWY | SANTA FE, NM 87505

505-983-5319 | WWW.BOBCATBITE.COM

TUE–SAT 11 AM–7:50 PM

CLOSED SUN & MON, AND TUE IN WINTER

A visit to the Bobcat Bite for a green chile cheeseburger results in what I like to call the "Whole Burger Experience." The restaurant, the people who work there, the relaxed environment, and a stellar burger all coalesce into a perfect hamburger moment.

I was tipped off to the Bobcat by my father-in-law, Don Benjamin, a man whose only red meat intake is at this burger spot. He had a perfect burger moment there, sitting on the porch watching the sunset. It was a perfect moment that turned into a decision to move to Santa Fe.

The Bobcat Bite is way out of town, southeast on the long, lonely Old Las Vegas Highway. The low adobe structure sits on a rocky washboard incline at the foot of what once was a large quarterhorse ranch. The interior is cozy New Mexican with a low viga ceiling and a large picture window that looks out toward the old ranch and a hummingbird feeder. Seating is limited—

there are only eight stools at the counter, five tables, and just recently added, three tables on the front porch (weather permitting). The restaurant got its name from the bobcats that used to come down from the surrounding mountains to eat scraps that had been tossed out the back door. Co-owner Bonnie Eckre told me, "People used to come down and watch the bobcats eat."

In 1953, Rene Clayton, owner of the Bobcat Ranch, turned a gun shop into a restaurant. Today, Bonnie and her husband, John, keep tradition alive by serving a green chile cheeseburger that has been on the menu since the place opened. Fresh chuck steaks are ground and pattied by Bonnie's brother nearby. In 2006, John decided to switch over to naturally raised antibiotic- and hormone-free beef. He made one of the best burgers in America even better.

A green chile cheeseburger at the Bobcat is a beauty. Steamed and diced Hatch, New Mexico, green chiles are held in place atop a nine-ounce patty by a slice of melted white cheddar. The well-seasoned cast-iron griddle creates a crunchy exterior and leaves the interior perfectly moist. John is also a master of cooking temperatures, so if you ask for your burger medium-rare it'll be medium-rare. He employs a complex system of bacon weights to manage the different temperatures of the burgers.

I beg of you, please do not pollute this burger with ketchup and mustard. The simplicity of the green chile cheeseburger should not be tampered with. The chiles, hot and flavorful, enhance the beefiness, creating one of the greatest marriages of flavors and textures in the burger world.

The decades-old cast-iron griddle is one of the secrets to the Bobcat's success. John Eckre once told me, "I've tried to find another like it, but it's impossible." John stands at the grill making perfect burgers while Bonnie takes orders, makes change, and delivers food to the tables. Bonnie knows just about everyone who walks into the restaurant and greets them by name with a smile.

The Bobcat has strange hours so check before you go. They are open 5 days a week (and only 4 days in winter), and only until 7:50 p.m. Why 7:50? "Apparently there was a curfew in Santa Fe years ago," Bonnie told me. "You had to be home by 8."

John Eckre

THE HAMBURGER AMERICA TEST KITCHEN

BOBCAT BITE COLESLAW

Turns out I was not the only one who has asked John and Bonnie Eckre for their amazing coleslaw recipe. Unlike most proprietary secrets restaurants possess, this recipe was adapted from a Depression-era recipe by a previous owner of the Bobcat, Shelba Surls. During America's economic dark days, the U.S. government issued recipes like this one that could be made with inexpensive ingredients (in this case, no cream).

MAKES A LOT OF COLESLAW
(THIS IS A DAY'S WORTH FOR THE BOBCAT)

2-3 heads cabbage, shredded

1 green bell pepper, chopped

1-1½ cups sugar

2 cups distilled white vinegar

½ cup canola oil

½ teaspoon salt

1 teaspoon ground black pepper

1 teaspoon celery seed

2 tablespoons prepared mustard

Place the cabbage in a large bowl. Place the green pepper on top of the cabbage. Pour the sugar over both (for 2 heads, use 1 cup sugar, for 3 heads use 1½ cups).

In a large saucepan bring to a boil the vinegar, canola oil, salt, pepper, celery seed, and mustard. According to Bonnie, the smell of the boiling vinegar concoction will drive you out of the kitchen. Boil until the mustard is dissolved (about 5 minutes). Pour the hot brew over the bowl of cabbage and peppers and let sit. When the bowl has cooled, mix the contents and refrigerate. Bonnie told me that the slaw tastes best when it has had time to marinate. Bobcat makes its coleslaw the day before serving.

OWL BAR & CAFE

US 380 | SAN ANTONIO, NM 87832

575-835-9946 | MON–FRI 8 AM–9:30 PM

CLOSED SAT & SUN

The Owl Bar & Cafe seems an unlikely candidate for producing a world-famous burger. The bar sits at a crossroads deep in the dry desert of central New Mexico. Its adobe structure has barely a window and is one of only a handful on the main drag in the tiny town of San Antonio. Even though you have to wait until your eyes adjust after entering, and there is a large supply of booze behind the bar, the Owl is a friendly place, a family saloon with an excellent burger on the menu.

The Owl Burger is what many call the "other great green chile cheeseburger in New Mexico." I drove 280 miles to eat this burger so my expectations were high. I sat at the bar at 11 a.m. and watched as burger after burger was dispatched to the booths opposite the bar. Thankfully, mine showed up in only four minutes—the smell of green chile wafting through the air was making me very hungry.

All of the burgers are served on plastic plates with a napkin between the burger and the plate. Their famous green chile cheeseburger starts as a patty of fresh ground beef that has been pressed flat on a flattop griddle (the Owl grinds its own beef daily). Cheese, onion, tomato, mayo, and pickles are standard, and the green chiles pack a punch. They come from Hatch, New Mexico, and are lovingly prepared by Pinto, the kitchen prep cook. Pinto has been preparing the green chile for the Owl for over 40 years.

The clientele is a mix of silver-haired motorhome enthusiasts and servicemen in fatigues. The bar's entrance celebrates its proximity to the infamous Trinity Site, the spot where scientists tested the first atomic bomb only 25 miles away. Large photos of the mushroom cloud and other missile-site ephemera are proudly displayed. Frank Chavez opened the Owl Bar in 1945, just in time to accommodate the entertainment-starved scientists who were frequenting the area. At the request of these scientists, a griddle was installed and the Owl Burger was born.

The shelves of the bar are covered with hun-

dreds of donated servicemen's uniform patches from all over the country. Current owner Rowena Baca, Frank Chavez' daughter, started the collection years ago. Bartender of 30 years, Cathy Baca, explained, "Rowena told a cop she liked the patch on his uniform so he ripped it off and gave it to her. Since then, we get patches from everywhere."

Another item tacked to the walls is money. Tourists are encouraged to sign and donate a bill of their choice and pick a spot on the wall. Once a year the money is taken down, counted, and given to charity. "We've collected over $15,000 in the last six years," said Cathy. The walls account for up to $2,500 a year, with the exception of a recent late-night robbery. "They stole $600," Cathy told me. "I don't know how they got it off the walls so fast—it takes us forever."

26

NEW YORK

CORNER BISTRO

331 WEST 4ᵀᴴ ST | NEW YORK, NY 10014

212-242-9502 | MON–SAT 11:30 AM–4 PM

SUN NOON–4 AM

For two decades the Corner Bistro in Greenwich Village, New York City, served my "hometown" burger. It's the burger that became the standard by which all others would be measured. I've eaten over a thousand burgers at the Bistro in different states of intoxication or sober, for lunch and dinner, and a few times I even ate them with friends at 3 a.m. on a Tuesday. For five of those years I lived a block away and secretly wondered if my motive for moving had been burger proximity. I knew the right times to visit to avoid the crowds, and their phone number was in the speed dial of my cell phone. I placed phone orders and used the quiet side door to sneak in, grab my waiting hot paper bag, and make a swift exit. My burger quest started here and ends here as well. I went forth into Hamburger America, ate well, returned, and was confident that the "Bistro Burger" really is one of the best in the nation.

Inside and out, the Corner Bistro defies its name and looks the part of the Irish pub. Carved-up wooden tables, well-worn, wide plank floorboards, and a long bar with a noticeable dip in the center create your lasting first impression. "The building is still settling," Bill O'Donnell said in defense of the sloping bar. Bill has been the owner of the Bistro for over 40 years and its famous burger has been on the menu just as long.

The building housing the Corner Bistro dates back to 1827 and before it was a bar it was an inn. The existing décor surrounding the bar (stained-glass cabinetry and mirrors) as well as the brass-foot-railed bar itself is said to date back to 1880. After Prohibition was repealed, the bar became Barney McNichols and attracted mostly the longshoremen who populated the neighborhood. After its short stint as a gay bar, in 1961 a Spanish woman bought it and attempted to put a European spin on the old tavern by calling it the Corner Bistro. It didn't last and went back to being what it has been for well over a century— a cozy dive with a great jukebox.

In 1977, Mimi Sheraton, the well-known food critic from the *New York Times*, wrote a favorable piece on the Bistro Burger that kickstarted the surge of popularity that has not slowed since. "I came in the next day and the place was packed," Bill told me. "I was shocked." Bill himself admits that there's nothing special about the burger and nothing has changed in 40 years. "We still use the same butcher around the corner. It's good meat, mostly chuck and sirloin but I think he puts some porterhouse in there too." Two hundred and fifty pounds of the fresh ground beef gets walked over by hand cart from 14th Street to the Bistro everyday. This was the way all restaurants received their meat in the first half of the twentieth

century, delivered by hand from a local butcher.

The Bistro Burger doesn't try to be anything but a great hamburger. It's a thick, 8-ounce burger whose only flourish is three crispy strips of bacon that have been flash-fried in the deep fryer (ever wonder why those fries taste so damn good?). It's served on a toasted, white squishy bun with lettuce, tomato, and a thick onion slice hidden beneath the burger. It's cooked in a tiny, postage stamp–sized kitchen staffed by two. They cook the burgers to your preferred temperature in a salamander broiler, a small, specialized oven that cooks the burgers slowly by indirect, overhead heat. Bartender of 40 years, Harold, explained, "It keeps the burgers soft and juicy."

Hard-working Louis has been the head chef and chief of burger operations at the Bistro for over 25 years. He is a man of few words but will always get your order right. Louis is in charge of the line that builds most nights for people waiting for a table and will take your order. The infamous line starts at the phone booth and can go all the way to the front door, so grab a beer at the bar first.

Many people try to bad-mouth this burger because they are embarrassed by its simplicity. In a city with no tangible burger identity (you really can find any type of burger in New York City, from the bloated wallet busters to tasty sliders), the Bistro Burger stands out as an unflappable success grounded in modesty. The success has spread to other bars in the neighborhood that claim to "know the secret of the Bistro Burger" and have even hired cast-off Bistro

kitchen staff to boost business. "There are no secrets," Bill told me laughing, "The recipe is 'good meat,' you idiots."

DONOVAN'S PUB

5724 ROOSEVELT AVE | FLUSHING, NY 11377
718-429-9339 | OPEN DAILY 11 AM–11 PM

Regulars, God bless 'em, show up at this Woodside, Queens, Irish pub at 11 a.m. daily to slowly drink their Guinness stout and just talk. They are cared for by Robert Kansella, bartender of 40 years who was at the pub before there was even a restaurant. The bar he tends to is an impressive one—long, dark, solid and with the type of patina that only comes with age. It's a great bar to sit at, drink a Guinness, and just talk, but even better to enjoy a burger, one of the best I've ever eaten.

I asked Robert how big the burgers were and his only response was, "They are pretty big." He was not far off. This pub has been serving half-pound burgers since 1970, and a lot of them. Artie Kardaras, head chef at Donovan's for over 35 years, told me they hand-patty 400 pounds of quality ground shell steak (New York strip) a day for their burgers. "I make every day fresh," he proudly explained with his thick Greek accent.

The Donovan's burger is a lesson in how a large burger should be prepared. It's cooked in a way that few burgers are in America—in a broiler used for cooking steaks. The loose-pattied burger is broiled to the temperature of your choice with little attention paid to it by the chef. "Too many people press them too much," Artie explained with big hand gestures and twisted facial expressions. Artie believes, and is correct, that the best burgers are left alone and touched the least.

When you bite into the inch-thick Donovan's burger, the first thing you notice is how loose the meat is. The delicate exterior char can barely contain the tender, steamy beef inside. A half-pound burger may sound tough to tackle, but the meat-to-bun ratio is nearly perfect, making the entire experience incredibly satisfying.

Other than a bar, burgers, and regulars, Donovan's also has an impressive dining room and a great menu loaded with comfort food. Go during the colder months and enjoy your burgers by the cozy fireplace in the dark-paneled dining room with Tiffany lamps hanging overhead.

The most obvious landmark you'll notice

outside Donovan's Pub is the undeniably old–New York elevated subway rumbling overhead every few minutes. What you may not pick out is the tavern's odd proximity to a church only a few feet away, directly across the street. "This place was here before the church so they were allowed to stay," regular Don Moran told me from his spot at the bar. According to New York City zoning law, no drinking establishment may be operated within 500 feet of a place of worship. So this may be the closest you'll get to a church to drink and eat great burgers in New York City—in fact, the stained glass windows do give the place a churchlike feel.

In 2004 *Time Out NY* called the burger at Donovan's the best in New York City. That's quite a claim in this town of diverse food possibilities and unlimited types of burger joints. Did the press increase sales at the sleepy neighborhood tavern? "Sure," bartender Robert admitted, "but we've been selling a lot of burgers forever."

HILDEBRANDT'S

84 HILLSIDE AVE | WILLISTON PARK, NY 11596

516-741-0608

WWW.HILDEBRANDTSRESTAURANT.COM

TUE–SAT 11 AM–8:30 PM | SUN 10 AM–4 PM

Densely packed suburban Long Island, New York, is a place where new malls and homes are constantly springing up and, unless protected, the past is unceremoniously swept away. In a part of the country where it's getting harder to find genuine nostalgia, locals embrace Hildebrandt's Luncheonette. This early-twentieth-century landmark soda counter, confectionery, and ice cream parlor offers a glimpse into the past. The counter, though, is not a washed-up has-been. It's as vibrant as ever and happens to serve some of the tastiest burgers this side of Manhattan.

Hildebrandt's opened in 1927 and was the only business in the newly developing dirt road suburb of Williston Park, 20 miles from New York City. Today, Hildebrandt's is owned by Joanne Strano and her son-in-law, Bryan Acosta. Joanne and her late husband, Al, bought the vintage luncheonette in 1974 when longtime owner and chocolate maker Henry Shreiver was looking to retire. The Acostas learned the chocolate-making trade from Shreiver and made a major improvement to the existing burger on the menu—fresh ground beef.

This classic luncheonette, with its checker-tiled floor and long marble counter with 13 stools, maintains a vintage look by making use of the soda fountain trappings of a bygone era. The seltzer and syrup dispensers are not vintage props. They all function daily, as does the long bank of ice cream chests behind the counter. Ice cream is a big draw at Hildebrandt's because it's made right at the restaurant.

But according to Bryan, most come for the food, which is a mix of classic diner fare and Italian specialties added by the Acosta family in the 1970s. Surprisingly, this amazing burger has been exiled to the bottom of the menu. Look for your cheeseburger in a section marked "sandwiches" at the bottom of the list, just after the meatball hero.

"We have the greatest burger," Bryan told me without pause, and added, "I've never really had a better burger. I really haven't." He can boast all he wants. It really is a great burger. The burgers at Hildebrandt's start as fresh-ground sirloin the restaurant receives from the butcher down the street. Bryan himself hand-patties the four-ounce burgers just before the lunch crowd shows up. The burgers are offered at the four-ounce size, or ask for the eight-ounce and get twice the meat. "We just take two four-ounce patties and smoosh them together on the grill," Bryan explained. On the flattop griddle, Alfredo presses the burger flat and places a bacon weight on top. It's served on a classic white bun with tomato, sliced onion, and a wedge of iceberg lettuce. Bacon is available, but not necessary (this meat is so good you won't want anything to hide the flavor). Ketchup is

king at Hildebrandt's (there's a bottle every few feet on the counter) but mustard has to be culled from the countermen in small pouches.

Hildebrandt's fries are a great addition to your hamburger lunch. They are large, hand-cut, deep-fried slices of potato that, if ordered well done, resemble homemade potato chips. Order a milkshake, listed on the menu in Long Island vernacular as a "frosted," and you'll get a tall glass and the obligatory metal cup the shake was made in. Since the ice cream is homemade, the shakes are superb.

The clientele at Hildebrandt's ranges from little old ladies to large families with kids. Bryan, waiting tables in the back, makes jokes as he takes orders. "These are the best seats in the house," he tells two older ladies looking for a table, "unless of course I'm waiting on you!"

In the vicinity of New York City, Hildebrandt's is not alone. The long-gone business model for this type of soda fountain survives at places like Hinsch's in Bayridge, Brooklyn, and Bischoff's in Teaneck, New Jersey. They too make their own chocolates, and in the case of Bischoff's, countermen still wear white paper caps and striped shirts. At all of these vintage soda fountains of German descent, you can take home hand-packed ice cream by the pint or quart, but the similarities end there. Only Hildebrandt's makes a top-quality burger. That, and the mocha frosted, will keep me coming back.

JG MELON

1291 THIRD AVE | NEW YORK, NY 10021

212-744-0585 | OPEN DAILY 11:30 AM–4 AM

The Upper East Side of Manhattan is known more for its high cost of living and less for good old places like JG Melon. The humble, dark, no-nonsense tavern should have been in the first edition of this book, and was prevented only by scheduling conflicts. When Mayor Mike Bloomberg saw my book, he told me, "JG should be in here. They make a great burger." He should know. The mayor lives only a few blocks away and is crazy about hamburgers.

Jack O'Neil and George Mourges (the *J* and *G* of JG Melon) were working at midtown restaurant Joe Allen when they decided they wanted to open a place of their own. In 1972 they leased Bar Central on 74th and 3rd and changed the name to JG Melon. The building dates back to the 1920s when the tavern was built by a local brewery to dispense its own products following Prohibition. Almost immediately, JG Melon became a watering hole for socialites and politicians, as well as locals and Wall Street types. Every sitting mayor for the last 40 years has felt comfortable at the tavern and the burger is at the center of it all.

Today, JG Melon retains its friendly broken-in pub ambiance thanks to the dapper Shaun Young, who plays the role of the New York City tavern proprietor perfectly. His clean-cut presence clearly sets the tone here and has done so for decades. After a stint as a bartender in the early 1980s at JG Melon, Shaun became a partner. "Jack and George made me the manager, and after 6 months I was ready to leave," he told me. They offered him a partnership and 30 years later he's still there. George passed away in 2003, leaving Jack and Shaun as partners.

I asked Shaun what kind of meat he used for the burgers and without missing a beat he shot

A cheeseburger and a Bloody Bull

back, "It's a secret," and looked away. JG Melon's burgers start as a special blend of cuts ground by the same butcher they've used for years. He added, "What I can tell you, though it's not really a secret, is that we have a hot grill, very hot." The burgers are portioned into 7-ounce balls then gently flattened on a large griddle, and Shaun pointed out, "Like a steak, we only flip them once."

The result is a substantially thick two-fister whose construction is perfect. No crazy toppings here, just a basic, beefy, uncomplicated burger that is truly satisfying. Because of the high heat and the steak-treatment, the exterior of the burger is seared to a serious griddle char that helps retain all of the moisture. You'll need a napkin—this one is juicy.

Equally famous at JG Melon are the cottage fries that have been on the menu since the beginning. At one point, Shaun convinced Jack and George to switch to shoestring fries. "There was a complete revolt!" Shaun remembers. "We had to switch back immediately."

Do not leave JG Melon without having a Bloody Bull. A drink you don't see often that hails from New Orleans, the Bloody Bull is like a Bloody Mary but half of the tomato juice is replaced with beef broth. What could go better with a beefy burger than a beefy drink?

There are a few tables in a rear dining room and 16 coveted seats on the sidewalk, but grab a stool at the bar if possible and listen to the burgers sear on the flattop adjacent to the bar. The sound is heavenly.

Shaun is a true New Yorker, having grown up only a few blocks away, and he knows that JG Melon's success is no mistake. "Why fix something that's not broken?" he asked me. He also pointed to Jack and George for the reason that simplicity and quality trump all. "I give them credit for staying on top of the product." And that's why people keep coming back.

★ ★ ★ ★ ★

P.J. CLARKE'S

915 THIRD AVE | NEW YORK, NY 10022

212-317-1616 | WWW.PJCLARKES.COM

OPEN 7 DAYS A WEEK 11:30 AM–3 AM

BAR CLOSES AT 4 AM

There are few taverns in America as steeped in history as P.J. Clarke's. All at once a neighborhood bar, broken-in dive, and a celebrity hang for decades, it's also a great place to find high-quality pub fare. Among that fare is the world famous P.J. Clarke's hamburger. P.J.'s has not been affected by its own celebrity status. It remains a comfortable place in the heart of a sometimes cold city—a friendly pub with a welcoming staff and a remarkably unpretentious hamburger on the menu.

The iconic corner saloon, in a two-story brick tenement-style structure, looks totally out of place surrounded by the tall glass and steel office buildings of midtown Manhattan. Irish immigrant Patrick J. Clarke started working at the cor-

ner bar in 1902, and in 1912 he purchased the business and changed the name to his own.

Before the skyscrapers, the neighborhood surrounding P.J.'s was mostly breweries and slaughterhouses. And those who are old enough will remember that the Third Avenue subway was elevated, giving the area a radically different feel. By 1960, the elevated tracks were down and the slaughterhouses were long gone. P.J.'s neighborhood has undergone a profound transformation in the last century but the tiny saloon remains, dwarfed by its neighbors.

The tin ceilings, faded mirrors behind the bar, and stained-glass windows in front remind the casual observer of the saloon's rich past. Sinatra made P.J.'s his last stop on nights out and even had his own table (#20). Affable young general manager Patrick Walsh told me, through his Irish brogue, "If there was anyone sitting there when

The Béarnaise Burger

Sinatra came in they'd get the boot." Buddy Holly proposed to his wife here and Nat King Cole once called the hamburger at P.J.'s "the Cadillac of burgers." Even the famed 1970s sports painter LeRoy Neiman put brush to canvas to create a portrait of the bar in full swing that proudly hangs in the dining room. There are many more stories, but you have to ask Patrick. He told me, "Every single day I learn a new story."

The meat for the burgers comes from cattle that are handpicked for P.J.'s. They grind chuck steaks in the kitchen and the fat-to-lean ratio is kept secret. The eight-ounce burgers are hand-pressed one by one, cooked on a flattop griddle, and served on a classic white squishy bun. Don't be surprised to find a slice of onion underneath your burger. Today's burgers are served on a porcelain plate, but Patrick told me, "They used to be served on paper plates and the onion was there to soak up the juices"—presumably to prevent the plate from falling apart.

I've been going to P.J.'s for decades and the burger has always been perfect. The bun-to-beef ratio, the slight griddle crunch, and the moist, meaty flavor are what burger dreams are made of. There are a few burger choices at P.J.'s, but I always get the "Béarnaise Burger." Imagine the simplicity of the elements—the perfect burger, a soft white bun, and a healthy dose of pure béarnaise sauce.

The dark dining room walls are covered with an amazing collection of New York City ephemera (including P.J.'s death certificate) and old photographs of past patrons. The 100-year-old men's

NOTABLE BURGER CHAINS ▶▶

In the corporate burger world, all burgers are created equal by design. Most are frozen, then shipped for miles to their intended fast-food outlet. There are, however, a few hamburger chains that buck the system and offer burgers made with fresh ground beef: places like Red Robin, Cheeburger! Cheeburger!, and the Northwest's own Burgerville. Here is a short list of my personal favorites:

urinals are as famous as the burgers and must be seen to be believed (they're over five feet tall with thick porcelain embellishment). Sinatra once said they were "big enough to take a bath in."

P.J.'s has been part of the collective uncon-scious of literally millions of former and present New Yorkers. Just like your favorite jacket or an old pair of shoes, the tavern has always been a familiar, unchanging place that many rely on for hearty comfort food, a drink, and good com-pany. The burger at P.J.'s is part of that legacy of comfort and hopefully will be forever.

Steak 'n Shake

Locations throughout the Midwest and the South

www.steaknshake.com

This classic drive-in burger stand opened its first location in Normal, Illinois in 1934. Since then, Steak 'n Shake has expanded to over 450 locations and still serves burgers made from fresh-ground strip steak, sirloin, and T-bone. A seat at the counter offers excellent views of the white paper-capped grill man preparing your "Steakburger." A wad of beef is smashed thin and seared on a super-hot flattop griddle. Within just a few minutes, a moist yet crispy patty is placed on a toasted white bun and delivered to you on real china. Get a double with bacon for an unforgettable meal.

Oh, and the shakes are pretty good too.

Smashburger

Locations throughout the United States

www.smashburger.com

How could I not love a burger chain that smashes fresh ground beef the old-fashioned way? In 2007 there was one Smashburger, in Denver. Today there are over 60 locations all over the country and many more on the way.

Five Guys

Locations throughout the United States

www.fiveguys.com

This relative newcomer to the burger scene is making quite a dent in the business corporate fast food is doing, across the country, especially since the Five Guys business plan calls for up to 1,000 new locations in the next few years. One college student I spoke to told me he'd never visit a Mickey D's if there was a Five Guys nearby. What's all the fuss about? Great burgers made in large portions from fresh ground beef, not to mention free refills and the bottomless bag of fresh-cut fries. Corporate burger biggies are in trouble when even drunken students can tell the difference between fresh and frozen burgers.

27

NORTH CAROLINA

CHAR-GRILL

618 HILLSBOROUGH ST | RALEIGH, NC 27603

(AND FIVE OTHER LOCATIONS IN RALEIGH-DURHAM)

919-821-7636 | WWW.CHARGRILLUSA.COM

Racing to catch a flight I was sure to miss out on Raleigh, North Carolina's own burger mini-chain, the Char-Grill. Fortunately, I did stop, but would have missed the flight had the service not been super-fast.

The set up is pure 1950s drive-in, but the ordering process is peculiar. No honking for service here. You park your car, walk up to the window, and fill out a cryptic order form. Once you have marked your choices, you shove the slim piece of paper into a thin slot in one of the large plate glass windows. Your order form slides down a stainless chute to the waiting grill cook. The lack of indoor seating and a glass-enclosed kitchen creates a sort of public hamburger laboratory—as you wait, you can peer inside and watch your burger being constructed according to the condiments you checked off on your order. Within minutes, your number is called and you are rewarded with a white paper bag full of hot food by a smiling employee.

The burgers are grilled over a flame and come in three sizes, the largest being the half-pound hamburger steak sandwich. Any combination of mayo, lettuce, tomato, onion, pickle, cheese, and bacon can be created. The staff all wear white paper caps and aprons and work at stations to keep this model of efficiency chugging along. The beef comes in fresh daily, as square preformed Angus chuck patties. The manager at the original Hillsborough stand, Scott Hobby, told me "All of the lettuce, tomato, and onion come from a local farmer's market."

Bruce Garner opened Char-Grill in 1959. In 1975, two fraternity brothers, Mahlon Aycock and Ryon Wilder, assumed ownership and over three decades later are still partners in the business. They have expanded from the one location they purchased in 1975 to five locations with more planned. All of the locations are in the Raleigh-Durham area but Mahlon plans to expand throughout North Carolina—and as he put it, "probably beyond."

By design, not much has changed at Char-Grill. The Hillsborough location is a piece of American architecture stuck in time. The deliberately oversized, overdesigned structure is almost sculpture—the enormous white wavy roof looks as if it could crush the floor-to-ceiling windows supporting it. The other Raleigh locations also serve their well-known Charburgers, but it's the original location that has that great drive-in feel. And for over 50 years Char-Grill has continued to serve the same tasty, flame-grilled burgers and creamy shakes.

All walks of life visit Char-Grill for a dose of nostalgia. Mahlon told me, "We get everybody from the governor of North Carolina to construction folk and anybody in between." And me. I'll be back. I hope my flight gets delayed.

PENGUIN DRIVE-IN

1921 COMMONWEALTH AVE | CHARLOTTE, NC 28205

704-375-6959 | MON–THU 11 AM–12 AM

FRI & SAT 11 AM–1 AM | SUN 11 AM–11 PM

When the doors open at 11 a.m. at the Penguin, people pour in. On most days, especially weekends, the seats are filled within 30 seconds and stay that way through lunch with a wait for a table before noon not uncommon.

The first time I visited, I sat at the bar and watched as longtime manager Rhyne Franklin unlocked the front door for lunch. At the same time the door swung open, a tattooed server named B-Mac flicked on the jukebox and out came the punk classic, "Sonic Reducer," at a decent volume. The Penguin went from zero to sixty in a matter of seconds and the first customer through the door was a gray-haired woman with a cane in a powder-blue suit. She was followed by a couple of guys with ties and a handful of other younger locals. I was shocked by the varied demographic and Rhyne just shrugged and said, "That's lunch." Everyone is welcome at the Penguin.

The Penguin opened in the early 1950s, first as an ice cream stand and then in 1954 as a drive-in with carhops, burgers, and fries. The neighborhood went into decline in the 1970s and the Penguin became a biker bar. "It was a complete hole in the wall," Rhyne told me. In 2000, two friends, Brian Rowe and Jimmy King,

bought the business from Jim Ballentine and spent months renovating the place. Ballentine retained the rights to the Penguin name and ownership of the property. Brian and Jimmy kept the overall integrity of the place intact and brought in chef Greg Auten to help them develop straightforward fare for the revamped menu. When they opened, the Penguin was reborn in a neighborhood that was on the rebound. The timing was perfect.

The burgers come in three basic sizes at the Penguin, the "Small Block," the "Big Block," and the "Full Blown Hemi." The names are probably a nod to NASCAR since the Charlotte area is where most of the race teams call home. The Small Block is a one-third-pound burger, the Big Block two one-third-pound patties, and the Hemi is a ridiculous three stacked one-third-pound patties. "Most people get the Small Block," Rhyne told me, and for good reason— it's a totally satisfying burger, and just the right size, especially if you plan on indulging in the Penguin's famous fried pickles. The Big Block uses the same sized bun, but the contents tend to slip and slide. The Full Blown Hemi is just a colossal mess, but a damned tasty one. "A lot of people ask for a knife and fork for the Hemi," Rhyne laughed, and B-Mac pointed out, "We really only sell one or two Hemis a day."

How do you want your burger? At the Penguin, the options are "all the way" (lettuce, tomato, onion, mayo, and pickles) or "Southern Style" (chili, mustard, onions, and cole slaw).

The Big Block with pimento cheese

Southern Style is the way to go because you can get lettuce and tomato anywhere. The chili that the Penguin uses is made in-house and is simple, beefy, and spicy. The coleslaw is also made at the Penguin and is shredded impossibly thin. You can get American cheese on your burger but the pimento cheese at the Penguin is incredible.

The burgers are cooked on a flattop and start as portioned wads of fresh ground chuck. The grillperson takes a wad, tosses it onto the griddle, and presses it into the shape of a burger. They are obviously not over-pressed because the resulting burger is very juicy.

The entire staff is young, energetic, and mostly tattooed. The tone at the Penguin was set by Jimmy and Brian, both ex-military, and both tattoo-covered themselves. Jimmy is a big fan of punk music and the jukebox reflects this. At first glance you'll see a bunch of Elvis and Johnny Cash in there, but check out the black folder to the left of the juke. It's loaded with hundreds of punk and hard rock tunes.

At the time of this publication, the Ballentine Family had no plans to renew Jimmy and Brian's lease, effectively pushing out the two guys that saved an icon and turned the Penguin into a destination burger joint. There's no guarantee that the soul of the Penguin will remain, but when your restaurant fills up within 30 seconds of opening your doors, you'd be a fool to change anything.

SNAPPY LUNCH

125 NORTH MAIN ST | MOUNT AIRY, NC 27030
336-786-4931 | MON–WED & FRI 6 AM–1:45 PM
THU & SAT 6 AM–1:15 PM | CLOSED SUNDAY

The Snappy Lunch sells one of the best pork chop sandwiches in America and it is "World Famous" according to the menu. But this is a hamburger book, and the restaurant does its part to offer a bit of hamburger history as well. Popular with the locals, the Snappy Lunch sells a curiosity called the "Breaded Hamburger." Sometimes referred to as the "No-Burger" or the "old fashioned," this throwback to the Depression was invented when meat was scarce. At the Snappy Lunch, the breaded burger still outsells the regular burger on the menu three to one.

"I don't even get into it with out-of-towners," said Mary Dowell, wife of longtime owner and local food celebrity Charles Dowell. "I don't even like them!" she told me with a smile. I tried my first Depression-era burger at the Snappy Lunch and really liked it. It kind of resembled a bland crab cake with ground beef inside. "What do ya think?" Mary asked. I told her it tasted like a biscuit and she informed me that I had named the main ingredient.

The breaded burger, referred to as just a "hamburger" by the staff (a nonbreaded burger is a "burger with meat") starts as a blend of ground beef, crumbled cooked biscuits, and day-old bread. The blend, which leans mostly toward bread, is then formed into patties and cooked on the flattop griddle. A finished burger "all the way" has on it coleslaw, mustard, onion, tomato, and chili.

The chili, a tasty, sweet, and chunky concoction, is ladled onto both the pork chop sandwich and the burgers. It was created by Charles in the 1950s by accident. "I was trying to make up something to put on the pork chops—the recipe has not changed since then and everyone wants it."

Charles was a fixture at the Snappy Lunch since 1943 when, at age 15, he was paid $10 a week. Eight years later his father, a local grocer, helped Charles negotiate the purchase of a share in the restaurant and in 1960 he became the sole owner.

The name Snappy is fitting for the turn-of-the-century post office turned lunch counter because the doors close most days at 1:45 p.m. Oddly on Thursday closing time is 1:15 p.m. "As part of the war effort," Charles told me, "restaurants were asked to choose a day to close early."

Mary and Charles met over twenty years ago when someone tried to set her up with Charles's son at the restaurant. Charles, now in his early 80s, is retired and Mary holds down the fort at Snappy Lunch.

In the recently renovated, gleaming kitchen at the rear of the restaurant, I met 16-year veteran cook, Diane. "I never thought a breaded burger could out sell the regular burger, but they do, every day."

Mount Airy, North Carolina, exists in the minds of *The Andy Griffith Show* fans as the inspiration for Mayberry, the setting of the popular 1960s TV show. Not only did Andy grow up in Mount Airy, he also ate at the Snappy Lunch frequently as a child. Because of this, and his massive fan base, you may want to avoid the restaurant in late September when thousands descend on the small country town for Mayberry Days. Diane told me "We'll actually stay open late those days just to make sure all those people are fed."

SOUTH 21 DRIVE-IN

3101 EAST INDEPENDENCE BLVD
CHARLOTTE, NC 28205
704-377-4509 I WWW.SOUTH21DRIVEIN.COM
TUE 11 AM–3 PM I WED & THU 11 AM–9 PM
FRI & SAT 11 AM–10 PM I CLOSED SUN & MON

Traveling along Independence Boulevard just east of downtown Charlotte, NC, you'll notice a vintage red neon sign that blinks with the words "curb service" and beckons you to pull in and float back in time. Slip into one of the many stalls, check out the menu, and push the order button. You are on your way to a classic South 21 Drive-In experience.

Since 1959, very little has changed at this Charlotte institution. Owned by the same family of Greek immigrants since the beginning, South 21 serves the same fresh, thin-patty burger that has come from the same local meat supplier for over 45 years. In 1955, George Copsis and his two brothers decided to open a drive-in on South Boulevard in Charlotte. The business boomed and the brothers opened another nearby in 1959. They leased the original location and made the Independence location their flagship. Over the years, the family would open and sell off other drive-ins across town, but offspring Maria and her husband, George Housiadas, have held on to the flagship icon.

You've heard the story before but it bears repeating—Greeks in the hamburger business. The Housiadas family is not alone. Many proud Greek families still own classic burger stands across America, namely the famous mini-chains of the Billy Goat of Chicago, Burger House of Dallas, and Crown Burger of Salt Lake City. Or the one-offs like Helvetia Tavern near Portland, Oregon, and Western Steakburger in San Diego. All of these restaurants were the result of hardworking Greeks finding their way in America.

Not surprisingly, most stories of Greek burger entrepreneurism in this country start the same way. "They came here with nothing," Maria told me. "They didn't know what else to do so they started flipping burgers and didn't stop!" She told me that in the beginning the brothers would sell a few burgers, take the cash, run down the street to the Winn-Dixie supermarket, and buy another few pounds of ground beef. "Can you imagine if we did that today?" Maria pondered.

South 21 is the real deal. Expect carhops, window trays, and tasty, classic burgers. The burgers start as preformed fresh-ground four-ounce patties and can be ordered as singles or doubles. Make it a "Super Boy" and you will get two patties on a toasted white bun with chopped lettuce, onion, mustard, and tomato. If you want cheese, you'll need to order the "Jumbo." The burgers show up on your window tray with a large pickle speared to the top bun.

The fries at South 21 are great, but it's the onion rings that have received decades of accolades. The kitchen at South 21 slices and breads fresh onion rings daily, tasty circles of deep fried goodness.

216

You'll also notice an item on the menu that sounds almost cartoonish but is anything but—the "Fish-O-Burger." Imagine two pieces of fresh (not frozen) lightly breaded and deep-fried trout served with tartar sauce on a toasted white bun. It's a heavenly sandwich, especially for those who want to partake of the drive-in culture without the red meat.

One thing you may find odd about South 21 is the black fedora your carhop will be wearing as he clips the tray to your car window. It was part of a uniform that was retired about 20 years ago according to Maria. "The uniforms used to be absolutely ridiculous." For years, carhops were required to wear what looked like a period carriage driver's getup—a long red coat with two gold buttons and heavy black pants. "They looked nice," Maria remembered, "but the carhops hated to wear them. The heavy material was really only comfortable in the three colder months of the year."

South 21 still employs a hard-working staff of four; some have been at the drive-in for over 40 years. One of those is Nick, the Greek griddle master who has been flipping perfect patties at South 21 since 1971.

Late-night cruising is a thing of the past, as the last burgers are sold at 10 p.m. on weekends. Check the drive-in's hours before you head out to South 21 to show off your '66 Corvette Stingray.

Maria is at the drive-in every day to take orders and manage the staff. She seems confident in the quality of their fare and understands why people continue to patronize South 21. "Diehard fans tell people, 'If you haven't eaten there, you haven't eaten.'"

WHAT-A-BURGER DRIVE-IN

210 SOUTH MAIN ST I MOORESVILLE, NC 28115

704-664-5455

(4 OTHER LOCATIONS IN KANNAPOLIS AND CONCORD, NC)

MON–SAT 11 AM–10 AM

This is not the well-known Texas burger chain you are thinking of. In fact, this What-A-Burger actually opened in 1950 in Virginia, the same year as the 700-store Whataburger chain, but both owners were unaware of the existence of the other. After a lawsuit brought more than 50 years later, the two chains agreed that they would not expand into each other's territory and that was that. Today, the Texas based burger chain has expanded into eight states and Mexico but has stayed away from North Carolina and Virginia where a handful of What-A-Burgers still exist.

Eb Bost opened the first What-A-Burger in North Carolina in 1955. At one point, through the ownership of many members of the Bost family, there were up to fifteen locations in the Charlotte area. Today, Eb's son Mike Bost is the president of the company and there are now five locations that still retain their original number in the chain (for example, the Mooresville location is still called No. 11). Some of the locations still offer curb service.

Built in 1965, the What-A-Burger of Mooresville is an authentic artifact of the drive-in era that sits just south of the main drag. Twenty-eight curb service stalls sit under a retro corrugated shelter and the dining room inside can hold up to a hundred hungry burger lovers.

The burgers at What-A-Burger are very wide, cooked on a flattop, and are made from fresh-ground beef. "The patties come in every morning from a butcher in town," employee of 25 years Diane told me. They are served on soft white buns that have been toasted on a large press. The thin patty and the squashed, toasted bun make for a very flat but satisfying burger. If you are hungry, go for the "Double What-A-Burger." Priced at under 4 dollars this half-pound burger could be the best deal going. There's also a kid-sized What-A-Burger, a smaller version of the original.

You'd have to be a local to understand the baffling burger combinations that What-A-Burger offers. The signature "What-A-Burger" comes with shredded lettuce, sliced tomato, mustard, and onion. The "What-A-Cheeseburger" adds cheese, but mysteriously takes away the mustard. The "What-A-Salisbury" has no mustard, either, and no cheese and, follow me here, the "What-A-*Ham*burger" comes Southern Style with mustard, coleslaw, and chili. In reality, you can get a burger any way you want it. Just ask.

On my first visit I was compelled to order a crazy sounding drink on the menu called the "Witch Doctor." When I asked what was in the drink, through the muffled vintage drive-in speakerphone, I could not make out what the kitchen was telling me. All I could hear was, "Wah, wah waah, wah waaah." When the drink appeared at my car I took a sip and tasted cherry and lime soda, and something savory. Then I opened the lid of the Styrofoam cup to find a wedge of lemon and three pickle slices floating in ice. The Witch Doctor, a drink that goes back five decades at What-A-Burger, is made by filling a cup with a little bit from each soda on the fountain. "There used to be a raw onion ring in there too," Employee Jeff told me, and Diane added, "Some people still ask for the onion. Yuck." Mike Bost told me, "The customers dreamed that one up a long time ago." The drink was amazing with a flavor that was complex and refreshing. Just don't make the mistake I made and take a sip hours later after the ice had melted and the pickles had marinated.

The Witch Doctor is a great drink, but the bestseller at What-A-Burger is the "Cherry-Lemon Sundrop." It's so popular that Mike told me, "If we couldn't sell those and burgers I think we'd go out of business."

Each curb stall is set up in twos and you'll need to follow curb service etiquette to park correctly. Imagine two gas pumps and you'll get the idea. In a row of two curb stalls, pull through to the second one so that someone can pull in behind you. I did not do this the first time I visited and received some quizzical looks from regulars.

For many years the curb service at the Mooresville location was not up and running. A lack of qualified carhops led Mike to shut down the talkback speakers and send all of the business indoors. But after pressure from regulars, three years ago the curb service returned. Thanks to that pressure you can now enjoy your What-A-Burger and Witch Doctor curbside.

OHIO

CRABILL'S HAMBURGERS

727 MIAMI ST | URBANA, OH 43078

937-653-5133 | MON–FRI 10 AM–6:30 PM

SAT 10 AM–5 PM | CLOSED SUNDAY

Crabill's is very, very small. What's amazing is that the original Crabill's was much smaller. Eight stools sit bolted to the floor at a small counter and there is barely enough room to pass behind them. "The old place was five times smaller," grill cook Andy Hiltibran told me. Andy is married to third-generation owner Marsha Crabill, the granddaughter of Forest Crabill, who opened this heartland burger stand nearly 100 years ago.

Crabill's started as a hamburger counter in picturesque downtown Urbana. It's the sort of town that Norman Rockwell would have painted in his depiction of everyday life in mid-twentieth

century America. Two men, Crabill and Carpenter, opened the minuscule six-stool counter in 1927. After only three days, Crabill bought out Carpenter for $75. The counter remained in operation, run by Forest's son and daughter-in-law, David and Joyce, until it closed in 1988.

Marsha and Andy decided to restart the family business soon after with the help of Marsha's parents. They were eager to leave their factory jobs (she worked at Honda, he worked at Bristol-Meyers) so they purchased a small motor home and dubbed it "Crabill's on Wheels." They made the rounds of county fairs and horse shows, and after three years on wheels the couple decided to go brick-and-mortar. Crabill's was reborn on the west side of town, just a few blocks from, and not much larger than, the original location.

The first time I visited the reincarnation of the burger counter, I sat next to a white-bearded regular named Will Yoder who for decades has

played the annual town Santa. Will had recently had his teeth removed and was on a soft food diet. Personally, I couldn't think of a better spot to dine on tasty, soft food. The tiny burgers at Crabill's, with their pillowy Wonder buns and healthy dose of burger grease, actually do melt in your mouth.

The burgers at Crabill's are cooked in a wide, shallow griddle. The griddle is filled with about a half inch of grease. "The griddle in the old place was much smaller," Andy told me, and showed me with his hands only a foot apart. "It was also much deeper." Small balls of fresh ground beef are tossed into the grease, then pressed once with specially made spatulas. The grillperson uses two of these spatulas at a time to systematically press and flip the dozens of patties floating in the grease with a sort of Benihana-like speed and dexterity. As your burger nears doneness, it gets a splash of grease from a spatula and is transferred to a waiting tiny Wonder bun.

Chopped raw onion, spicy mustard, and relish are standard, but cheese and ketchup are also available. There is a sign on the wall menu that explains that ketchup was introduced in 1990. That's right, it took ketchup 63 years to be accepted at Crabill's.

On a busy Saturday Crabill's can move up to 300 burgers in ten minutes. When someone walks in with an order for 20 doubles, the griddle is quickly filled with the balls of meat and the spatulas start whacking at lighting speed.

Don't waste your time with singles; go for doubles. Twice the beef, twice the grease, and half the bread. If you are feeling brave, do what some regulars do—ask for yours dipped and you'll get the top of your bun dipped in the grease. "Some people even like theirs double-dipped," Andy told me. "That's where we dip the top and bottom of the bun." A double, double-dipped anyone?

GAHANNA GRILL

82 GRANVILLE ST I GAHANNA, OH 43230

614-476-9017 I WWW.GAHANNAGRILL.COM

MON–SAT 11 AM–10:30 PM I SUN NOON–8:30 PM

"This used to be all farm fields out here," owner of the Gahanna Grill Jimmy Staravecka told me, waving his arm. He pointed to a photo that shows the bar in 1900, not surrounded by much of anything. Looking at the restaurant today in this busy suburb of Columbus, it's hard to imagine its former surroundings. No one seems to know the age of the building, but supposedly the business dates back to the days of mud streets and horse-drawn carriages. This means the tavern has been pouring drinks for well over a century and makes the Gahanna Grill one of the oldest restaurants in the area.

The nondescript exterior of the tavern yields to a comfortable interior. The wood-paneled walls are covered with photos of the tavern's past (one depicting the former Gahanna Lanes, a bowling alley on the premises) and the large bar is surrounded by televisions. The surface of the bar is a potpourri of advertisements for local services— from real estate to a hair salon—laminated directly into the finish. One corner of the bar is dedicated to the Beanie Burger Hall of Fame. Floor-to-ceiling photographs show the brave souls who have ingested the burger that has made the Gahanna famous—the "Double Beanie Burger."

The regular Beanie Burger itself is a monster, with its patty of fresh ground beef weighing in at about half a pound. The Double gives you two half-pound patties, a photo on the wall, and a free T-shirt for your efforts. But the Beanie Burger, named after the cook who invented it decades ago, does not just contain a perfectly griddled patty. The burger is also piled high with lettuce, tomato, grilled onions, bacon, cheese, and a hearty scoop of homemade coleslaw. The burger is a sloppy, tasty mess that is barely contained by its toasted, soft kaiser roll. For that reason, the kitchen staff takes great pride in stabbing the vertical burger with a large steak knife. I know of no frilly toothpick that could keep this beast together.

Beanie Vesner still mans the grill and turns out hundreds of burgers for the lunchtime crowd consisting mostly of construction workers and faithful regulars. Jim Ellison, a friend who alerted me to this hamburger destination, calls the Beanie Burger "A good, manly lunch," referring to the nearly 100 percent male population at noon. "Dinnertime is different, mostly families,"

Jimmy, the newest owner of the restaurant, told me. "This used to be mainly a lunch crowd with the bar busy at night." Since he purchased Gahanna in 2005 he has updated the kitchen and added steaks and pastas to the menu.

I asked Beanie how long he had been making burgers at Gahanna and he refused to give me a straight answer. Smiling, with a toothpick in his mouth, he told me, "Maybe 20 years, maybe?" But by other accounts, the figure is more like 30 years.

To make the burger, Beanie grabs a half-pound wad of ground beef measured by hand and presses it flat, also by hand, onto the hot griddle. The burger is flipped once and a bacon weight is placed on top. I asked him how he knew the burger was a half pound and his deadpan response was, "Because I've made up probably about three million of them." I ordered my Beanie Burger cooked to the chef's specs and ended up with a medium-well, but moist, burger. Beanie told me later, with a shrug, "Most people around here like their burgers well done."

Jimmy is far from the typical Midwesterner or Ohio native. That's because he was born in Albania and lived in Brooklyn, New York, for 17 years. He attended cooking school in New York City, owned a pizza parlor, and for a few years was Mayor Rudolph Giuliani's chef at Gracie Mansion. He came to Columbus for opportunity and the quality of life it promised. "In Bensonhurst, we lived in a studio apartment on the sixteenth floor. Here, I live in a mansion, wife, two kids, two-car garage, backyard, and a pool." All that, and he owns a restaurant that makes one of the best burgers in America.

★ ★ ★ ★ ★

HAMBURGER WAGON

12 EAST CENTRAL AVE | MIAMISBURG, OH 45342

937-847-2442 | WWW.HAMBURGERWAGON.COM

MON–SAT 10:30 AM–7 PM | SUN 11 AM–7 PM

Every day of the year two dedicated employees of the Hamburger Wagon open a small garage door and drag a tiny spoked-wheel lunch cart 50 feet to a spot across the street. "It's pretty awkward to pull," an employee told me once, "but if you get a running start it's okay." The wagon has been selling burgers in roughly the same spot for almost 100 years to faithful regulars from the center of this picturesque town south of Dayton. I asked former owner Michelle Lyons if the Hamburger Wagon would be around for a while and she told me, "I think there would be civil unrest if they tried to get rid of the wagon."

Born of necessity, the Hamburger Wagon was started by Sherman "Cocky" Porter just after the devastating Dayton Flood of 1913. Miamisburg was evacuated and in shambles, left without power or water. Cocky served burgers from a cart to relief workers and locals who were put to the task of rebuilding the town.

Today, the Wagon still sells the one thing it

has sold for almost a century—hamburgers. It's as basic as you can get. The burger comes one way only, on a bun with pickle and onion, no cheese. You can always tell when someone in line has never been to the wagon when they ask for cheese. Various cranky old men have owned and worked on the Wagon through the decades and Michelle told me, "If you asked for cheese, they'd tell you, 'If you want cheese, get yer ass over to the McDonald's!'"

The small patties, around three ounces apiece, come as singles or doubles on tiny Wonder buns. Chips and pop are offered, but that's about it. If you were looking for variety, you came to the wrong place. If you were looking for one of the tastiest burgers in America, dig in.

The burgers at the Wagon are unique. The first thing you'll notice upon first bite is the extraordinarily crunchy exterior and the pleasantly moist interior. Think chicken-fried burger. You also probably watched your burger being deep-fried in the enormous skillet through one of the Wagon's windows. The reason for the super-crunch of the burgers is kept secret, but I'd venture to guess that one of the ingredients is some sort of breading. Adding bread to ground beef was a government-sanctioned method for stretching food during the Depression. It's a method that a few old-time burger stands in America still operate successfully with.

An average order at the wagon is four burgers. A customer of over 60 years named Glenn makes the 40-mile round trip twice a week for four of the tasty deep-fried burgers. One day when I was there he added a Diet Coke to his order. Rubbing his belly, he told me, laughing, "I'm watching my figure!"

Two employees work at lightning speed to prep, cook, and bag over 200 burgers an hour. One stands at the skillet managing the tiny bobbing and bubbling patties while the other preps buns and makes change. This sounds entirely ordinary except that it is accomplished in a space that is no more than four by five feet wide. The illusion of the small cart is perpetuated though by a large commercial kitchen across the street where the meat, onions, and buns are prepped and stored.

New owner Jack Sperry bought the Hamburger Wagon in 2007 and changed virtually nothing, except that now the Wagon is open year round. Jack told me, "Unless there's a 10 foot snow drift we're dragging out the Wagon." This is a big change from the previous owners who would close down for the month of February much to the dismay of the regulars.

Jack is also working on building a second wagon that he can send out to fairs and festivals. Even though the new wagon will have the same menu, it'll be twice the size and totally tricked out. Jack explained, "It'll be like the Hamburger Wagon on steroids."

JOHNNIE'S TAVERN

3503 TRABUE RD | COLUMBUS, OH 43204
614-488-0110 | MON–SAT 11 AM–10 PM
CLOSED SUNDAY

On my first visit to this semi-suburban burger destination I was invited into the kitchen to interview the chef and I was sort of shocked by what I found. Although Johnnie's is a tiny out of the way tavern they do manage to crank out a ton of burgers during the lunch hour and all of those burgers are prepped, cooked, cheesed, and placed on buns by the one-man hamburger machine Joe Lombardi.

"When I get real backed up it can take me a while," the twenty something fourth-generation Lombardi told me. "I'm alone back here." As he jumped from griddle to prep surface and back again with lightning speed, the band Phish poured out of a beat-up boom box. The only other employee during lunch, the bubbly server/bartender Brittney, burst into the kitchen with the next large order of burgers and announced, "You're gonna HATE this order." The order contained about nine burgers, all with different types of cheese and different toppings, not to mention that the order was hard to read. When I asked why she thought Joe would hate the order she told me, "Just because it's a bunch of mumbo-jumbo."

Joe's grandfather, Dominic, opened the comfortable, broken-in bar in 1948 by turning his family's local grocery store into a tavern. Joe's great-grandfather emigratcd from Italy to open the grocery store around the turn of the century. Johnnie's sits near a busy freight rail crossing in the old-world Italian neighborhood of San Margherita, an attractive spot to Italian immigrants at the time due to its proximity to a large, nearby marble quarry.

As I stood talking to Joe in the kitchen at Johnnie's, I saw him reach somewhere and toss what looked like perfectly pressed frozen burger patties on the griddle. My heart sank and I shouted out in disbelief, "Are your burgers frozen?" Fortunately, my trip to Johnnie's was not in vain and Joe explained with a chuckle, "No, that's fried bologna." The fried bologna, which is clearly linked to the strong Ohio roots in European sausage making, is a local central Ohio favorite.

The "Super Burgers" are the only burger on the menu and they come in one size—huge. Every morning Joe and other family members hand-patty enough burgers for lunch and dinner. Joe told me, "I usually don't weigh them but they are around a pound." These burgers are beasts and after cooking they are still just north of three-fourths-pound. The fresh-ground chuck comes from two local sources and blended in the kitchen. Why two sources? "That's just the way it's always been done," Joe told me with a straight face. I love those answers.

A burger with everything comes on a seeded, white squishy bun with your choice of cheese

(six to choose from), raw onion, a slice of tomato, and lettuce. The regular's cheese of choice is Pepper Jack, which has a decent kick and is the perfect cheese for the Super Burger. Fried onions are also available, but you'll have to ask for them.

On my first weekday visit to Johnnie's, the place was full by 11:30 a.m. and there were beers on every table. A pool table dominates the dining area, leaving only enough room for about 28 hungry patrons. The bar is also an option with its 13 stools but a wait seems inevitable after 11:45. On one wall is a poster of grandpa Dominic standing at the bar, a mug of beer in front of him with a strange contraption protruding. I asked local friend and burger expert Jim Ellison about the beer and he explained that more than once Johnnie's has been awarded the

"Coldest Tap Beer in Columbus." The thing sticking out of the beer? A thermometer.

People who love Johnnie's really love the place. A guy in the booth next to me announced, unprovoked, "I've been coming here for 25 years." That's the kind of burger-love I'm looking for across America. Jim pointed out that for most people who live in Columbus a trip to Johnnie's is not serendipitous because it's way out by itself in a quiet part of town surrounded by homes with perfectly trimmed lawns. "If you are coming here you are making a choice to be here."

Joe plans to keep Johnnie's in the family and eventually buy the place from his dad. When his dad asked him to step into the business, Joe told me, "I took about a month to decide." Let's hope a Lombardi runs this American icon for at least another four generations.

KEWPEE

111 NORTH ELIZABETH ST | LIMA, OH 45801

419-228-1778 | MON–THU 5 AM–10 PM

FRI & SAT 5 AM–MIDNIGHT | SUN 3 PM-10 PM

In the center of Lima, Ohio, sits a slice of Americana that is impossible to ignore. A well preserved Art-Deco restaurant with a big history, this 1920s hamburger tradition once existed throughout the Upper Midwest with over 200 locations that competed with White Castle and outlived White Tower. Today there are only six Kewpees remaining, and of those, three are in Lima.

Owner Harry Shutt hasn't done much to his enameled-brick burger restaurant that was built in 1938 (and replaced a version built in 1928). "We have tried to maintain our image and not change much." That's a good thing because this Kewpee has been turning out tasty square-patty burgers for over 80 years.

Yes, the burgers at Kewpee are square, not

round. Sound familiar? In 1969, Dave Thomas, the founder of the ubiquitous Wendy's chain, introduced a square burger to America. It may have been a new concept to some, but both Kewpee and White Castle have been serving square burgers since the 1920s. Dave was clearly influenced by the local Kewpee in his hometown of Kalamazoo, Michigan. But unlike both White Castle and Wendy's, the burgers at Kewpee are made from fresh ground beef, not frozen.

Step into the Kewpee of downtown Lima and instantly step back in time. Very little has changed from the food to the 1930s fast-food décor. The restaurant's original curved white enamel steel wall and ceiling panels look as clean as if it were opening day. Newish orange plastic booths, a low counter with stools, and random tables fill the small terrazzo-floored restaurant. In the dining area two large Kewpee dolls stand watch over customers enjoying their burgers and thick shakes. Fortunately, Harry has held on to these icons of a forgotten age and has even had the priceless dolls refurbished recently. The Kewpee name comes from the popular early twentieth–century doll of the same name (but different spelling), the Kewpie doll.

The burgers are fresh. "I buy boneless carcass beef and grind it here," Harry told me. The beef comes from a Lima slaughterhouse that uses local cows only. Harry said it best when he explained, "The worst thing you can do to meat is haul it. These animals have never been more than 40 miles from Lima." This makes Harry

and Kewpee an anomaly in fast-food America. The hamburger über-chains today, with their cross-country shipments and city-sized warehouses, could not even begin to imagine this sort of localized business plan.

Two separate griddles work full-time during the lunch rush; one services the drive-thru and the other walk-up customers inside. All of the women working behind the counter slinging patties and dressing burgers have been at the Kewpee for over 30 years. Amazingly, grill cook Nancy has been employed at Kewpee since the Kennedy administration.

The burgers are super-thin and so fresh they are almost falling apart. The usual condiments like mustard, ketchup, and pickle are available, but most order "The Special," which is a burger with mayonnaise, lettuce, and tomato. The produce for Kewpee comes from a local farmer and is hydroponically grown. One menu item, the vegetable sandwich, appears to be a late addition for a health-conscious America, but this is not the case. On the menu for decades, the sandwich was probably added during World War II to make up for the lack of available burger meat. "We've had a vegetable sandwich for over 70 years," Harry pointed out. Harry has been at Kewpee for over 50 years and owns the rights to the franchise, as well as two other "contemporary" Kewpees in Lima. He started flipping burgers at the downtown Kewpee when he was 25 and became the owner in 1980. Harry has a lot to say about the "Wal-Marting" of America.

He feels the crush of commercial fast food and the lack of support for small business in America. Coincidentally, one of his Kewpees is threatened by highway expansion designed to accommodate . . . a new Wal-Mart! Regardless, Kewpee does a brisk business and is hardly fazed by the seven McDonald's restaurants in Lima.

You owe it to yourself to visit Kewpee. It's a part of American hamburger tradition that remains vital in the face of a homogenizing fast-food culture. Pay homage to a burger chain that preceded Burger King and Wendy's by almost 40 years. Look for the wide-eyed smiling Kewpee doll over the front door and remember the Kewpee slogan, "Hamburg pickle on top makes your heart go flippity-flop."

THE SPOT

201 SOUTH OHIO AVE | SIDNEY, OH 45365

937-492-9899 | WWW.THESPOTOEAT.COM

MON–SAT 7 AM–9 PM | SUN 8 AM–9 PM

The Spot has been a fixture in the center of downtown Sidney, Ohio for over a century. The large, gleaming neon sign over the front door is a beacon to those in search of genuine diner food and one of the best burgers in the country—the "Big Buy."

The first time I stepped into this updated time-warp diner with its two-tone leather booths and vintage Coke signage I thought the place may have lost its way. Then an old-timer got up from his booth, approached the vintage jukebox and put on Little Anthony's "Tears on My Pillow" and the whole place was transformed. The ownership had not fallen prey to '50s kitsch. They had merely embraced it. A major remodeling effort in 1976 updated the interior of The Spot to a wood-paneled "country kitchen" look and it took sixth owner Michael Jannides to rescue the diner and restore it to its original character. "I wanted to bring the place back to the way it looked in the '40s," Michael explained, and he did so with amazing detail.

Don't let the sock hop décor fool you. The Spot actually dates back to a time well before Elvis was King. In 1907 Spot Miller was selling food from a cart on the location where the restaurant now sits. The cart eventually became a permanent structure that burned down in 1940. A year later, the second owners rebuilt The Spot in the Art Moderne style that remains today.

Michael was no stranger to The Spot when he assumed ownership of the Ohio hamburger icon in 1999. In 1989, Michael took a part-time job at The Spot and liked what he saw. His grandfather owned an ice cream parlor in Sidney when he was growing up, and this most likely influenced Michael's decision to buy The Spot.

There are many diner favorites on the menu like the BLT, the tuna salad sandwich, the seasonal mincemeat pie, and a house-made tenderloin sandwich. Michael confessed, "We've added things to the menu over the years but people come in for the burgers." For sure, the burger remains the number one seller at The Spot. The restaurant can go through up to 1000 on a busy Friday.

I had blinders on when I saw the best seller on the long burger menu—the "Big Buy." Advertised as a triple-decker, the Big Buy is actually a double patty burger with one of those bun inserts in between the patties (like you'd find on a Big Mac). Cooked on a flattop griddle, the Big Buy is served on a toasted, white squishy bun with shredded lettuce, pickles, American cheese, and a house-made tartar sauce. The taste of this thing is phenomenal, although you'll find lifting the Big Buy to your face a challenge. The two quarter-pound square patties slip and slide in the tartar sauce and make a mockery of the bun. If you can manage to get a solid bite that includes all of the ingredients, you are in for a treat. The tartar, tangy and sweet, plays to the beefiness of the burger with the cheese lending a salty hand.

The Spot grinds and patties their own burgers and have done so for years. Michael showed me the patty maker he inherited with the purchase of the restaurant, a strange looking contraption with many parts. From what I could tell, the burgers are not "pressed" or "stamped" like most patty machines, rather they are extruded sideways through a narrow opening and cut into squares. The patty, when cooked, stays loose and almost crumbly, most likely from not being pressed in the patty-making process.

Grab a booth or a spot at the counter along the window, then place your order at the register in the rear of the restaurant. When your order is ready, listen for your number to be called over a loudspeaker and pick up your burgers at the counter. At The Spot you can also enjoy traditional carhop service in one of the restaurant's 21 parking spaces. Regulars have enjoyed carhop service for decades and as Michael put it, "It never went out of vogue here!"

After six owners I have a feeling this place will be around for a while. Almost everything at The Spot is fresh and made to order, which is a tough claim for most diners today. Michael is committed to keeping the dream alive and continues that spirit by sticking to the basics.

SWENSON'S DRIVE IN

658 EAST CUYAHOGA FALLS AVE | AKRON, OH 44310

(6 OTHER LOCATIONS IN AKRON, CANTON, AND CLEVELAND)

330-928-8515 | WWW.SWENSONSDRIVEINS.COM

SUN–THU 11 AM–MIDNIGHT

FRI & SAT 11 AM–1:30 AM | CLOSED MONDAY

I was happy to find that classic carhop drive-in culture is alive and well in Ohio. Anyone who has ever visited the Cuyahoga Falls Avenue location of Swenson's can tell you that. There are other large burger chains in the United States that employ carhops but I've never seen anything like the energy displayed by the carhops at Swenson's. For these carhops, delivery of a burger to your car is a true sport.

My first impression of Swenson's, with its young men and women in white polo shirts darting back and forth, was that something was wrong. These carhops were moving way too fast for college-age kids. A half-dozen carhops crisscross with trays of burgers and drinks at lightning speed, often running into each other entering and leaving the kitchen area. When a car pulls up to the 58-year-old drive-in, the driver barely has to flash lights before a carhop is sprinting in their direction. And when a regular pulls up, the carhops all shout out their name in singsong fashion, "Angela's here!" or "Omar's here!" It's pretty incredible to witness and a great show to watch. Swenson's hires only college students for their youth and their flexible schedules. "It's a rigorous, hard job," Patty Palmer from Swenson's main office told me. "It takes a special person to do that."

The Cuyahoga Falls Avenue location is the oldest physical structure dating back to 1952 but the local chain now boasts seven locations in Akron, Canton, and Cleveland, all drive-ins with carhops, or "curb-servers" as they are referred to at Swenson's. Wesley "Pop" Swenson opened his first drive-in in 1934 after he had success selling burgers from his station wagon to high school students as classes let out. The Swenson family sold the business in the late '50s to the Phillips family who in turn sold it to current owner Steve Thompson in 1974 (a former curb server himself at Swenson's in the '60s). He was responsible for expanding the business by adding five additional locations, as well as rebuilding the original 1934 West Akron drive-in. The Phillips family probably ran the drive-ins well, but Steve had an added advantage. Friendly with Pop's granddaughter, Steve was able to get the original Swenson recipes making the drive-in today as authentic as it could possibly be.

The menu at Swenson's is large and offers Ohio classics like the fried bologna sandwich and the Sloppy Joe, but the burgers are the star attraction, headlining the top of the menu. The signature burger at Swenson's is the "Galley Boy," a double cheeseburger with two special sauces. I deduced that one sauce was mayonnaise and the other was barbecue sauce. "You are sort of right but not quite," Patty told me. Clearly the sauces are a secret. There are many condiments available at Swenson's, but if you ask for everything, you'll get mustard, pickles, and raw onion. But the Galley Boy, with its two sauces, two 3-ounce patties, and cheese, is perfect.

All of the burgers are served on buns that are a special recipe and been made exclusively for Swenson's by the local Massoli Italian Bakery. Fresh ground beef is delivered daily to each of the locations in the chain, pattied and shipped out from their central commissary location in North Akron.

Swenson's is also known for its shakes and the incredible chocolate peanut butter is one of the most popular. There are 18 flavors to choose from with "limitless combinations," Patty explained. Swenson's also offers seasonal flavors, like the immensely popular pumpkin shake in the fall.

People are crazy about Swenson's and the restaurant has a solid legion of fans. "It's bizzaro!" Patty explained of the lengths some fanatics go to enjoy their Swenson's burgers. "We just sent two burgers to a wedding for the bride and groom," Patty explained. That's right, the newlyweds ate Swenson's burgers, and the guests ate the catered food. That is my kind of wedding.

THURMAN CAFE

183 THURMAN AVE | COLUMBUS, OH 43206

614-443-1570 | WWW.THETHURMANCAFE.COM

OPEN DAILY 11 AM–2:30 AM, SUNDAY TO 1 AM

The quaint, historic German Village in Columbus, Ohio, with its low, ancient buildings and streets paved with red brick, is the perfect setting for this broken-in, dark and cozy tavern. The menu at Thurman Cafe is loaded with great food from decades-old family recipes like the Coney sauce for the hot dogs and terrific French fries. But it's the burger you came to eat, so settle into one of the odd-shaped booths and prepare to feast on one of the tallest burgers in the land—the "Thurman Burger."

Thurman Cafe has all the trappings of a typical time-tested favorite local hang—walls covered with the obligatory license plates, beer ads, and old photos. But look a little closer and discover the amazing ceiling covered in vintage Budweiser wallpaper and the thousands of signed dollar bills dangling over the bar area like party decorations. Chances are, while you are waiting for your Thurman Burger to arrive, one will pass by on its way to another customer. Your first glance at the famed burger will result in an audible gulp that signals either fear or hunger. This is because the Thurman Burger is enormous.

Macedonian immigrants Nancho and Dena Suclescy opened the Thurman Cafe in 1937. Today, more than 70 years later, the café is still in the Suclescy family, run by third-generation siblings Mike, Paul, and Donna.

There are many different burgers on the menu, but it's the Thurman Burger that outsells them all. The creation starts with a three-quarter-pound patty of griddled fresh ground beef that is topped with (follow me here) grilled onions, lettuce, tomato, sliced sautéed mushrooms, pickle, jalapeño slices, mayonnaise, and a half-pound mound of sliced ham. The pile of ingredients is then covered with both mozzarella and American cheese, capped with a toasted bun, and speared with extra-long toothpicks. When I say tall, I'm guessing this burger stands no less than seven inches high. Get your mouth ready.

"The best way to eat this thing," local burger expert and friend Jim Ellison told me, "is to press it down and flip it over. The juices have already destroyed the bottom bun." He was right, and flipping worked, but after the first few bites something went wrong and my burger imploded.

The combination of ingredients and sheer size beg for your patience. Take your time and enjoy this pile of goodness. It's a sloppy burger.

On a busy Saturday at Thurman, the kitchen will prepare and serve up to 500 of the famed burgers. "We go through over 1,500 pounds of beef a week," Mike Suclescy told me. Good meat too. Mike buys only top-quality 85/15 ground chuck and told me, "We ran out once and went over to the Kroger Supermarket for ground beef. The taste just wasn't the same."

The "Blue Cheeseburger" (for which the Suclescys go through over eight gallons of blue cheese dressing a week) is also a big seller as is the "Macedonian," served on Texas toast with sweet red peppers. Or try the new "Thurmanator," a Thurman Burger on top of a cheddar cheeseburger. You heard correctly, it's basically a double Thurman Burger. A regular cheeseburger has been banished to the bottom of the menu, clearly a lightweight choice at this tavern.

My favorite-sounding concoction was the "Johnnie Burger." Invented by a chronic tequila-quaffing regular, the Johnnie is a three-quarter-pound burger with bacon and blue cheese that's drizzled with a shot of top-shelf 1800 tequila. No lettuce, tomato, or mayo is offered because, as Johnnie once explained, "If I wanted a salad, I'd order one!"

WILSON'S SANDWICH SHOP

600 S. MAIN ST I FINDLAY, OH 45840

419-422-5051 I MON–THU 7AM–10PM

FRI–SAT 7AM–MIDNIGHT I SUN 2PM–10PM

It's hard to miss Wilson's as you roll through downtown Findlay, Ohio. The restaurant is on a busy crossroads in the center of town with the word WILSON spelled above the front door in large black letters. Across the street sits the impressive former Marathon Oil world headquarters: a beautiful glass, steel, and concrete monument to the automobile age.

Wilson's has walls of windows on three sides. From inside, the sun-drenched space makes you feel like you're in a huge fishbowl. Grab a stool at one of the long counters lining the windows, watch small town America unfold, and enjoy a fresh-ground hamburger and a chocolate malt.

The building is the second constructed in the restaurant's long history. The first, built in 1936, was a stunning example of enamel steel road food culture. It was replaced with a greatly expanded Wilson's in the mid-sixties. During construction of the new Wilson's, the tiny yellow restaurant was pushed to the back of the parking lot and remained open. The original Wilson's was as narrow as a subway car and held only 32 people. Today's newer building seats over 130 hungry patrons in a wide dining room filled with a combination of booths, tables, and counters. Expect to find a line to the door at lunch and dinner.

Stub Wilson opened Wilson's Sandwich Shop in 1936. A few years earlier, Stub had opened two Kewpee restaurants in nearby Lima, Ohio and decided to open another in Findlay. Finding another Kewpee already in Findlay (the restaurants were independently owned), he chose to name the new restaurant after himself. When Stub Wilson died, he passed all three restaurants onto his managers—the Kewpees in Lima went to Harrison Shutt and Wilson's went to three managers, Woody Curtis, Wilber Fenbert, and Lance Baker. Today, Wilson's is part owned and run by Lance Baker's widow, Pat. After a few years of decline, Pat stepped in to take charge of the situation. "I got everybody back on track and back in uniforms." She was wise not to change the menu and she told me, "The burgers are still hot, juicy, and good!"

There's no question that the burgers at Wilson's are fresh. Three times a week the restaurant receives a delivery of 600 pounds of beef from a slaughterhouse in Lima. Every morning the staff grinds and patties enough for the day's burgers. A patty machine attached to the grinder forms them into square patties, a shape that Wendy's popularized in the late 1960s but actually hails from the original Kewpee restaurants.

The basic, three-and-a-half-ounce griddled burger comes with mustard, pickle, and onion. Make it a "Special" and you'll also get lettuce, tomato, and mayo (for only 40 cents more). Just think; it only takes 40 cents to make your burger special.

236

Similarities between the Kewpees of Lima and Wilson's still exist, but the most notable is the historically significant vegetable sandwich. Listed on the menu as the "Veggie," this meatless sandwich (a Special without the patty) is a product of the WWII years when meat rationing forced many burger stands to adapt or shut down. White Castle temporarily embraced the grilled cheese sandwich, many others went to fish sandwiches, and Wilson's (and the Kewpees of Lima) introduced the vegetable sandwich.

Wilson's is the type of happy place that you remember from your youth. People come from all over to eat the burgers they ate growing up in Findley. Mark Metcalf, an actor from Findley best known for his role as the R.O.T.C. commander Neidermeyer in the film *Animal House*, recalls Wilson's burgers fondly. He told me by phone, "My grandfather used to go down to Wilson's and bring back bagfuls of hamburgers." Pat is aware of the restaurant's popularity and its place in the memory of anyone who was raised on Wilson's burgers. And I for one am overjoyed that she had the good sense to step in to basically rescue Wilson's. She told me, "We want to stick around for a while. We have a seventy-fifth anniversary coming up."

29

OKLAHOMA

CLAUD'S HAMBURGERS

3834 SOUTH PEORIA BLVD | TULSA, OK 74105

918-742-8332 | TUES, WED, & SAT 10:30 AM–4 PM

THU & FRI 10:30 AM–8 PM | CLOSED SUN & MON

The hours posted in the window at Claud's are correct but slightly loose depending on the number of people waiting outside for the 56-year-old hamburger counter to open. "Depends on how I feel that morning," Robert Hobson said with a smile after opening a few minutes early. "Every day is different."

Robert and his brother, Cliff, own the tiny, bright diner in the neighborhood of Brookside, just south of downtown Tulsa. In 1985, Claud Hobson passed the business to his sons, who had already put in plenty of years behind the counter. "I was four months old when he moved to this location [in 1965]," Robert told me. "I guess you can say I've been here all my life."

The interior of Claud's is clean and utilitarian, with white walls and a long counter lined with short green and chrome swivel stools. The Hobsons have only the absolute basics behind the faux-wood Formica counter: a flattop griddle, refrigerators, and a deep fryer, everything in gleaming stainless steel. Large picture windows allow ample daylight to stream in and passing cars on South Peoria send flashes down the counter.

The burgers at Claud's are a lesson in simplicity. When Claud was at the griddle your options were only mustard, pickle, and onion. Today, his sons have expanded options slightly to include lettuce and tomato. American cheese reigns supreme but as Robert told me with a sigh, "We also offer pepper jack cheese, but I think I made three yesterday." Robert is a man after my own heart. "Our main focus is the meat," He told me standing at the griddle. "When you cover it up

with all that stuff you lose the taste."

The burger to get at Claud's is the double cheeseburger with onions. The onion is not just a slice tossed on cold or grilled to limp. When you order yours with onions watch what happens. To the right of the flattop is a small piece of white marble embedded in the countertop. Robert takes a patty, slaps it onto the marble, and works a handful of chopped raw onion into the patty with the back of a stiff spatula. He then takes the flattened patty and plops it, onion-side down, onto the hot flattop. If you require a double, Robert takes two patties and stacks them on the marble and works them together with the spatula. The result is a very flat, wide burger that hangs far outside the white squishy bun, a style that has been Claud's for decades.

The only change Claud's burger has seen over the years was an increase in the size of the patty from 2 to 3 ounces and a switch from balled-beef to pre-formed patties. After two decades of balling ground chuck to smash into patties, Claud finally purchased a patty machine in the early seventies. "He used to say," Robert told me, "if someone is smart enough to make a machine to make my life easier, I'm smart enough to buy it."

Before it was Claud's, the burger counter was well known as Van's Hamburgers, part of a mini-chain in Tulsa. Claud opened his original burger joint in 1954 about 2 miles west of downtown but moved to the Van's on South Peoria in 1965. "He was actually 'chosen' to take over this loca-

tion," Robert told me. The busy thoroughfare has its share of burger joints with the 80-year-old Weber's Root Beer Stand directly across the street and a Sonic Drive-In just two doors down from Claud's. Amazingly, the Sonic has not affected their business.

Robert is 45 years young and plans to run the business for a while. "I plan on being here until our seventy-fifth anniversary!" he told me with a chuckle, which would be in 2030. "Maybe longer."

FOLGER'S DRIVE-INN

406 EAST MAIN ST | ADA, OK 74820

580-332-9808 | MON–FRI 10:30 AM–7 PM

CLOSED SAT & SUN

If you didn't know what you were looking for, you could drive right by Folger's. The unassuming little '50s prefab on the east end of downtown Ada has only two neon signs in the window—one that reads FOLGER'S, the other OPEN. A short flight of red concrete steps leads directly into hamburger heaven. Inside you'll find a bright, sunny, clean restaurant filled with the friendliest people. I'm not kidding. Within 15 minutes of my visit to Folger's, I knew everyone in the place.

Folger's is definitely a family-run business. In October 1935, G.G. and Christine Folger opened a hamburger concession in the local movie theater

just up Main Street. They opened the current location in 1950 and eventually turned over operations and ownership to their two sons, Jim and Jerry Folger. Today, Jim and Jerry spend the better part of their day behind the large flattop griddle and Jerry's wife, Wanda, works the tiny 12-stool counter. Orders to-go come in on the pay phone by the front door and Jim makes change at the register between burger flips.

"We have a few other things on the menu but hamburger baskets are 90 percent of our business," a very busy lunchtime Jim told me. I stood and watched him methodically flip and manage 12 quarter-pound burgers on the griddle at the same time. The Folger brothers engage in a sort of silent culinary dance in their open, narrow kitchen—Jim flips burgers, Jerry dresses them, and Wanda delivers. The dance is repeated over and over again for hours at lunch until hundreds of burgers have been dispensed to happy customers.

"We've been open 75 years now," Jim told me. "We have quite a bit of loyalty and now five generations of families are coming in." A regular customer named Mike, smiling and rubbing his belly joked, "You can tell I've had a bunch of them." The burger at Folger's comes with mustard, onion, lettuce, and tomato. Ask for an "Educated Burger" (not on the menu), and you'll get a burger that replaces the onion with mayo. Make it a "basket" and you'll get to experience the other reason you came to Ada—for their outstanding fries. Every day, Folger's manages to go through over 200 pounds of potatoes for their fresh-cut fries.

"The produce and meat are fresh, every day," Jim told me as he flattened another hand-formed patty on the griddle with a long spatula. Jim uses large Wonder buns that are perfectly toasted on the griddle. The finished product is a wide, flat burger that is bursting with greasy goodness and flavor.

"The grill used to be right behind the counter, and was smaller," Bill Peterson, the district attorney in Ada, told me. If it had not been for Bill and mutual friend Tom Palmore, I may never have found Folger's. Both Bill and Tom grew up in Ada and were classmates of Jerry Folger's. They agreed that Folger's was not to be missed on the hunt for great burgers in America—they were right.

HAMBURGER KING

322 E. MAIN ST | SHAWNEE, OK 74801

405-878-0488

WWW.HAMBURGERKINGOKLAHOMA.COM

MON–SAT 11 AM–8 PM | CLOSED SUNDAY

Legend has it that there used to be two Hamburger Kings in Oklahoma, one in Shawnee and one in Ada, and the Ada location was lost in a craps game. The owners of both were George "The Hamburger King" Macsas and his brother, Joe. The Macsas brothers emigrated from Beirut to Oklahoma and opened the successful hamburger venture in 1927. Today, more than 80 years later, the Hamburger King still stands in Shawnee and proudly remains in the Macsas family.

Dusty downtown Shawnee, Oklahoma, feels proudly American. A restaurant named Hamburger King is almost required in this setting, along with the Rexall Drug store, the furniture store (with layaway plans), and the enormous grain elevators on the edge of town. The Hamburger King exists in its third location in Shawnee; the other two were only steps away and the previous one burned down in a grease fire in 1965.

Soon after the fire, the Macsas family rebuilt a much larger version of their burger restaurant a block up Main Street. Today's Hamburger King is a large, airy diner awash in pastels. The walls are pink-and-white striped Masonite panels. Two long rows of booths and a small counter in the rear service customers and there are the

constant sounds of sizzling burgers and the whir of the milkshake machine. Since 1965, at least, nothing has changed. "We switched to Pepsi once and the people rebelled," Colleen Macsas told me. Colleen is the restaurant's manager and met her husband, owner Michael Macsas, at the Hamburger King in 1975.

The burgers at Hamburger King are fantastic. Fresh 80/20 patties are delivered to the restaurant daily and cooked on a large, well-seasoned flattop griddle. Quarter-pound singles and doubles are offered. Order a double and you'll get double the cheese as well. Waitress Beverly pointed out, "Most men order the double meat burger." I was not about to let my manhood be challenged and naturally ordered a double, a half-pound burger loaded with lettuce, tomato, onions, pickles, and mustard on a toasted, white squishy bun. This burger is not small. Order a "basket" and you'll get deep-fried potato wedges or tater tots, not fries.

The method for ordering your burger at Hamburger King is one of the most unique in America. If you sit at the counter, expect normal interaction with a counterperson. Sit at one of the many booths and you'll need to place your order by phone. That's right, each table is equipped with a red phone and a single button—your lifeline to the kitchen. On the other end of the red food phone is a switchboard operator who relays your order to the grill cook. The funny thing is, the restaurant is not so large that you can't just call out your order, but the quirkiness of the phone system can't be beat.

Regulars in a place like Hamburger King are as expected as good burgers. "See those guys over there," Colleen said to me, pointing to a group of older men at a booth in trucker hats, overalls, and plaid shirts, "they come in here every day and they bring in their wives on Saturday." Naturally, I had to approach and ask them the obvious, "Do you guys phone in your order?" One guy, smiling, told me, "Naw, they know what we want."

HARDEN'S HAMBURGERS

432 SOUTH SHERIDAN RD | TULSA, OK 74112

918-834-2558 | WWW.THEHAMBURGERSTORE.COM

TUE–SAT 11 AM–8 PM

As I savored the first bite of my "Men's Burger" at Harden's, owner Rick West said in his quiet Oklahoma drawl, "That's what you want, isn't it?" This smiling, intense burgerman with piercing blue eyes wasn't asking about the specifics of the burger in my hand. And he wasn't asking my opinion of this glorious pile of beef and cheese either. I could tell by the tone in his voice that his question had a larger meaning, as if to say, "Isn't this what everyone really wants?" Oh yes, most certainly.

Rick started his career in burgers at the age of 12 working at the long-gone Tanner's Drive-In on Admiral Place and Garnett Road. "I knew that I wanted to be in the hamburger business after working for Tanner," Rick told me. But it wasn't Tanner that had the largest influence on Rick. In 1987, after spending many years outside the restaurant business, Rick bought the decades-old burger joint from the hamburger icon Johney Harden. Johney taught Rick the secrets to his success.

As my friend (and local hamburger expert) Joe Price clicked off names of past and present Tulsa burger flippers, Rick said with a serious tone, "Johney trained a lot of those guys." His influence today is far reaching and can probably be felt in every corner of Tulsa. At one point, Johney even consulted for Wendy's founder Dave Thomas and designed his first hamburger kitchen.

A large sign hanging underneath the menu at the register says "We cook 'em with a light pink center." The burgers come in four sizes. The Girl's Quarter Pound, the Men's Double, the Triple, and the 4-patty, one-pound B.O.B. which stands for "Big Old Burger." "If you are a guy and order a Girl's Burger, you're gonna get flak," Rick warned, "but I love it when a girl orders the Men's Burger."

The most popular burger on the menu is the Men's Burger, two quarter-pound patties neatly

Rick Harden

stacked on a toasted, white squishy bun. The burger is cooked on a flattop and is actually cooked with a bit of pink in the middle. The large, well-seasoned burger explodes with flavor and is incredibly moist. Just after the patties of fresh beef hit the griddle, they are sprinkled with a top-secret seasoning. Rick is one of the only people who actually know what is in this seasoning and the company that blends the spices for Harden's has strict orders to keep it to themselves. "People actually call the spice company all the time for the recipe," Rick told me.

The onion rings at Harden's are legendary. Size alone would be a reason to order and ogle these rings. They are so large that they resemble bangle bracelets. They taste amazing. Where most battered onion rings separate on contact, these stay together. Whatever process Rick uses has the batter sticking to the onion like glue.

In 1997 Rick moved Harden's from its second location, setting up shop in a former truck rental business that he owned. This incarnation of Harden's is a virtual museum of mid-century Americana. Authentic enameled steel gasoline and soda signs are everywhere and display cases are full of vintage scale-model cars. Large, detailed model airplanes hang from the ceiling and Rick's collection of restored pedal cars are spread around the dining room. You could spend hours in Harden's and still not see everything.

When you place your order at the register, you are handed an oversized playing card as your "number." Listen for your suit to be called out over the loudspeaker (i.e. "King of Hearts!"). There is a drive-up window on the north side of

the building but Rick dissuades most people from just driving up. "We prefer that you call an order in to pick up at the window." He explained that he can't guarantee how the experience will go and recommends that you park and come inside to order. It's a drive-up, not a drive-thru.

Burger making is part science and part art and Rick West is clearly at peace with both. He told me, "I watched what Johney did and do it exactly the same way." Okay, part fear, too, I guess.

J&W GRILL

501 WEST CHOCTAW AVE | CHICKASHA, OK 73018

405-224-9912 | MON–WED 6 AM–2 PM

THU–SAT 6 AM–9 PM | CLOSED SUNDAY

"Just down from the courthouse in Chickasha there's a little place that makes a *great* burger," was the advice Bill Peterson gave me. Bill is the district attorney for the area, and a man to be trusted with hamburger knowledge. It was Bill who had led me to the amazing burger at Folger's in Ada, so hopes were high. Not only was the burger at J&W first-rate, but unbeknownst to Bill, I had stumbled upon one of the most historically important burger joints of the Oklahoma onion-fried burger phenomenon.

Onion-fried burgers are to this part of Oklahoma what cheesesteaks are to Philadelphia. The epicenter of the onion-fried burger world is 35 miles north from Chickasha in El Reno. This

small town near Oklahoma City boasts three of the best burgers in America, served at counters that are only a few hundred feet from each other. The onion-fried burger craze, started in the 1920s, was created in an effort to stretch meat and feed laid-off railroad workers cheaply.

Restaurants serving the tasty local burger popped up all over town and competition was fierce. But in 1957 a man named Richard Want moved down to Chickasha to open the J&W Grill. He was not alone in his venture though. Johnnie Siler, already successful with Johnnie's Grill in El Reno, helped to finance the new onion-burger counter.

In an effort to avoid confusion when attempting to figure out the rich histories of these Oklahoma burger joints, let's just say that they are all connected in some way. Many owners and employees of the remaining burger stands have all worked at each other's stands, though most worked for and learned from Johnnie Siler. Current owner Darren Cook seems to be the only burger man in this part of Oklahoma who did not work in El Reno. "I started at J&W when I was 12 years old washing dishes," Darren told me, "I had to use a milk crate to reach the sink." When he was 19, he purchased a share in the restaurant, and in 1981, when he was only 23, bought the restaurant outright. Understandably, J&W is his life and he has been at the burger counter for over 35 years. A restaurant in El Reno made a few offers to buy J&W from Darren, but he told me, "I'm only in my forties, what would I do?"

The *J* in J&W stands for Johnnie, the *W* for Want. "I think it was supposed to be 'S&W' for their last names but the sign people made a mistake," Maryann Davis, wife of past owner Jim Davis, told me.

J&W has everything you'd want in a burger joint—meat ground fresh on premises, onions hand sliced in back, a basic menu, and fast service. The concept is simple. Order a "hamburger" and it comes with onions. A quarter-pound wad of fresh ground beef is pressed onto a hot flattop griddle and sprinkled with a large amount of sliced (not diced) onions. The stringy onions go limp, and the burger is flipped and pressed again, forcing the onions into the cooking beef. The result is a mess of beef and caramelized onions that create a moist burger with an intense onion flavor. At J&W, if you want a double, two wads of beef are pressed together and twice the amount of onion is dispensed.

The restaurant sits on the busy thoroughfare of Choctaw Avenue near downtown Chickasha. It's a very visible red and white cinder block structure with a large American flag painted on one side. The long, low, wood-grain Formica counter has sixteen swivel stools that are never empty at lunchtime. "It gets crowded in here at lunch. The line goes out the door," counterperson Brandi told me. The good news is that the average time at a stool is 10 minutes and, Brandi said with a smile, "We can move them in and out of here in fifteen."

Brandi knows just about everyone who walks in the door and calls out their order to the grill cook before they even take a seat. Biscuits and gravy are a big seller in the morning, but she told me some customers order burgers first thing. "We'll start making burgers at 6 a.m. if someone wants one."

When I visited J&W there was no music playing, just the sounds of the exhaust fan, regulars talking about just getting off a night shift, and the sizzle of burgers on the griddle. It was refreshing to enjoy my burger without music for once, just the mesmerizing sounds of America.

JOHNNIE'S GRILL

301 SOUTH ROCK ISLAND | EL RENO, OK 73036

405-262-4721 | MON–SAT 6 AM–9 PM

SUN 11 AM–8 PM

Steve Galway is a dedicated man. The first time I visited Johnnie's to taste an onion-fried burger, the pride of El Reno, Oklahoma, Steve was not there. "He comes in every day at two," a counterperson told me. But it was 3 p.m. and he was nowhere to be found. That's because Steve comes in every day at 2 *a.m.* to prep the restaurant for the day and is gone by 11 a.m. Now that's dedication to burgers. When I finally caught up with him we had a long talk about what it takes to keep a restaurant successful. "Give the best you've got and the people will come back," are the words he lives by. He must be doing something right because every time I've

been there the place has been packed—the people most definitely come back.

Don't be fooled by the fairly nondescript exterior of Johnnie's Grill. Located on one of the main drags in downtown El Reno, the simple, brick-faced restaurant is set back from the street by a small parking lot. The only windows are the glass in the front door and a small drive-up on one side of the building. The inside is bright and clean with a sea of tables and booths, a fact you could not imagine from a parking lot assessment. There's also a short counter with seven stools and a clear view of the large flattop griddle that's usually loaded with onion-fried burgers.

This version of Johnnie's is new as of 2005. Prior to that, Johnnie's was a narrow burger joint at the same location with a counter on the left and four booths on the right. Prior to that, the original location was across the street, but, collapsed under the weight of snow in 1986. Today's Johnnie's could easily seat up to a hundred. There's even a "party table" in the new Johnnie's that seats twenty.

But for all its newness, Johnnie's remains one of the most historically important purveyors of the El Reno onion-fried burger, important because it seems that all roads lead back there. Sid and Marty Hall from the popular Sid's (only two blocks away) both worked at the counter and Johnnie himself brought the onion-fried burger south when he opened the J&W Grill of Chickasha in 1957.

Order a hamburger at Johnnie's and it comes

standard with onions smashed in. In the old days, onion was used in a burger to stretch the day's meat and to add flavor, but Steve told me, "Back then it was a lot of onion and a little meat."

The grillman takes a ball of fresh-ground chuck, slaps it on the grill, covers it with thin-sliced onions, and starts pressing the patty until the onion and red meat are one. The thin patty cooks on the hot griddle until the beef has a crunchy char and the onions are caramelized. As it nears doneness, a white squishy bun is placed on the burger, softened by onion steam. The burger is served with pickles on the side only. All other condiments are self-serve.

Steve started working at Johnnie's for then owner Bruce Otis at age 12, over 40 years ago. He and Marty (from Sid's Diner) worked at the grill at the same time and have remained friends. "It's not like it used to be," Steve said, referring to the cutthroat competition in the early days between rival burger stands in El Reno. "If I need some sacks (paper bags), I'll call Marty. We try to help each other."

If you really want to experience El Reno at its peak, show up in town on the first Saturday in May. That's when this proud town just west of Oklahoma City celebrates Burger Day. Thirty-thousand people descend on El Reno for live music, a car show, and a public construction of the "World's Largest Onion-Fried Burger." The three main burger outposts, Sid's, Robert's, and Johnnie's, all within a block of each other, operate at beyond capacity. "That day we'll have a six-block line for burgers and forty employees," Steve told me.

Steve has three sons and plans to bring them up in the business if they are interested, but makes a point to tell them his secret to success. "I tell them if you are going to own one of these you have to come down and talk to the people." But he doesn't plan on ceding control to anyone just yet. "If I'm going to do something the rest of my life, I want it to be here." Like I said, Steve is a dedicated man.

MY FAVORITE SIDES

On my ten-year journey to the best hamburgers in the nation, I came across a few regional treats that I just could not pass up. Here's a short list of the not-to-be-missed sides you'll find while burgering your way through America. I didn't include fries because most burgers come with them anyway. These are the sides, drinks, and desserts you would likely miss out on if I didn't alert you to their greatness.

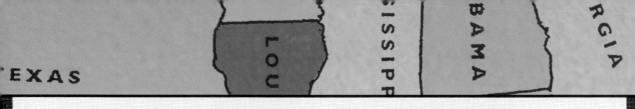
Steak Fingers—Harden's Hamburgers, Tulsa, OK

Owner Rick West made me do it. After polishing off his double cheeseburger, he presented his battered steak fingers and I somehow managed to finish them too. The best I've ever had.

Frickles—The Meers Store & Restaurant, Meers, OK

Joe Maranto is constantly adding things to his menu and this one is a winner. I sat with him recently, a basket of his new deep-fried pickles between us and he said, "I can't stop eating them!" Neither could I.

Banana Cream Pie—The Apple Pan, Los Angeles, CA

This is the king of all banana cream pies. Reserve your slice with one of the countermen before you bite into your burger.

Cheese Curds—Dotty Dumpling's Dowry, Madison, WI

These are a must-have on a burger tour of Madison. Skip the fries and get some curds, a treat whose distant cousin is the over-processed mozzarella stick. You'll never look at hot cheese the same way again.

Flan—El Mago De Las Fritas, West Miami, FL

This is, unquestionably, the BEST flan I've ever eaten, period.

Onion Rings—Crown Burger, Salt Lake City, UT

Made by hand in a private, windowless basement room. Amazing dipped in Utah's favorite fry sauce.

Fried Pies—Phillips Grocery, Holly Springs, MS

Basically a skillet-fried, fruit-stuffed piecrust. Owner Larry Davis is tired of making these tasty Southern treats—so get them soon before he gives up.

Witch Doctor—What-A-Burger Drive-In, Mooresville, NC

A sweet and savory soda drink that is topped off with sliced pickles. Sounds gross but it's so good.

Peanut Butter Chocolate Shake—Sid's Diner, El Reno, OK

After inhaling two of Marty Hall's beautiful onion-fried burgers, this was the last thing I needed. I managed to finish it though, knowing that it would be a while before I'd taste something this great again.

Cinnamon Coke—Zaharakos Ice Cream Parlor and Museum, Columbus, IN

Mixed by a real soda jerk at this perfectly restored ice cream parlor, this drink has no equal.

Onion Rings—Bobo's Drive-In, Topeka, KS

Lightly greasy oniony goodness. In a word—sublime.

Raspberry Lime Rickey—Mr. Bartley's Burger Cottage, Cambridge, MA

A mix of seltzer, sugar, raspberry, and lime syrup. Refreshing, crisp, and cool, it's the perfect accompaniment to Bartley's large, flavor-packed burgers.

LINDA-MAR DRIVE-IN

1614 WEST 51ST ST | TULSA, OK 74107

918-446-6024

WWW.FACEBOOK.COM/LINDAMARDRIVEIN

MON–SAT 11 AM–8 PM

Oklahoma has no shortage of great burger joints and Tulsa is no exception. It was very difficult to choose from the bounty of burger options in Tulsa but this tiny, bright yellow and red painted cinderblock box stood out. That may be because their signature burger, "The Westside," is a double-meat double cheeseburger served on Texas Toast and is a sight to behold.

Linda-Mar sits just outside the cloverleaf where I-44 meets Route 75. The neighborhood is called the Westside and when I asked manager Tiffany, "What is The Westside?" referring to the burger, she told me, "We're just a close-knit group over here."

The place is spotless and the décor is NASCAR-themed with an image of Winston Cup champion Rusty Wallace's Blue Deuce taking up one entire wall of the dining room. There are also framed shots of dirt track racecars everywhere, some bearing the Linda-Mar logo. Owner Mike McCutchen, who at one point was an owner at Tulsa Speedway, used to sponsor a Sprint racecar team. Not coincidentally, his brother, Danny, was the driver and the entire McCutchen family worked on the team. Today, Mike owns two bars, an automotive shop, and Linda-Mar.

The restaurant opened as Warren's in the early '60s and around 1970 was sold to the bun supplier, Walt Cook. He named the restaurant after his two daughters, Linda and Margaret, and eventually sold it to his son-in-law, Jerry McCutchen. Various members of the McCutchen family have owned and run Linda-Mar over the past 40 years, with Danny nearly running it into the ground. In 2009, Mike stepped in to take the reins at the restaurant because, as he put it, "He was sick of it. He had let it go downhill." Under Danny it had been

open for business only 2 hours a day, 5 days a week. "Everywhere people were bitching about the hours and asking why it was not open on Saturdays," Mike told me, "So I said, 'To hell with that,' and took it over from Danny. I went in, gutted it, and cleaned it up." Mike also expanded the menu, the hours, and changed the work ethic in the kitchen. "I always tell the kids [that work at Linda-Mar], 'Every time you cook something, make it like you would for yourself.'"

Linda-Mar uses fresh beef from Tulsa's favorite meatpacker Tulsa Beef and they make quarter-pound patties at the restaurant every morning with their own patty machine. The machine makes the patties wide and flat so on the well-seasoned flattop they cook quickly. "The Westside" comes with tomato, shredded lettuce, pickles, mustard, and mayo by request. It also comes with diced onion that is cooked

next to your patties on the flattop.

The Westside is a colossal pile of cheesy, greasy goodness. The major difference between a regular double cheeseburger and The Westside is in the Texas toast. The thick-sliced, regional favorite is brushed with butter on both sides and toasted directly on the flattop with the patties. A burger bun only gets toasted on one side whereas the Texas toast gets toasted on both sides. The Westside also comes with not two but four slices of gooey American cheese. It's a lot to handle but not as much of a mess as you would think. If the half-pound grease and cheese intake from The Westside doesn't frighten you, indulge in Linda-Mar's deep-fried sides, like fries, tater tots, onion rings, cheese balls, and mushrooms. They are all great, but the real winner here is the jalepeño chicken—deep-fried bits of chicken in a butter-milk jalepeño batter. Mike told me, "We marinate the chicken in the batter overnight. Makes a huge difference."

One curious element to the Linda-Mar experience is a small television that plays episodes of *The Andy Griffith Show* non-stop. "My mom loved *Andy Griffith* and that sumbitch would play until I whistled myself to sleep," Mike told me. It has become an integral part of the restaurant, so much so that when an employee recently tried to put on something else (*The Addams Family*) the customers rebelled.

I was tipped off to Linda-Mar by friend and local burger expert Joe Price. As we were leaving we spotted an ancient milkshake mixer behind the counter and almost fell over. "Do you still use that?" I asked, not because it looked like its best days were behind it but because I was fully aware of its historical significance. "We use it every day," Tiffany told me as she reached over to start it up. The mixer slowly came to life and I could hear the whir of the friction-driven mechanics inside. This was the same mixer, the Multimixer, that Ray Croc sold as a traveling salesman in the '40s, the same mixer that led him to McDonald's for the first time and the rest was history.

"Have a very Linda-Mar day!" Tiffany shouted out as we left. "That's just what we say here." I wish I could have a Linda-Mar day more often.

THE MEERS STORE & RESTAURANT

HIGHWAY 115 | MEERS, OK 73501

580-429-8051 | WWW.MEERSSTORE.COM

MON, WED, THURS, SUN 10:30 AM–8 PM

FRI–SAT 10:30 AM–8:30 PM | CLOSED TUESDAY

The Meers Store is way out in the country. About two hours from Oklahoma City and four from Dallas, the "Meersburger" had better be good because it's the only reason you got in the car this morning. The burgers are better than good, they are excellent, and the drive is beautiful. Joe Maranto, the latest owner of the 95-year-old burger mecca, put it best when he told me, "We're out in the

middle of nowhere, but the good thing is we're the only thing in nowhere." Meers is not as desolate as it sounds. The restaurant is a short drive from the entrance to the Wichita Mountains Wildlife Preserve and the next town over is Medicine Park, former hideout of Bonnie and Clyde and turn-of-the-century resort for Oklahomans.

The restaurant is made up of a bunch of cobbled-together old buildings and newer ones, the older left behind when Meers did not produce the copious amounts of gold it promised. Remnants of the tiny post office have been incorporated into the newer buildings, all of them strung together like a pile of shoeboxes. Joe is responsible for the larger additions. The expansion is a result of the popularity of his Meersburger and the need to accommodate the 500 plus daily burger seekers, bike tours, and other backcountry tourists.

It's no secret what goes into a Meersburger. Joe proudly displays, inside and out, the key ingredient to his success—the lean Texas longhorn cattle. What's better, Joe raises the longhorns himself (with the help of his son, Peterhood) at a ranch nearby, and they are free of antibiotics and hormones. During the summer, Peterhood and Joe send at least 2,500 pounds of longhorn to slaughter every six days. "We sell A LOT of Meersburgers. They wait in line for the burgers," one of the grill cooks told me. On a busy day, Joe can sell over 400 burgers. That's quite a feat, considering the burger is a half-pound of lean Texas longhorn beef served on a specially made seven-inch bun. Joe claims, and is correct, that longhorn beef is lower in cholesterol than chicken or turkey, especially since he is raising them the old-fashioned way—on grass, not grain.

Joe Maranto and Bonnie

Recently, Joe decided that the Meersburger was not large enough to feed his hungry patrons. The "Seismic Burger" was created to fill this need. The Seismic is a gut-busting one pound of ground longhorn beef on the same seven-inch bun, topped with cheese, onions, lettuce, tomato, sweet relish, pickles, jalapeño slices, and bacon. Whoa. I finished one without trouble, just some sweat and a full belly. The grease was in the bacon, not the burger.

The store's proximity to the Wichita Mountains Wildlife Preserve, where the Texas longhorn was saved from extinction in the 1920s, is a little odd. But the cattle in the preserve and on Joe's ranch have quite the life. Joe said it best when he told me once, "These are happy cows. Happy cows taste better."

PAK-A-SAK

429 EAST MAINE | ENID, OK 73701

580-234-6499 | MON–FRI 10:30 AM–6:30 PM

CLOSED WEEKENDS

On a Saturday in early May, 2008, Kent Crook, the owner of the Pak-A-Sak, put a sign on the door saying that he was retiring. He then locked the door and walked away. Fortunately, an electrical engineer named Terry Washburn drove by two days later and read the sign. Terry had included his e-mail address on the sign and within a day they had struck a deal. Five weeks later, the restaurant reopened and the only thing that had changed was the ownership. "It was kind of a fluke," Terry admitted. But this "fluke" saved a landmark hamburger joint. "Enid went into a panic when this place closed," Terry told me. "There were people cheering when they walked in the door on opening day."

"Enid is a hard place to start a new business," Terry told me, "but buying this place was a no-brainer." He should know since he grew up in this sleepy northern Oklahoma town. "It was this little bitty stand right here on the corner," Terry explained. Crook's grandparents had opened the burger stand in 1954 and after 2 years of success built a larger building on the same corner. When Terry bought Pak-A-Sak he was wise to have Crook stay on for a while until Terry had the business figured out. Kim, an employee and longtime friend of Terry's, told me, "[Crook] wanted to make sure everything was cooked and prepped the exact same way. We've kept the burger the same. Shoot, all of us have grown up eating here!"

The burgers at Pak-A-Sak basically come in two sizes, the regular and the bigger burger. The regular starts as a 10-1-pound patty and the bigger as a 5-1-pound patty. The regular was the basis for the name of the restaurant because seven of them would "pack a sack." Today all of the burgers still go out in white bags and are the equivalent of a "basket." Ask for a "white bag" and you'll get burgers, fries or tater tots, and a

drink. A burger comes standard with mustard, pickle, and fried onions. "This place was founded on onions and I hate onions," Terry admitted.

The most popular burger on the menu is an American classic—the double with cheese. The burger is perfect, cooked on a very seasoned flat-top griddle and served on a toasted, white squishy bun. The patty is pressed thin, cooked fast, and develops a crunchy exterior. The simplicity of beef, bun, pickle, mustard, and onion is hard to beat. I couldn't stop eating them. Add tater tots and you'll be in burger heaven.

A guy walked into Pak-A-Sak once and asked for everything on his burger and Kim explained that everything meant pickle, mustard, and onion. "But he wanted everything so we gave it to him," Kim told me. "We put bacon, lettuce, ranch dressing, honey mustard, you name it on there. We watched him, in his truck, take the first bite and he gave me thumbs up."

Pak-A-Sak is strictly takeout so you'll have to eat in your car or at one of the picnic tables outside. "A lot of people take them to the park," Kim told me. I broke the rules and ate right at the order window.

Like most places of its ilk across America, Pak-A-Sak has dedicated regulars that stop in on a daily basis. "We have about eight or nine customers that come in every day," Terry told me. Kim added, "At eleven thirty Delvert comes in, at noon, Richard, then Heather after him . . ." Kim knows what they all eat and places their order as they are stepping out of their cars. Delvert has been such a devoted regular that his absence can trigger worry. "If he doesn't show up at eleven thirty, there's something wrong," Terry told me. "Once he didn't show up so I drove by his work and, sure enough, he was in the hospital."

The walls near the order window are covered with photocopies of Bible passages that are for sale behind the counter. My first thought was that Terry was clearly a missionary spreading the word of God to people in search of greasy nourishment, a bit of a disconnect. "Oh no, those came with the place," Terry pointed out. He really didn't want to change a thing about Pak-A-Sak and still sells about $4 worth of the passages a week (at 25 cents a pop). There are also romance novels for sale on a rack near the photocopies.

"People call all the time to tell me how much they love the burgers," Terry told me. My guess is that they are actually calling to tell him how much they love Pak-A-Sak and that they are happy to see that someone saved this hamburger destination from the wrecking ball.

ROBERT'S GRILL

300 SOUTH BICKFORD | EL RENO, OK 73036

405-262-1262 | MON–SAT 6 AM–9 PM

SUN 11 AM–7 PM

tep into Robert's and step back in time. Much like the Texas Tavern in Roanoke, Virginia, or the Cozy Inn of Salina, Kansas, very little has changed at Robert's Grill in the last 80 years. Maybe the stools and the red Formica counter are new, or the front door was moved about a half-century ago, but Robert's is a perfect example of what all hamburger stands looked, felt, and smelled like in the 1920s. Robert's is, historically speaking, one of America's most important treasures.

Don't expect warm hellos, pictures on the walls, or a large menu. Robert's is a tiny, clean, utilitarian place—a counter with fourteen stools facing a flattop griddle surrounded by a wall of stainless steel. It's the kind of counter where you don't linger long, and the burgers come fast and go down even faster. The exterior is sparse as well. The building is a bright-white box with

small windows and red trim—the visual effect may be off-putting to the untrained gourmand but believe me, you have come to the right place.

Robert's menu is limited to Coneys (chili dogs), grilled cheese, fries, tater tots, and the burger that made El Reno famous, the onion-fried burger.

Located in the burger belt of El Reno, Robert's is only a few hundred feet from Johnnie's and Sid's, and across the street from the spot where the onion-fried burger was born. "The Hamburger Inn was right where that bank is now," owner of almost two decades, Edward Graham, told me. It was at the eight-stool Hamburger Inn that a man named Ross Davis tried to stretch his burger meat by pressing in sliced onions, appealing to cash-strapped, out-of-work railroad men. The Hamburger Inn was situated on old Route 66, an outpost at the onset of the auto age, so you can imagine the brisk business. Imitators were born and a legendary burger was embraced.

The hamburger at Robert's, as it is all over town, is an onion burger. Edward smashes a ball of fresh-ground chuck on the hot griddle with a sawed-off mason's trowel, and a pile of shredded onions is placed on top. The onions are pressed hard into the patty. The contents fuse, creating a beautiful, caramelized, onion-beef mess. Edward places a white squishy bun on the patty as it finishes so that the bun soaks up the onion steam. The result is a flat, odd-looking burger that tastes incredible.

When Robert's opened in 1926, it was called

Bob's White Rock. The front door was on the Route 66 side only steps from a trolley stop. Edward told me, "People could get off the trolley here, get burgers at the window, and jump back on again. The grill used to be in the front window." Edward started working at Robert's in 1979 and purchased the counter in 1989.

For locals, there is an abundance of great onion-fried burger options in El Reno. When I asked a regular named Troy at the counter why he chose to patronize Robert's, he seemed to fall back on brand loyalty. "I've been coming here for 50 years. I remember when they were eight for a dollar." Now that's a good customer.

SID'S DINER

300 SOUTH CHOCTAW | EL RENO, OK 73036

405-262-7757 | MON–SAT 7 AM–8:30 PM

CLOSED SUNDAY

"Do you know what the definition of a diner is?" Marty Hall, part owner of this El Reno burger destination asked me. "It's a place where the grill is in view and I can turn around and talk to the people." And he does, making Sid's one of the friendliest places I have ever set foot in. But it doesn't stop there—Sid's also makes one of the best onion-fried burgers anywhere.

Sid's is named after Marty's father, who passed away just before the restaurant opened in 1989.

Bob and Marty Hall—truly dedicated burgermen

Marty had planned to work side by side with Sid, a retired highway employee. When he died, Sid's brother, Bob, asked if he could take his spot. This sounds like a customary role for a family member to play, except that Bob left a six-figure job at Chevron in Houston to flip burgers. El Reno, Oklahoma, is famous for one thing—onion-fried burgers. Invented just across the street from Sid's at the long-gone Hamburger Inn.

Sid's is not alone in El Reno. At one point there were over nine onion-fried-burger joints within five blocks of downtown. Today, Sid's, Johnnie's, and Robert's, the three remaining diners, are just a few hundred feet from one another.

If you choose a seat at the counter, you'll have a great view of the construction of an onion-fried burger. Sid or Bob grab a ball of fresh-ground chuck from a beautiful pyramid of beef balls at the side of the griddle. Gobs of thinly sliced onions are piled onto the ball of beef on the large flattop griddle. The ball is pressed thin and the onions are worked into the soft meat. The burger is flipped, and after a few minutes, the caramelized onions have fused to the griddle-charred beef. Prepare your mouth for a taste explosion.

The burger is served on a white squishy bun with the meat and gnarled onions hanging out of it. Nothing is served with a regular burger except pickles (on the side) but you may find condiments unnecessary. If you require lettuce and tomato, ask for a Deluxe. Make yours a King Size and the meat and onions are doubled. The King is the most popular burger and makes

for a perfect meal, especially if enjoyed with Sid's excellent hand-cut, homemade fries. "I learned how to make fries down at J&W," Marty told me, referring to another not-to-be-missed onion-fried burger further south in Chickasha.

One of the more unique features of Sid's is their impressive decoupage countertop, sealed in poured resin. "The history of El Reno starts on that end," Marty told me, pointing to the far left side of the counter. The patchwork of vintage El Reno photography includes everything from early shots of downtown to color photos of local baseball teams. "I wanted people who came in who weren't from here to know something about my town."

Even though Sid's is technically a newcomer

to the onion-fried-burger phenomenon, Marty has been involved just about his entire life. "I used to work at Johnnie's and my father helped out there as well." Sid's, he told me, was modeled after the old Johnnie's.

Bob and Marty take turns flipping and pressing a lot of onions into their burgers. When the pyramid of beef balls next to the griddle gets low, a new, perfect pyramid miraculously appears. Every once in a while Marty will turn and dispense life lessons with a smile to anyone at the counter. "Be good to your daddy," he says to some teenaged girls picking at their fries, "I should know. I have three daughters."

SLICK'S

107 SOUTH LOUIS TITTLE AVE | MANGUM, OK 73554

580-782-2481 | MON–SAT 8 AM–6 PM

I receive e-mails daily telling me where to go (literally) and I love them all. Following the publication of the first edition of this book, an e-mail came in that said simply (in all caps), "LOVED YOUR BOOK. SOMEDAY I HOPE YOU CAN TRY HAMBURGER SLICKS IN MANGUM, OK. SLICKS IS THE BEST." I think it was the all caps that got to me and I started planning a trip to western Oklahoma immediately.

Mangum, Oklahoma is not on the way to anything. It is a true destination deep in rural ranch and oil country and is a solid 35 miles south of I-40, hours from Oklahoma City. If you decide to venture off the interstate into the Oklahoma interior I guarantee that you will be rewarded with one of the greatest burgers in America.

Slick's is located on the main artery in and out of the dusty city of Mangum. It's hard to miss the tiny white shack with its red-and-white striped roof. There's barely an identifying sign and no place to sit, just a little window with a sliding screen to place your order. When I arrived for the first time, grillperson Helen told me, "Come around back." Inside I found a griddle and fry area adjacent to a small table with mismatched stools. What I assumed was a table for the kitchen staff turned out to be a table for regulars that prefer to eat in. It was equipped with a roll of paper towels and a tip jar. Imagine a chef's table at a hot restaurant where you can watch your favorite chef make magic. This is my kind of front-row seat, inches from a flattop griddle loaded with sizzling burgers.

The burgers at Slick's are phenomenal and the choices somewhat confusing. You can order a regular hamburger or cheeseburger, which is around 3 ounces and comes on a toasted, white squishy bun. Or order the Giant, which adds twice as much meat and a larger bun. Anything can be doubled, and sure enough the most popular burger is the Giant Double Cheeseburger. From what I could tell, the Giant Double included 2 seven-ounce patties making this beast, after condiments, a one-pound burger.

A regular named Chris who has lunch at the kitchen table every Friday told me, "I usually get the regular double. Anything larger than that and I won't be worth a damn back at work." Undeterred, I polished off, with ease, the Giant Double with two slices of American, pickles, mustard, raw onion, lettuce, and tomato. How? Because it was so damned good.

The small flattop griddle is darkened with decades of seasoning. The burger at Slick's starts with a ball of fresh ground beef, a special 73/27 chuck blend from the local supermarket down the street. Helen grabs a few balls from a nearby fridge, tosses them on the griddle, and presses them into the shape of a burger with a heavy spatula. A not-so-secret blend of salt and pepper is sprinkled on the patties and they are cooked over high heat until a decent crust forms. Large, soft buns warm on the griddle as the patties cook and they pick up some residual grease.

Like many of the places in this book the grillperson at Slick's uses a non-traditional, custom-made spatula. In this case, a sawed-off concrete trowel with a handle re-fashioned from molded fiberglass resin is the grill tool of choice at Slick's. Owner Mike Avery told me, "I used a toilet paper tube for the mold and just held it in place until it set."

Mike left 10 years in the oil exploration business to take over Slick's from his dad in 2009 and as a third-generation owner understands his duty to the regulars. "Some people are here every day," Mike told me. As I sat at the community table in the kitchen I noticed something slightly incongruous with the setting—an 8 x 10 glossy of 2007 Miss America Lauren Nelson signed over to "The gang at Slick's." "Oh, that's my cousin," Mike shared nonchalantly.

The tiny burger shack started as a Dairy Queen back in 1959 and was built and owned by Mike's grandfather, Audry Mills Avery, and their uncle Slick Avery. Audry was a blind carpenter and built Slick's from the ground up. When I asked Mike how this was possible he said with a smile, "You tell me."

About a year after running the place, the relationship with Dairy Queen soured. "They were trying to tell Slick what to cook and wanted him to use frozen beef," Mike's younger brother, Joe, told me. Slick only wanted to use fresh ground beef, and as Joe put it, "They told him 'You can't do that,' and Slick said, 'The hell I can't.'" And that was the end of that. Thankfully, 50 years later Slick's continues to avoid the temptation to use frozen beef and will only serve quality food to a faithful clientele.

30

OREGON

GIANT DRIVE-IN

15840 BOONES FERRY RD | LAKE OSWEGO, OR 97035

503-636-0255 | SUN–THU 10 AM–9 PM

FRI & SAT 10 AM–10 PM

Hooray for the mom-and-pop hamburger stand. Giant Drive-In is quite literally a mom-and-pop—owned and operated by a husband and wife team that is dedicated to bringing quality comfort food to the neighborhood and have done so for 30 years.

Bill Kreger and his wife, Gail, bought Giant in 1981 after Bill had burned out on a mechanical engineering career. "We had planned to fix it up and flip it, but here we are!" Bill told me enthusiastically. The odd looking A-frame ski chalet structure was originally part of a failed '60s chain called Mr. Swiss. In 1970 it became Giant and was open for 10 years until a Burger King opened across the street. "The previous owner just gave up, locked the doors, and walked away," Bill told me. But today, the

Burger King is gone. When I asked Bill what happened, he just smiled and shrugged. I gathered there's only room for one burger stand in this stretch of suburban Portland.

Starting the business was not easy for the Kregers. "You have to keep your hand in it or you are not going to have it," Bill explained. "We spent seventeen hours a day, seven days a week for the first seven years to get this place up and running." The time invested shows—the burgers are excellent.

The list of hamburger concoctions is vast. You can order a standard quarter-pound burger or choose from an eclectic selection of burgers like the "Teriyaki," the "Hawaiian," or an "Avocado Burger." But the burger that gets its own neon sign is the enormous "Filler." The Filler is almost too big to put in your mouth, but I managed. Its contents are similar to nearby Stanich's signature burger, but the Filler contains two quarter-pound patties instead of one. The burger also contains a slice of ham, cheese, a fried egg, bacon, lettuce, onion, pickles, tomato, and mayo. All this piled neatly on a locally baked seeded sourdough roll. I was speechless (and dazed) for hours after I consumed this thing. Amazingly, Gail told me it was her burger of choice, but said, "Believe it or not, I actually put an extra patty on it."

The fresh hamburger patties are delivered daily and come from local grass-fed Angus sirloin. The Kregers request a 90 percent lean grind. "Any less fat and the burger breaks up on the griddle. Any more and the burger shrinks to

nothing." The cheese is also local Tillamook, purchased in 40-pound blocks and sliced on premises. Bill explained, "We try to only use local, fresh ingredients," and added, "In the summertime Oregon tomatoes can get to be this big," making a shape with his hands the size of an invisible grapefruit.

The interior of the Giant is a classic retro burger drive-in. Bright, clean, and inviting, the Giant has floor-to-ceiling windows on three sides, booths for seating, and a yellow-and-brown checkered linoleum floor. Hanging over the cash register is a photo of a half dozen UPS trucks lined up in the Giant parking lot. "Once a week the local UPS guys converge on Giant," Bill explained. "Sometimes there are over fifteen trucks out there."

I watched the Kregers greet familiar faces, pleasantly take orders, and flip burgers. They make the business of selling hamburgers look easy. But as I left, Gail gave me some sage advice, "Keep your sanity and stay out of the restaurant business!"

HELVETIA TAVERN

10275 NW HELVETIA RD | HILLSBORO, OR 97124
503-647-5286 | SUN–THURS 11 AM–10 PM
FRI & SAT 11 AM–11 PM

 estled in the rolling farm country of western Oregon, a short distance from Portland but a world away, sits

a restaurant and bar that amazingly turns out over a thousand burgers on a busy Saturday. The restaurant is the comfortable Helvetia Tavern (pronounced Hel-VAY-sha) and is way out in the country. Regardless of how far it is from anything, burger lovers gladly make the trek to the Helvetia for their signature "Jumbo Burger" and great selection of microbrews on tap.

"It's a pretty simple menu and nothing has changed since we opened," part owner Mike Lampros told me. "We did add salads, though, two years ago." There are a few sandwiches on the menu and a grilled cheese, but I looked around and saw mostly burgers being consumed. A lot of them too—the grill stayed full the entire time I was at Helvetia. They easily served over 200 burgers in the hour that I sat at the counter.

The Jumbo is just that—two thin quarterpound patties of fresh ground beef are cooked on a large flattop griddle and served on a toasted six-inch bun with bacon, cheese, lettuce, onion, tomato, and the ubiquitous and tasty Pacific Northwest condiment, "Goop" (see sidebar on page 346). The bun is larger than the patties, which are arranged slightly overlapping so the burger is presented wider, not taller. "That's the way we've always done it," Mike explained. "The single patty is served on a smaller bun." As a finishing touch, the Jumbo is stabbed in the center and delivered with a plastic knife, as Mike explained, "to keep the contents from sliding around." The burgers are moist and exploding with flavor, thanks to the mustardy-mayo Goop holding the large burger together. Wash your burger down with the tasty and hard-to-find RC Cola, on tap at Helvetia.

The building that houses the Helvetia first opened in 1914 as a general store. In 1946 a bar was added to one side and burgers were served. Mike's father, Nick Lampros, bought the tavern in 1978 and changed nothing until the late 1990s when he and his son turned the old general store into a dining room. "Up until then it was a twenty-one-and-over bar crowd," Mike told me, taking a break from the grill. "The dining room allowed us to start attracting families." And they do, and those families have the benefit of dining at Helvetia with a picture-perfect view of the sheep grazing across the street. The dining room tables are actually enormous foot-thick blocks of timber with a high-gloss finish. Mike pointed out, "They came from a tree that fell in a neighbor's yard."

The tavern side of Helvetia is a comfortably dark, broken-in bar with a 1950 Brunswick pool table that still costs only a quarter to play. A strange collection of baseball caps hangs from the ceiling, some signed by pro athletes. Mike explained that the thousand of caps were up there to hide the ugly ceiling. "We take them down twice a year to clean them."

If there was any doubt as to how accommodating this place was to regulars, just take a counter seat at the last stool in the back of the restaurant. That's Grant's seat. Then look over the food prep area directly in front of you. Hanging on an air duct is a mirror positioned perfectly to read the TV behind you in reverse. "He comes in here at three everyday, like clockwork," the grillman told me. Then Mike explained, "We blocked his view of the TV across the room with a new sign. This was his solution."

STANICH'S TAVERN

4915 NE FREMONT ST | PORTLAND, OR 97213

503-281-2322 | MON–THU 11 AM–10 PM

FRI & SAT 11 AM–11 PM

Once upon a time in America, the "sports bar" was merely a neighborhood bar where you could guarantee that the game you wanted to watch would be on the TV hanging in the corner over the bottles of booze. If there were two games on at the same time, the TV at the other end of the bar would be tuned in. At some point, the sports bar concept went corporate and today it is not uncommon to find many with stadium seating and games on up to 30 screens, some of them full-sized movie screens. The sports bar became a soulless, unfamiliar place where the only reason to go was to ensure you'd see your game. Stanich's is a real sports bar, one that is oozing soul. It's an unquestionably comfortable, welcoming place that also happens to make one of the tastiest burgers I've ever eaten.

"Sometimes the wait for a burger can be an hour, but we have a great jukebox," Debbie Stanich told me as she sang along to Sonny and Cher. Debbie manages Stanich's and is married to Steve Stanich, the owner and son of the couple who opened the tavern in 1949. Serbian immigrants Gladys and George Stanich opened this Portland tavern and put a burger on the menu. "Gladys cooked and George was out back playing pinochle," Debbie says. It was Gladys who invented what the menu still today bills as the "World's Greatest Hamburger," the sloppy two-fister "Special."

The Special is large. Gladys must have had the very hungry in mind when she dreamed up this burger. The grillperson swiftly assembles the impressively diverse ingredients that go onto the Special, which include a quarter-pound patty of fresh chuck, an egg, bacon, ham, cheese, lettuce, red onion, and tomato. All of this is piled high on a large five-inch toasted bun with the obligatory mustard, mayo, and "burger relish" that seems to adorn all burgers in the Northwest. "There's no 'special sauce' here at Stanich's, just mayo, mustard, and relish," Debbie explained.

There's a two-napkin limit per burger, so use them wisely. The moment the juices, hot cheese, and mayo start running down your arms (and they will) resist the urge to reach for a napkin. "We don't like to hand out napkins," Debbie told me, "but if you really need one, okay."

When you first walk into Stanich's, you'll be shocked by the décor. Every inch of the walls at this decades-old tavern is covered in those felt triangular pennants and pretty much nothing else. There could be a thousand, and all were donated by regulars. The bar is one of the deepest I've ever seen, lined with cozy leather swivel stools that take practice getting into. There is no way to look cool getting into one of these seats, Debbie pointed out laughing, "It's kind of a 'slide 'n twirl' move," and as she demonstrated, she looked like she was dancing with an invisible partner.

Steve Stanich, an ex-pro football player for the 49ers, believes in giving back. Among the sea of pennants that lines the walls of his tavern are more than a few accolades of his philanthropic efforts. On the fiftieth anniversary of Stanich's, Steve brought the price of his family's signature burger back to its original 25 cents. The proceeds built a gymnasium for a local school. He also sponsors numerous local teams and every year gives out scholarships to college-bound kids. Steve told me, "It comes back to you tenfold."

"It's a bar, but people don't come in here to drink. They come in here to eat," Debbie pointed out. Or maybe for a burger and a scholarship? It all sounds good to me.

31

PENNSYLVANIA

CHARLIE'S HAMBURGERS

ACADEMY AVE AT KEDRON (ROUTE 420)

FOLSOM, PA 19033

610-461-4228 | MON, WED, THU 11 AM–9 PM

FRI & SAT 11 AM–10 PM | SUN 1–8 PM

CLOSED TUESDAY

If you prefer your burgers with ketchup, Charlie's is the place to go. A "loaded" burger at this decades-old hamburger spot comes with onions, ketchup, pickles, relish, and cheese, creating a sweet burger experience that is hard to find among the more staid and traditional burger stands of America. "Pretty much everyone orders them that way," a teenaged prep girl told me. She wasn't kidding—just about every person who walked in during the hour I spent at Charlie's ordered burgers with ketchup. Of course the burgers can also be ordered with mustard and tomato, but not lettuce.

Charlie's is a real place with real food. A menu of hamburgers, hot dogs, and milkshakes keeps things simple. Some may see a greasy spoon. Others see a haven for grease lovers. You get the point—this is not health food. Fortunately, the burgers are made from fresh-ground chuck (pattied in the kitchen with a small patty former) and the shakes are made with great ice cream and real milk. In fact, people frequent Charlie's more for its shakes then for its burgers. The milk for the shakes still comes out of a large vintage aluminum milk dispenser.

The crowd is a mix of airport employees from nearby Philadelphia International, kids from the local schools, and a blend of salty regulars. When I visited, the better part of a girls volleyball team had landed in search of nourishment.

Charlie's location is relatively new, though the business dates back to 1935. Charlie Convery operated the restaurant nearby at an intersection of the Baltimore Pike until 1984, when an expansion of the road spelled the end of Charlie's. Through a confusing set of purchases and sales, the restaurant relocated a mile away to a former fruit stand next to a defunct miniature golf course (the concrete skeleton of the weeded-over course is still visible behind the restaurant).

Colorful character and part-time manger of 11 years Mike Goodwin once explained to me, "After they moved, changed owners, and reopened, they still went back to Charlie's original butcher." The small burgers are cooked on a very seasoned flattop griddle, smashed thin, and cooked in the bubbling grease of previous burgers. They are served on a toasted, white squishy bun. "No lettuce, no bacon, no tofu, no pineapple," Mike joked, emphasizing the simplicity of the burgers at Charlie's.

One important note: Charlie's is closed on Tuesdays. In a vestige of wartime America, the restaurant still observes "meatless Tuesdays," a day that most burger joints closed during World War II for meat rationing. "Are you familiar with Wimpy?" Mike asked me. "I'll pay you

TUESDAY for a hamburger today?" A lightbulb went off in my head—Wimpy was a lot smarter than I thought.

TESSARO'S

4601 LIBERTY AVE | PITTSBURGH, PA 15224

412-682-6809 | MON–SAT 11 AM–MIDNIGHT

CLOSED SUNDAY

For years, the incredible ground beef that Tessaro's used for its burgers came from a butcher shop directly across the street called House of Meats. When the shop closed one day, Kelly Harrington, former part owner of this Pittsburgh burger destination, did what seemed the most sensible—he hired the butcher.

Dominic Piccola, a retired Pittsburgh fireman, is now employed by Tessaro's as their in-house butcher. He has become their link to hamburger perfection. Six days a week, at 7 a.m., Dominic grinds hundreds of pounds of chuck shoulder for the day's burgers. "Since I'm the only one grinding, the consistency is always the same," Dominic told me through his classic fireman's bushy handlebar moustache.

I was interested in Tessaro's because of its stellar reputation among hamburger cognoscenti, but it was the method of cooking the burgers that put me on an airplane to Pittsburgh. I had to see for myself the fabled hardwood grill that many had talked about. Unique to the burger world, the hamburgers at Tessaro's are grilled over a fire made from west Pennsylvania hardwoods, not the charcoal or the blue propane flames that seem standard for indoor flame grilling. Tessaro's uses a mixture of yellow maple, red oak, and walnut, all indigenous to the area. "We stay away from hickory because it's too strong," Kelly pointed out, "and no fruit trees because they are loaded with pesticides." Hardwoods produce a flame that is far hotter than gas or charcoal. Grillman of 23 years Courtney McFarlane told me, "The fire can get up to 600 degrees in there."

Courtney invited me into the grill area, a section of the restaurant adjacent to the bar that was once the dance floor and is now a small room with a big picture window. I stood about three feet from the grill and the heat was so intense it felt like my eyebrows were burning right off my face. Every few minutes, Courtney tossed a small cup of water onto the flames and told me, "That's just to slow the heat down a bit."

The burgers at Tessaro's are unmeasured but somewhere near a half pound. Courtney grabs a wad of Dominic's fresh ground beef and tells me, "After a while it's easy to guess the size." He then swiftly forms the ball into a patty, slaps the beef onto a stainless steel surface next to the grill, and does this move where he spins the patty to form an edge. The entire process takes seconds. He is a master burger maker and the finished product strangely resembles a large, machined-pressed patty.

The burgers are served with many cheese options and just about any condiment you can think of from barbecue sauce to three types of mustard. To be honest, this burger is so amazing it'd be foolish to cover it with anything. Served on a soft, Portuguese-type roll from a bakery down the street, the hefty burger is a sight to behold. It's perfectly charred on the outside and juicy and moist on the inside. And thanks to the hardwood, the burger has a taste like no other—a woodsy, barbeque essence that manages not to overpower the flavor of the high-quality beef.

In 1984, Kelly, his sister, Ena, and their mother, Tee, bought the bar and restaurant from

Richard Tessaro. It was Richard who began the tradition of flame grilling burgers that the Harringtons perfected. He started by grilling on the street in front of the bar on a makeshift barbeque made from halved 55-gallon drums. He eventually moved the operation to the backyard, once starting a fire that burned part of the building and finally moved the grill indoors.

The restaurant is dark and cozy with a long vintage bar running along one side. The walls are wood paneled and the aroma of the burning hardwoods is arresting. The building has been a bar for 75 years, but previously housed a dry goods store and a nickelodeon as far back as the turn of the century.

In 2009, Kelly passed away due to complications from cancer and a stroke. His imprint on the burger business was enormous and he will surely be missed.

Ena once told me that if they run out of ground beef on a busy night, they'll call Dominic the butcher back in to grind some more. I asked her why the burgers were so good and she told me bluntly, "Not everybody can afford a butcher."

32

RHODE ISLAND

STANLEY'S HAMBURGERS

535 DEXTER ST | CENTRAL FALLS, RI 02863

401-726-9689 | WWW.STANLEYSHAMBURGERS.COM

MON–THU 11 AM–8 PM | FRI & SAT 11 AM–9 PM

CLOSED SUNDAY

Stanley's is an absolute gem of a burger destination in a neighborhood about 10 minutes north of downtown Providence. The tiny restaurant is so picture perfect that it looks completely out of place in an area that has clearly seen better days. From my experience there's usually only one reason burger joints like Stanley's survive—someone came along and saved the place. That's exactly what happened and we should all be thankful.

Meet Gregory Raheb, a man who bought a fading diner and didn't simply grab the keys and continue making burgers. He actually gutted the entire place at one point and rebuilt to exact specifications and amazing detail, sending the décor back to opening day in 1932. "When I took over it was rundown," Greg remembered. "It had dark wood paneling and old vinyl floor tiles. But the food was great so I knew it had potential." The centerpiece of the menu then as it is now is the Depression-era American standard in hamburgers—one that is loaded with onions.

The "Stanleyburger" is a classic. Not in the bloated half-pound-lettuce-tomato sense but something closer to the birth of the hamburger in America. In the beginning, burgers were small.

The patties were anywhere from 1 to 2 ounces and almost always loaded with steam grilled onions. The Stanleyburger is a perfect nod to the past and a primary example of burgers from the first half of the twentieth century. As you step out of your car in the lot next door you are immediately enveloped in the intoxicating essence of grilled onions pouring from the restaurant's exhaust. It is a sign of good things to come.

The burger to get is the double Stanleyburger, or two of them. The burgers start as fresh-ground beef that is machine-formed at the restaurant into "plugs," or tiny two-ounce tall patties. The wad of beef is tossed on the flattop and a pile of paper-thin Spanish onion is thrown on top. With great force the onions are smashed into the burger and the whole comingled mess cooks to perfection. When the patty is flipped, the bun is placed on top to steam. The same practice of smashing onions can be found at primary source burger joints across America, and personally it is my favorite way to enjoy a hamburger. Places like the White Manna, Cozy Inn, and Town Topic, as well as all of the burger joints in El Reno, Oklahoma are still making burgers this way.

If you ask for a double, watch what happens. The grillperson takes two wads of beef and presses them together on the griddle. Cheese is available and it seems that ketchup rules the counter at Stanley's, but neither is necessary. This little burger, thanks to equal amounts of beef and onion, absolutely explodes with flavor. "Some people ask for extra onions," longtime manager and counter person Nancy told me.

The menu is not limited to burgers and offers a vast selection of diner favorites, all of it homemade from the freshest ingredients. In 2008 Greg opened a second Stanley's in downtown Providence, a larger version of the original. Not surprisingly, the new location is also an amazing example of '30s/'40s retro design and he obviously spared no expense.

I was stunned at how spotless Stanley's was. "We keep it clean!" Nancy told me. Greg bought the restaurant in 1987 from the Kryla family, renovated, and renovated again in 2002. Polish immigrant Stanley Kryla opened the burger counter back in 1932 in the early days of the Depression. Most burger joints failed during this time in American history and if they didn't, they were wiped out by meat rationing during World War II. It's a miracle that Stanley's survived. "In 1932 the burger at Stanley's was 5 cents, can you imagine?" Greg told me. "And they made money!"

33

SOUTH CAROLINA

NORTHGATE SODA SHOP

918 NORTH MAIN ST | GREENVILLE, SC 29609

864-235-6770 | WWW.NORTHGATESODASHOP.COM

MON–FRI 9 AM–8 PM | SAT 9 AM–3 PM

CLOSED SUNDAYS

Just up the hill on Main Street in Greenville, South Carolina where the high-rises give way to trees and homes, I discovered an excellent spot to enjoy a Southern favorite—the "Pimento Cheeseburger."

Longtime owner of 41 years Jim DeYoung was looking to retire, and sold the shop to a lawyer with an office just 20 feet away named Catherine Christophillis. A few years later, she sold it to one of Jim's friends, Iris Hood-Bell, in 2009. I was sitting at Jim's round table once (that the former owner installed for daily visits with his friends) when Jim told me, "I wanted to sell the shop to someone who would keep everything almost the same." That sounds like a simple request, except that just about every square inch of the Northgate is covered in four decades of collectibles. It resembles an antique shop that happens to have a soda fountain, with signed 8 x 10s, extensive bottle, can, and cigar box collections, beer and soda neon, a vintage Ex-Lax sign, and an impressive church fan collection. This is the real deal—no fake made-in-China

reproduction crap here. When Catherine bought the shop, she bought the stuff too. "Where was I going to put it?" Jim said of his antiques. "It belongs here anyway." And when Iris bought Northgate, the stuff was again part of the deal.

The menu at the Northgate is classic soda shop diner fare—tuna, peanut butter and jelly, hot dogs, grilled cheese, and egg sandwiches, but the big seller is their fantastic Pimento Cheeseburger.

"You'll either love it or hate it," longtime waitress Brenda warned me before I bit into my burger. I have to admit I had never had one, even though my mother is from South Carolina. Fortunately, I fall into the "love it" category.

The pimento cheese for the Northgate's sandwiches and burgers is a tangy mix of mayo, cheddar, and diced pimentos. "We make it right here, fresh every day," former waitress Maudie told me once of the over 40-year-old recipe. The beef is also fresh, picked up daily from a butcher just up Main Street (this fact is also proudly announced on the menu, complete with the butcher's name and address).

The burger starts as fresh ground beef that is pressed in a vintage burger press. The press produces a three-and-a-half ounce patty that is cooked on a flattop griddle. The burger comes to you on a toasted bun with tomato, lettuce, and a large dollop of pimento cheese. I also had a cherry smash, a drink made from cherry syrup and soda water, dispensed from the Northgate's venerable soda fountain. A few years ago, Jim's cherry syrup supplier stopped making the syrup, so he started making it himself. "I found some extract so we started making it in-house."

Today, Iris's husband, Ren, works at Northgate and nothing has changed much since the days when Jim owned the soda fountain. "Same burgers, same sodas, same butcher." And Jim still comes in to hang out at his round table. Ren told me, "He's here every day!"

ROCKAWAY ATHLETIC CLUB

2719 ROSEWOOD DR | COLUMBIA, SC 29205
803-256-1075 | OPEN DAILY 11 AM–11 PM

I swear I drove by the place five times before accidentally turning into the parking lot. There are no signs of life from the street side of the Rockaway Athletic Club, an imposing brick structure with armored windows. As I was pulling out of the lot after checking the map, I noticed a small piece of cardboard by a back door with the words BOILED PEANUTS TONIGHT scrawled in black Sharpie. I figured this must be the place.

"We've always been sort of low key," part owner Forest Whitlark said, describing the 29-year-old hang out in this quiet neighborhood in Columbia. The fortress-like building is a some-what recent addition in the history of The Rockaway. "The original burned to the ground," Forest told me. In 2002, it was the victim of a faulty air conditioner. The Rockaway opened in 1982 by brothers Paul and Forest Whitlark and friend David Melson. The original bar occupied three storefronts of a 1940s strip mall at the same location. My guess is that when they rebuilt they wanted to make sure that the Rockaway could withstand anything.

I was there to sample their often talked about "Pimento Cheeseburger" (pronounced "pimena" in these parts). The Rockaway Pimento Cheeseburger has so much gooey cheese on it that it's almost impossible to pick up. Fortunately the burger comes cut in half, and each half has a large toothpick to keep the contents together. The second you pull the toothpick, hold on as the contents have a tendency to slip and slide.

Pimento cheese is a Southern staple and is traditionally made with only three ingredients—cheddar cheese, mayonnaise, and diced pimentos. In his book *Hamburgers & Fries*, burger scholar John T. Edge points out that the marriage of pimento cheese to the burger may have actually happened in Columbia by J.C. Reynolds at the now-defunct Dairy Bar. I believe the claim. There are more pimento cheeseburgers available in this town than anywhere else on the planet.

The burgers at Rockaway start as eight-ounce handformed patties of fresh ground chuck. They are cooked on a flattop and the large seeded buns are warmed nearby on the griddle until they are soft as a pillow. In keeping with tradition, Rockaway only uses the three basic ingredients to make their pimento cheese and it's amazing. If you're not too pimentoed out, the Rockaway also offers a plate of fries with a copious amount of hot pimento cheese dumped on top.

In 2005, George W. Bush visited Rockaway on a swing through South Carolina. He ordered two burgers and two pimento cheese fries to go, then made a point to shake a few hands. Forest remembered, "I think he spoke to everyone in here." A comfortable bar will do that to you.

Rockaway is huge. With the University of South Carolina only 5 minutes away with its 30,000 students, it's a good thing they have a capacity of almost 300. There are booths and tables everywhere, an air hockey table, a pool table, and a very long bar.

So if you can actually find the Rockaway and make it through the throngs of students, you will be rewarded with a great pimento cheeseburger. The Rockaway Athletic Club did not invent the pimento cheeseburger but they are doing something just as important: perpetuating a great Southern food tradition.

34

SOUTH DAKOTA

HAMBURGER INN

111½ EAST 10ᵀᴴ ST I SIOUX FALLS, SD 57104

605-332-5412 I MON–SAT 10 AM–2 PM

CLOSED SUNDAY

On a corner in the heart of downtown Sioux Falls (which is in the midst of a revitalization) sits the tiny Hamburger Inn. It is a classic '30s burger joint specimen—eleven stools, a single counter, minimal menu, and a griddle in the front window. When I visited, the small TV on the wall was tuned to *The Price Is Right* and the first customer of the day was a blind regular who found his stool without help. This is my kind of place.

The Sioux Falls favorite "Eggburger" is served here—a fried egg is placed on top of a finished burger, the yoke popped and cooked through thanks to health department rules.

"Can't decide on breakfast or lunch? Have an Eggburger!" Maria Poulsen, the current owner, exclaimed when I asked about the origins of the strange pairing of chicken and cow. If you've never had one, fear not—the combination works well. It's basically steak and eggs on a bun.

Many past patrons have fond memories of Mel Nelson, the longtime proprietor of the Hamburger Inn. Sadly, Mel is no longer pressing balls of ground beef into a puddle of grease, cooking burgers the "old-fashioned way." But the good news is that three months before he died, local chef Maria offered to buy the place. This is always great for the burger world, especially when the plan is to keep a similar menu and scrape up some of the caked-on grease. Maria said, "It was a mess when I took over. Grease up to here!" and she made a gesture about two feet from the floor.

The burgers are no longer cooked in a tray of grease like Mel did for 32 years and previous owners did for close to 75 years. Now, one-third-pound balls of fresh ground beef hit the hot griddle, are flattened with a spatula, and cooked until the fresh meat has an exterior crunch.

The menu at Hamburger Inn is sparse but focused. Burgers are the star attraction here and can be ordered with cheese, bacon, or the afore-mentioned fried egg. Standards such as onion rings and fries are also on the menu, as is a curiosity called "cheeseballs." This Midwestern treat is also known as the deep-fried cheese curd, one of my all-time favorite side dishes.

For those old-timers who may miss Mel's tasty sliders, there is no need to fret about the state of burgers here. The Hamburger Inn is still turning out great burgers and your clothes will still smell of grease all day. Maria also refurbished the decades-old neon-and-glass sign that hangs over the front door, using all of the original let-tering. "It was falling apart but I didn't want to change much," she told me. In keeping with the integrity of the old place, the Hamburger Inn still looks like a shoebox with a door, a burger bunker whose only window faces 10th Street.

Maria understands good food, service, and simplicity. She runs a catering business in the Sioux Falls area and this is the second restaurant she currently owns. "I'm looking for an old stainless steel diner to buy and fix up," she said as I was leaving. "Got any ideas?"

NICK'S HAMBURGER SHOP

427 MAIN AVE I BROOKINGS, SD 57006
605-692-4324 I WWW.NICKSHAMBURGERS.COM
MON–FRI 11 AM–7 PM I SAT 11 AM–4 PM
CLOSED SUNDAY

Dick Fergen is my kind of guy. He left a job in farm management in Texas to return to his hometown of Brook-ings, South Dakota. Upon his arrival, he inquired about the landmark burger joint, Nick's, and soon after purchased it from the notorious and sometimes volatile third owner, Duane Lar-son. In his nearly three decades at the grill, Duane was known to close early because he ran out of buns, and refused to sell the business to just anyone, saying that he'd burn the place down before he sold it to the wrong person. Duane was also involved in a spat between the Coca-Cola Company and Nick's that led to a dramatic photo in *Time* magazine of Duane pouring Coke into the street.

The good news is that, Dick Fergen is now in charge and he will never run out of buns or Coke. I watched Dick at the grill for one-and-a-half hours, waiting patiently to speak to him. He was in a zone, pressing small balls of ground round into a puddle of bubbling grease, transfer-ring them to buns, and serving them at a rate of about 700 per hour. When I finally got his atten-tion, he was taking a break and eating, not sur-prisingly, a burger. "I eat mine dry," he said. This meant he had squeezed some of the grease out, "Makes it a little bit healthier." Amazingly, Dick creates his own "solution" for the deep-frying of his burgers. This is not just any old grease. He starts with solids and adds seasoning according to a recipe that has been handed down for decades.

Dick doesn't really look like your typical hamburger stand owner. He is a sixtysomething, impossibly fit, tanned, and a self-described Harley nut. What brought him to and keeps him at Nick's is pure nostalgia. Nick's was started by Harold and Gladys Nickalson in 1929 and was later passed on to their son, Harold Jr., in

1947. When Duane Larson bought Nick's in 1972, much to the dismay of the old-timers, he added the cheeseburger to the menu. The small burgers come with a secret relish whose recipe goes back to the beginning. It's a mustard based pickle-and-onion relish that has "other seasonings," waitress Laurie told me.

Orders are not taken, they are yelled. "We just holler at Dick what we need," Laurie said. First, you tell the counter person what you want. When your burgers are ready, you tell them what you want on them. They arrive at your counter spot on a square of waxed paper and can be consumed at a rate of roughly one every 20 seconds, which is good, because you will need to make room for the 30 people waiting for your stool.

In 2008 Dick bought the barbershop next door and doubled the size of Nick's. The new counter wraps around the griddle, which is in the center of the restaurant, and the burger joint can now seat many more hungry burger lovers.

A man named Stewart sitting to my left told me that he had been coming back to Nick's every time he visited his alma mater, South Dakota State University. "I've been coming ever since I graduated in '52." Old-timers refer to their visits as getting their "Nick's fix."

"If you are not from South Dakota, then you wouldn't understand." Dick pondered seriously while gazing at the ceiling. "There's something about these people. I wouldn't trade them for anyone in the world."

★ 35 ★

TENNESSEE

BROWN'S DINER

2102 BLAIR BLVD | NASHVILLE, TN 37212

615-269-5509 | MON–SAT 10:45 AM–11 PM

SUN 11 AM–10 PM

It may not look like much, but Brown's may be one of the most historically significant burger joints in this book. The fact that it survives is a miracle, and a testament to the power of hamburger culture in this country. It has lived through more than one fire and withstood many facelifts.

To the untrained eye, Brown's appears to be a dump—an unimpressive double-wide with a drab grey/beige exterior. But to American cultural historians it is a treasure. There was a time in this country when hamburgers were not king.

They were considered dirty food for wage earners, and were served in establishments much like Brown's. The only difference is that places like this, which once dotted the Americna landscape in the thousands, and were mostly found in close proximity to factories and urban areas, are just about gone.

What makes Brown's Diner special is that its core is made up of two retired trolley cars, mule-drawn cars that were left at the end of the line in the early 1920s as the automobile became ubiquitous in city life. The trolleys are arranged in a T shape, one making up the bar, the other serving as the kitchen. Terry Young, the bartender and manager, told me, "The wooden wheels are still on it, though I wouldn't suggest going down there." The practice of converting trolleys and diner cars into eating establishments was so popular in the early part of the twentieth century that companies emerged to fabricate the restaurants without the wheels—and the modern diner was born.

Today, Brown's is a beloved spot in Nashville and has numerous regulars, famous and not. Vince Gill loves the burgers, as do Marty Stuart and Faith Hill, among other members of Nashville's country elite. Johnny Cash dedicated an album to the place and John Prine was as comfortable there as you will be. According to a regular, Prine was at the bar one night when someone recognized him and put one of his songs on the jukebox. Apparently, Prine stood up and mimicked himself continuing to sing along to his own music and giving the bar patrons a twisted, impromptu karaoke performance.

Randy, a 25-year veteran of Brown's, told me, "This is a good anti-anorexia place." I'm assuming he was referring to the gloriously unhealthy menu that includes, beyond burgers, grilled cheese, Frito pie, hush puppies, and a catfish dinner. The only salad on the menu is coleslaw. The burger at Brown's has been on the menu since it opened in 1927. It's made from a daily delivery of fresh chuck, hand-pattied to around five ounces. A cheeseburger comes with mayo, tomato, lettuce, and onion on a white squishy bun with pickles speared to the top. If you ask for a cheeseburger, you don't get mustard. If you ask for a hamburger, you do. I'm confused too—just read the menu and have another Budweiser.

Charlie Brown demonstrates the new "electric" coffeemaker, mid-1930's.

Photo courtesy of Brown's Diner

DYER'S BURGERS

205 BEALE ST | MEMPHIS, TN 38103

901-527-3937 | WWW.DYERSONBEALE.COM

SUN–THURS 11 AM–1 AM | FRI & SAT 11 AM–5 AM

No hamburger restaurant in America flaunts the method of deep-frying a burger like Dyer's in Memphis, Tennessee. There are other burgers out there that are cooked in skillets of bubbling proprietary, blended grease, but Dyer's goes to the extreme and employs a two-foot-wide skillet that I'm guessing holds more than three gallons of grease. But that's not all. Dyer's claims the grease has never been changed since the restaurant opened almost a hundred years ago.

I know this sounds nuts, but according to previous owner Tom Robertson, the grease has never been changed, just added to. "We'll top off the grease but never throw it out and start over," he told me as I interviewed him for my film, *Hamburger America.* As I sat there in disbelief, he produced one photograph after another documenting the police-escorted moving of the grease from the old location to the new. On some news footage I obtained for the film, you can hear someone say, "As soon as the mayor gets here we'll go inside and make some lunch!" Now I've really seen it all.

The burgers are not deep-fried in just any old grease. Dyer's uses beef tallow, or rendered beef fat to add to the decades-old skillet. You'd think your burger would emerge from the grease

a sludgy disaster, but quite the opposite occurs. The grease of course adds flavor, but the burger turns out being no greasier than a regular, griddled burger. It's probably because of this that some regulars ask to have their bun dipped, which is where the top half of the bun is returned to the skillet for a dip in the grease.

The method for cooking a burger at Dyer's is the most peculiar of any burger counter in America. A quarter-pound wad of fresh ground beef is placed on a marble surface. A large spatula rests atop the meat as the cook pounds the beef into a paper-thin patty nearly eight inches wide. The

flat beef is then scraped off the surface and slid into the nearby skillet of bubbling, brown grease. Within a minute, the patty floats to the top and it's done. Ask for cheese and watch what happens. The cook lifts the patty out of the grease with the spatula, places an orange square of American cheese on it, and the patty is quickly dipped back into the grease to melt the cheese.

Mississippi native Elmer Dyer opened Dyer's Restaurant in 1912 in the midtown section of Memphis. The burger shack proudly served both blacks and whites, though in the Southern tradition before the civil rights movement, they had to enter though separate doors. At some point, Dyer's moved around the corner to Poplar and North Cleveland, and from there made its historic move to Beale Street. The North Cleveland location became a Vietnamese restaurant that curiously continued to sell deep-fried burgers among a selection of traditional Vietnamese dishes.

The Dyer's of Beale Street comes off as a tourist trap, but maintains the fabled grease and uses only fresh ground beef for the burgers. If you want to broaden your horizons, order the second most popular sandwich at Dyer's—the deep-fried bologna sandwich. Previous owner Tom once told me bluntly, "If you are watching your health, I recommend going next door."

FAT MO'S

2620 FRANKLIN PK | NASHVILLE, TN 37204

615-298-1111 | (17 OTHER NASHVILLE METRO LOCATIONS)

WWW.FATMOS.COM | TUE–SUN 10 AM–11 PM

MON 10 AM–10 PM

Ask any current or former Nashville area college student about Fat Mo's and most likely they'll tell you they've been there. That may be because in the Nashville metro area there are eighteen Fat Mo's locations. It also may be because people in Nashville love burgers and Fat Mo's makes one helluva burger.

At first glance, anyone of the Fat Mo's outposts look like a standard roadside burger joint, some of them nondescript, brightly painted cinderblock boxes near highway interchanges. But to those who know Fat Mo's, there is something entirely unique at play here. Opened in 1991 by Iranian husband and wife Mohammad Ali and Shiva Karimy, the burgers at Fat Mo's have a very distinct flavor that is unmistakably Middle Eastern.

The story of how Mo and Shiva came to found a burger empire in Nashville is right out of a storybook. After the Shah of Iran was deposed in 1979 the lives of any remaining supporters of his regime were in danger under the new ruler Ayatollah Khomeini. "After the revolution I escaped," Mo told me, "I was for the Shah and if I had stayed I'd be killed. They had no mercy." Mo was a prominent businessman in Iran prior to the revolution and owned a number of restaurants, four of them burger joints.

Inspired by the success of McDonald's in his country Mo saw potential in the burger business. He opened his own burger joint and called it "Mamad Topol," which translated from Farsi means "Fat Mo's." "The Iranians loved American culture," Mo explained, "and they still do! Don't believe what you see on the news."

Mo and Shiva have made their name with a unique twist to the all-American hamburger. The basic construction of the burger is the same but a very important step in the cooking process sets these burgers apart from the rest. When you bite into the half-pound Fat Mo you'll be struck by the subtle spices at work. Black pepper, salt, and garlic are all present, as well as other spices, but none of this overwhelms the beef-and-cheese profile of the burger. The secret is in the marinade, an old family recipe.

All of the burgers at Fat Mo's come from bulk fresh ground beef that is hand-pattied daily. "We weigh it on a scale then flatten into patties on a hard surface," Mo explained. The burgers are cooked on a flattop griddle, and just before they are finished, the patties are dipped into the marinade then returned to the griddle. "That's how we do it," Mo explained proudly. "But the marinade is a secret. I cannot tell you what is in that." Whatever it is, it makes the Fat Mo one unique, tasty burger.

The menu is vast but the burger options are pretty basic at Fat Mo's. The biggest seller is the "Fat Mo," which is a half-pound patty on a toasted sesame seed bun. Unless you specify what you want on your burger the Fat Mo comes with everything, which is shredded lettuce, tomato, raw onion, pickles, mustard, ketchup, mayonnaise, and American cheese. Mo's personal favorite burger on the menu (and coincidentally mine as well) is the half-pound Double Mo. Instead of one large half-pound patty the Double Mo comes with two quarter-pound patties, more griddle char, and an extra slice of cheese. There's also the Little Mo, a quarter-pound burger that Mo says, "Most of the ladies get that one." If you are feeling adventurous (or really hungry) go for the Super Deluxe Fat Mo, a twenty-seven-ounce patty that comes with everything plus grilled onions, barbeque sauce, bacon, and jalapeños. It may be your only meal of the day.

Fat Mo's Locations are a mixed bag of restaurant types because each location is an independently owned franchise. A handful of them are sit-down restaurants with drive-thrus, a few are sit-down with no drive-thru, and some are tiny roadside drive-up windows. Five of these have a curious double drive-up system with two lanes, one on either side of the building. When you pull up to the large menu in the parking lot there is no speaker asking you for your order. You make a selection and drive up to a window to order, or an employee will emerge from the rear of the restaurant to take your order to bring to the kitchen. It's all very low-tech but everything is made to order and very fresh.

Although most of the locations have been franchised, Mo and Shiva have retained the Smyrna location for themselves. They spend much of their time in the restaurant because as Mo put it, "People in Nashville want to see me, see that I'm alive, that I exist." Mr. Mo, as he is affectionately known, most definitely exists and so do his amazing burgers.

ROTIER'S RESTAURANT

2412 ELLISTON PLACE | NASHVILLE, TN 37203

615-327-9892 | MON–FRI 10 AM–10:30 PM

SAT 9 AM–10 PM | CLOSED SUNDAY

Nashvillians are proud of Rotier's and the burger that is served there on French bread. At first glance, the burger looks impossible to eat, a tower of edible elements that defy gravity, thanks, only to those, feathery sandwich toothpicks. And that bread—why the big loaf of French bread? "My father ordered some loaves of French bread from Sunbeam one day in the '40s to serve with our spaghetti," owner Margaret Crouse told me. One thing led to another and the famous Rotier's cheeseburger on French bread was born. Despite how tall the burger looks, it's a breeze to eat and the supersoft bread cradles the burger patty and condiments perfectly.

It should be a good burger. It has been on the top of every best burger list in Nashville for decades. Loretta Lynn, Tim McGraw, and Faith Hill are all fans of the cozy dive. Jimmy Buffett used to sit at the bar and write songs and eat burgers regularly back in the late '60s when he lived in Nashville, prompting many to assume that he penned the famous "Cheeseburger in Paradise" at Rotier's. Alas, he did not.

Evelyn and John Rotier opened their tavern and restaurant in 1945 just steps from the esteemed Vanderbilt University. Today, the giggly, effervescent Margaret Crouse, daughter of the Rotiers, owns the dark, comfortably broken-in tavern with her brother, Charlie Rotier. "I've worked here for 38 years," she told me, but many of her employees can boast similar claims. Pamela has been in the kitchen for over two decades. Her mother gave her the job after she had flipped burgers there for over 30 years, starting in 1951.

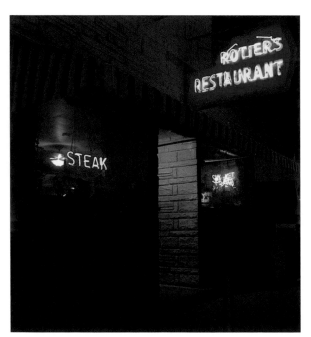

There are three burgers on the menu at Rotier's and the descriptions can be somewhat confusing. The well-known "cheeseburger on French bread" is self-explanatory, but order a grilled cheeseburger and it comes on white or wheat toast. Order just a cheeseburger and you'll get the same patty on a white squishy bun. The six-ounce burgers are hand-pattied every morning from over 200 pounds of fresh-ground chuck. A burger with everything comes with lettuce, onion, and tomato. Order a "half & half" and you'll get a plate with both fries and onion rings.

Other than hamburgers and the surprisingly good spicy fried pickles, Rotier's is also known for its plate dinners that come with Southern sides, like lima beans, broccoli casserole, and fried okra. And don't miss Eddie Cartwright's Lemon Ice Box Pie, a tangy, creamy dessert similar to key lime pie with a buttery graham cracker crust. Jack-of-all-trades Eddie and his pie recipe have been at Rotier's for over twenty years.

My good friend from Nashville, Vadis Turner, told me once, "My dad took me here for my first burger. It is the kind of place where you bring your kid to get them their first real hamburger."

Pamela, taking a break near the bar, smoking a cigarette, and waiting for the next rush told me, "This place is a home away from home for a lot of people. Once you sit down, you don't want to get up."

ZARZOUR'S CAFE

1627 ROSSVILLE AVE | CHATTANOOGA, TN 37408

423-266-0424 | MON–FRI 11 AM–2 PM

CLOSED SAT & SUN

Zarzour's is one of the places I visited where I had wished this book wasn't just about hamburgers. In addition to serving up one of the best burgers I've ever had, Zarzour's also provides a meat-and-threes menu that the locals love. But even if burgers were the only draw, it's worth a trip to this South Chattanooga food gem.

Until recently, Zarzour's burgers were not even listed on the menu. Local lunch patron Blythe Bailey told me, "I came here a few times before I realized they even made burgers." I asked Shannon Fuller, a Zarzours family member, grill chef, and master of ceremonies, why the burgers were not advertised. "Because I hate making them!" she said laughing hard, "Just kidding! But in the summertime it gets real hot in here because of the burgers."

It couldn't be a friendlier place. Everyone knows one another and some descendant of Zarzour is always in the restaurant either eating or working. "They come here to eat and I put every damn one of them to work—go clear that table," Shirley Fuller told me.

Shirley is the matriarch of the family, owner, and third-generation Zarzour. Her grandfather, Charles Zarzour, a Lebanese immigrant, opened the café in 1918. Shirley is in charge of the desserts for the three hours a day the restaurant is open. If a pie is running low, she'll spot a regular with a favorite and tell them so.

The burgers are large. How large? Shannon made an air patty with her hands "about this big" and burst out laughing. "And the large burger is this big!"and she made a bigger air patty. Each burger is pattied to order. Shannon scoops ground chuck out of a Tupperware dish next to the grill, hand-forms a patty and places it on the small, flattop griddle in the front part of the restaurant, surrounded by customers. No burger is the same, though she gets pretty close. If you ask for grilled onion, a thick slice is cooked like a burger patty on the griddle. A cheeseburger with everything comes with pickles, lettuce, tomato, onion, mayo, and mustard on a bun that comes from a bakery across the street.

From the outside, Zarzour's doesn't look like much. Look for the small painted-brick structure with heavily fortified windows. The only warmth on the exterior is the red-checked curtain hanging in the window of the front door. Inside you'll find just the opposite—a warm country café with tables of all sizes covered with the same red-checked fabric and a capacity crowd happy to be there.

Besides burgers, I watched plates of great Southern food be dispatched to tables. Butter beans, collard greens, and skillet corn bread are on the menu, as is the local favorite, lemon ice box pie.

The tables all have clear bottles filled with odd science experiments: things like homemade chow chow relish and pickled okra. One bottle's contents even the waitress could not identify, but I'm sure it was tasty.

It would be easy to miss out on a lunch at Zarzour's if you showed up, for example, after 2 p.m., or on a weekend. I asked Shirley why they are only opened for fifteen hours a week and she explained succinctly with a smile, "That's all I want."

36

TEXAS

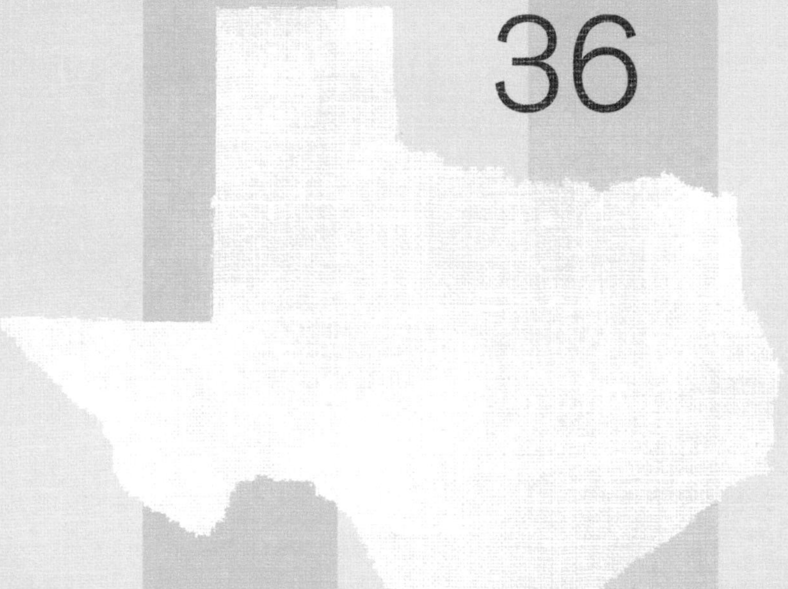

105 GROCERY

17255 TEXAS 105 | WASHINGTON, TX 77880

936-878-2273 | MON–THU 11 AM–7:30 PM

FRI & SAT 11 AM–8 PM

This is not a burger joint. It's not really even a well-stocked grocery store. 105 Grocery is a tiny country store, a place to meet and buy beer, lotto tickets, and a bag of chips. They also happen to serve one of the best burgers I've ever had in Texas.

105 Grocery is way out there. Far beyond the sprawl of Houston and a healthy 80-mile drive northwest is a burger spot that is barely on the map. Inside and out, the 105 is a friendly, classic, functioning rural country store. Mismatched chairs and tables fill the area by the register and people come

and go, paying for gas and hauling away beer by the 12-pack. At the 105 Grocery, the beer in the coolers far exceeds the space allotted for soda.

The best-looking seat in the house is a community table in the rear of the store near the beer coolers. The table is surrounded by a bunch of random chairs and one comfortable, high-backed leather office chair on wheels. As I eyed the chair at the empty table I heard a voice say, "Nobody better sit in that chair." One of the grill cooks, Sherrie, explained to me that, like clockwork, the owner's brother, Sam, shows up every day at 8 a.m. and 4 p.m. to sit in that chair. Sure enough, at exactly 4:01 a guy in a dusty John Deere hat walked in, helped himself to a can of Miller Lite and slipped into the chair. A friend in suspenders, jeans, and cowboy hat joined him with a Bud in hand and all I could think of was how fortunate I was to be in this authentic joint. Most people never get to see this side of the country.

Your choices for burgers are with or without cheese and single or double patty. As tempting as a double sounds deep in the heart of Texas, beware. The fresh, hand-pattied burgers seem to be close to half a pound, making a double-meat burger one full pound of beef. I opted for the half-pound single patty and that was sufficient. The girl on the grill, Beaujolais, told me, "Some folks come in and order double meat with bacon . . . that's big." A burger with everything comes with mayo, pickles, mustard, iceberg lettuce, a slice of tomato, and raw onion. The whole package is delivered on a toasted, buttered, soft white bun in a plastic basket and is an absolutely tasty belly bomb.

The flavor was peppery and I'm assuming that Beaujolais (named by her mother, who worked in a wine store) sprinkled a liberal amount of seasoning on the patties. Customers and employees pointed out that Beaujolais was the one who makes the best burger at the 105. Everyone who works here does it all, and Sherrie said it best: "Cook, cashier . . . whatever." The tiny flattop griddle can be seen though a small pass-thru behind the register and on busy days there's a wait due to the limited capacity of the griddle.

An older, outgoing regular named Donald, sitting at a table sipping a beer, told me that the 105 has been around forever and remembers the place from his youth, when it was called Jensen's Store. "I damn near own the place," he declared. "I'm here every day!"

The actual owners are Betty and John Eichelberger, who own a ranch nearby. Betty's aunt and uncle Minnie and Melvin Jensen opened the grocery many decades ago. The progression of ownership still exists in the signage outside, making the 105 look like it has an identity problem. One sign reads B&J's Gas and another across the parking lot calls the place D&K General Store. When you call, they answer the phone, "105." My favorite sign, though, is on the front door and lists two rules— No Smoking Cigars—No Sagging Pants. I wonder if they are enforced.

As Sam sat in his leather office chair and watched the activity at the register, he told anyone who would listen, "Can't get a bad burger here." He then turned to me. "I eat burgers here every day," he said, then added with a chuckle, "I eat all my meals here."

ADAIR'S SALOON

2624 COMMERCE ST | DALLAS, TX 75226

214-939-9900 | WWW.ADAIRSSALOON.COM

OPEN DAILY, 11 AM TO CLOSING

Down in Deep Ellum, a section of Dallas just north of downtown known for its honky-tonk nightlife, is a comfortably broken-in bar called Adair's Saloon. If you walk in off the street out of the blazing Texas sun, it'll take a while for your eyes to adjust to the darkness. But when they do, you'll find a place that is hard to leave. There are happy hour specials all day, old-timey country tunes on the jukebox, instant friends lining the bar, and they just happen to serve one of the best burgers in Texas.

Adair's is full of beer neon and other signage but most noticeable is the graffiti, which is everywhere. It's on the floor, walls, and tables and there's a lot of it. Cute bartender Tarah, who has a tattoo that spirals up her leg, told me, "We encourage it," and handed me a few black Sharpies. Adair's is the perfect spot if you need to let loose with a pen after a few beers. Just ask the bartender for a marker.

Settle into a booth or belly-up to the bar and order a burger and a local favorite beer (one of my favorites), Shiner Bock. If you need a menu there's one posted behind the bar but the choices are limited. You can order a cheeseburger or hamburger, and at Adair's they only come in one size—huge.

This classic Texas burger is a thing of beauty.

It comes in a plastic basket, wrapped in checked wax paper and speared with a fat, whole jalapeño pepper. The contents are bursting from its wrapping, begging you to grab hold and take a bite. A burger with everything comes with a thick slice of tomato, shredded lettuce, a slice of raw onion, pickles, and mustard. They also offer grilled onion, available upon request. The whole thing is sandwiched between two halves of a soft, white squishy bun that has been warmed in a steaming tray. A bite that includes all of these elements is blissful.

Like all classic Texas hamburgers the burger at Adair's weighs in at a half pound. The way the grill cook arrives at this measurement is one of the more unique methods I have ever seen. Fresh ground beef arrives at Adair's in long tubes that just happen to share the same circumference as Mrs. Baird's enriched buns. Sergio Perez, who has

manned the griddle at Adair's for a decade, lays out the beef tube and slices, with the plastic still on, half-pound patties. Each slice is identical (thanks to years of practice) and when the plastic is peeled off —voilà!—perfect patties! There's an art to slicing the patties and as bartender Tarah put it, "If I had to do it, it'd be a mess."

The burgers are cooked on a flattop in a spotless kitchen that in no way resembles the rest of the grungy bar. "I keep it very clean in here," Sergio told me with a smile. The only piece of graffiti in the spartan kitchen is over the door and reads, "Sergio's burgers are the best!" When he showed me the bun steamer, I remembered that the bun on my burger had been toasted. "Only for special people," Sergio pointed out. Everyone else gets a steamed bun. The fries are peculiar, long potato wedges that resemble truck stop jo-jos. Even though they are frozen and come out of a bag they are not bad. There is no deep fryer in Sergio's kitchen so the jo-jos get tossed onto the flattop to cook, making the exterior very crunchy.

Seven nights a week patrons enjoy live music at Adair's with no cover charge. There is a full-sized tabletop shuffleboard that is addictive and will allow you to channel your inner-Olympic curler. The walls are covered with framed photos and one very large one stands out. Look for the enlarged snapshot of Elvis Presley in a deep embrace with former owner Lois Adair. Apparently, during a live show in the '50s Lois broke through security to lay a big hug on the King.

Thankfully, someone had a camera.

Friend and local burger expert Wayne Geyer led me to Adair's when I told him I was looking for a quintessential Texas burger in Dallas. I caught him mumbling to himself as we enjoyed our burgers, "There's something about a Texas burger. . . ." And he's right. There is something special about burgers in Texas, and it's not just because Texas is the land of beef. I think it's because a true Texas burger is a simple thing, but it's large. Simplicity and size are what make a burger a Texas burger, and Adair's has it right.

ARNOLD BURGER

1611 SOUTH WASHINGTON ST I AMARILLO, TX 79102
806-372-1741 I WWW.ARNOLDBURGERS.COM
MON–FRI 9 AM–5:45 PM I CLOSED WEEKENDS

Arnold Burger's reputation far exceeds its physical size. The tiny, beat up burger joint may look worn out, but this burger destination has cranked out very large, tasty burgers to happy customers for decades.

Owner Gayla Arnold is a hoot. Loaded with energy, this transplanted Hoosier took over when her parents had finally had enough 10 years ago. Ann and Dinzel Arnold opened the restaurant in 1985, moving into an old barbeque joint in the center of Amarillo. The Arnold family today is huge and it's not uncommon to find a few family members helping out around the

burger on the menu—the "Arnold Burger."

The restaurant's namesake burger is not to be taken lightly. This burger is a monster. Assuming you were hungry when you walked in, you most certainly will not be when you leave. The Arnold starts with two, three-fourths-pound patties that are stacked with four slices of American cheese on a toasted, wide, white squishy bun slathered with mayo and mustard. Lettuce, tomato, raw onion, and pickles are standard but come on the side.

The Arnold floored me. Most of the time when someone leads me to a burger almost too big to consume, the finished product turns out to be flavorless, poorly cooked, and too much to handle. I was amazed because the Arnold was as flavorful and juicy as any of my favorite "slimmer" burgers and surprisingly easy to handle. The Arnold is really just a cartoonishly large all-American burger. The secret, I believe, may be in the griddle. In plain view directly behind the register is a beautifully seasoned freestanding flattop griddle. The jet-black surface reminded me that this is where some of the best burgers get their flavor.

If that wasn't enough, you can actually get a burger in the shape of Texas in four different sizes. A local bakery supplies Gayla with specially made buns that are also in the shape of Texas. Other shapes are available including a guitar, a boot, and the popular heart-shaped burger for two. Choose a shape from the outlines drawn on the wall in actual size. Some of the shapes I could not identify. "That's a snowman," Gayla told me pointing to a bulbous outline. I had to believe her.

restaurant. Gayle's nephew Perry, who worked at Arnold's as a teenager and is now a chef at a nearby Olive Garden told me, "Everything I know about the kitchen I learned here."

The menu boasts a dizzying selection of patty-and-cheese combinations, over 30, and the choices are based on patty size and quantity. The standard-sized patty at Arnold is three-fourths of a pound but to add to the confusion you can also order a Junior, a Baby, or a Small burger. Naturally, I had to ask how much each patty weighed and Gayla explained with a straight face, "The Baby is smaller than the Junior, the Small is smaller than the Baby . . . ," and so on. Each size can come in up to four patties, with or without cheese. "It looks like a lot of burgers but it's really not," Gayla assured me. When I asked why the menu was like this, Gayla said in her defense, "Our customers have dictated our menu. It's their fault!" My advice would be to stick to the basics, avoid the confusion, and get the most popular

Arnold is also the home of the "Family Burger," an ingenious invention dreamed up by Gayla's parents. "My mother was trying to figure out a way to feed a family, like a pizza." It sounds crazy, but they have sent Family Burgers to bachelor parties and weddings. Gayla added, "We've even sent them to funerals." The largest Family Burger is 24 inches in diameter, feeds a family of 10, and takes up most of the space on the flattop to cook. The grillperson uses a pizza peel to flip the Family Burger, and it's served on a huge, custom-made bun. If you want one of these, you'll need to order it a day in advance.

Arnold Burger gets a delivery of fresh beef daily and whatever family is around in the morning helps hand-patty the wide array of patty sizes. Nothing is actually measured and as Gayla put it, "We just grab the meat and start pattying." She added, "My dad had the perfect hand size for making the patties." The tiny restaurant has been known to move through hundreds of pounds of beef a day and once set a one-day record of 500 pounds following a TV appearance.

I asked Gayla about the limited hours at Arnold Burger, which is not open on weekends. The restaurant closes at the peculiar time of 5:45 p.m. and as Gayla explained, "It's a great time to go home!"

BLAKE'S BBQ AND BURGERS

2916 JEANETTA ST | HOUSTON, TX 77063

713-266-6860 | WWW.BLAKESBARBQ.BIZ

MON–SAT 10:30 AM–8 PM | CLOSED SUNDAY

I can always count on my good friend and Houston food critic Robb Walsh to dig up the obscure. Robb thankfully put this burger joint on my radar and I am forever grateful. Robb also introduced me to Don Blake, the man behind the burger. Don't call him Don, though. I tried a few times and he didn't respond. Finally he told me quietly, "My mom called me Don. Everybody else calls me Blake."

Blake didn't always serve the best, freshest burgers in town from his dream-come-true barbeque joint on the west side of Houston. "When we first started we were serving frozen," Blake admitted, but he knew the burger could be better. As fate would have it, when a truck didn't show with frozen patties one day, Blake ran to a local grocery store to buy fresh ground 80/20 chuck and the rest was history. "It was like a phenomenon," Blake told me. "Word got out and people were asking 'What are you putting in there?'"

There was no turning back, and after 28 years Blake is still using the same 80/20 chuck for his burgers that he picks up from a local butcher.

I had my first burger at Blake's with Robb Walsh and noticed right away that it seemed loaded with butter. "You have a problem with that?" Robb shot back. No, I most certainly did not. The burger to get at Blake's is the cheeseburger with everything. The griddleperson takes a measured eight-ounce ball of ground chuck, presses it between two sheets of wax paper, then plops it onto the well-seasoned flattop. A liberal amount of "secret" seasoning (that looked like salt and pepper) is sprinkled on top and the burger is pressed again. A very complicated bun-toasting procedure ensues where a five-inch white squishy is sent through a buttering toaster press and then transferred to the griddle to finish. "The key is the bun cooking on that griddle," Blake pointed out. The bun is prepped with pickles, mayo, mustard, shredded lettuce, and tomato. It ain't a picture-perfect burger, with its squashed bun and erupting contents, but don't let that fool you. The butter, beef, mustard, pickles, and soft bun make for an enormously satisfying burger experience (I added bacon and grilled onions, too). Add some jalapeños to remind yourself that you're in Texas.

There's a curious burger on the menu called the "Kick-Burger," designed by one of Blake's biggest fans, Houston mega-developer Vincent Kickerillo. The Kick comes with pepper jack cheese, jalapeños, and a splash of barbeque sauce. Even Frank Sinatra became a fan (thanks to his good friend Kickerillo) and had Blake frequently ship raw patties to his home in Malibu. "He and Kick loved the seasoning so I'd overnight 15 to 20 pounds to them."

There are many other things on the menu like sandwiches, baked potatoes, and burritos,

Don Blake

but I've never tried them. I have not even tasted the world-class barbeque that Blake is known for. I've only indulged in his amazing burgers.

There is no signage indicating a drive-up window but at Blake's you can order from your car. Look for the tiny window on the right side of the building and place your order. "twenty-five percent of our business is by drive-up," Blake told me.

The idea for a barbeque and burger restaurant was born of necessity. As a young salesman for an office supply business, Blake was constantly on the search for decent, affordable barbeque and decided to open his own place. Blake's sales beat had him in on the west side of Houston daily and he discovered his current location by accident while taking a shortcut. "This street was a two-lane dirt road back then," he told me, which is hard to imagine given the unstoppable urban sprawl of Houston. It turned out to be the perfect location.

Blake's stands out on Jeanetta Street thanks to its design. "I wanted it to look 'cowboy,'" Blake told me, and pointed out the horse hitch that completes the Alamoesqe façade. The dining room has a floor-to-ceiling painted mural depicting a dusty Old West version of his hometown of Brownwood, Texas. "That's not really what it looks like," Blake confessed. He grew up in a town where being black was an anomaly. He showed me his high school reunion picture and said with a chuckle, "See if you can find me!" As I scanned the sea of white faces it was not hard to spot Blake.

Every year, just before Thanksgiving, Blake smokes 100 turkeys and donates them to underprivileged families and a shelter for homeless vets in the neighborhood. Blake explained, "I grew up poor and know how it feels to get food during the holidays."

BURGER HOUSE

6913 HILLCREST AVE | DALLAS, TX 75205

214-361-0370 | WWW.BURGERHOUSE.COM

(OTHER LOCATIONS AROUND DALLAS AND ONE IN AUSTIN, TX)

OPEN DAILY 11 AM–9 PM

Any visit to Dallas, Texas, warrants a stop at this tiny, beloved burger stand. Impossibly small and showing its age, Burger House (aka Jack's from a previous owner) serves excellent, fresh-meat burgers to hungry college students and locals in this wealthy Dallas suburb. Constantly topping best-of lists, Burger House, opened in 1951, has been a favorite of Dallas natives for generations.

Jack Koustoubardis built Burger House and worked at the Hillcrest location flipping burgers for over 30 years. Even though there is no mention of his name anywhere in the restaurant's signage, dedicated regulars still refer to the restaurant as Jack's Burger House. In 1982, friends of Jack's, Angelo Chantilis and Steve Canellos, bought the burger stand and the recipe

for its now famous "seasoned salt." The salt goes onto all of the burgers and fries and creates the taste that regulars crave.

The restaurant is split in two—one part a tiny, fluorescent-lit diner (no more than two hundred square feet) with a few stools and a narrow counter, the other an alleyway dining room with a sloped concrete floor and carved-up picnic tables. Of curious note, the stand closes every night at 9 p.m., but the dining room side stays open all night. Manager Nicholas told me,

"That's just the way it was. Jack kept it open all night." Angelo, aware of the extremely low crime rate in this suburb, confirmed the policy, but said of would-be thieves, with a chuckle "Let 'em walk in instead of breaking the damn glass."

The most popular burger at Burger House is the double cheeseburger. Every morning Burger House gets a delivery of large, flat quarter-pound patties of 80/20 chuck. Angelo told me, "We buy from a local purveyor of meat and they only give us the best." The burgers have been cooked on the well-seasoned, original griddle from opening day at Burger House, a griddle that's over 50 years old. A wide, toasted sesame-seed bun is standard, as are shredded lettuce, tomato, onion, pickles, and mustard. The double with cheese is a large, two-fisted wad of greasy goodness that will fill you up and have you dreaming about your next visit even before you take your last bite.

The seasoned salt, a garlicky secret recipe invented by Jack's brother, Jerry, is so popular that in the 1990s Angelo and Steve decided to bottle and sell the stuff. "People would walk off with the shakers of the salt that we put out," Angelo told me, "so we figured we should just start selling it." Now you can attempt to re-create Jack's burger at home.

Today, Burger House is a mini-chain with seven locations around Dallas and more to come. The enormous Mockingbird location (with its large dining room and drive-thru) does the most business, but it's the original Hillcrest location with its red, white, and blue neon sign that burger lovers visit to get their dose of Americana. I asked Angelo if there were plans to keep expanding, and he responded with an emphatic. "Hell yeah." Angelo's confidence in the franchise led me to believe that there might just be one near you in the future.

CASINO EL CAMINO

517 EAST 6TH ST | AUSTIN, TX 78701
512-469-9330 | WWW.CASINOELCAMINO.NET
OPEN DAILY 4 PM–2 AM

Casino El Camino is not a burger joint. It's a dark punkabilly rock bar with tattooed and pierced patrons that maintains one of the best jukeboxes just about anywhere. People go to Casino to drink and listen to great tunes at this bar on the Sixth Street party strip in downtown Austin, Texas. I was in a rock band for 10 years so I feel at home in a place like Casino. But it wasn't until my third visit that I realized they offered amazing burgers to the buzzed clientele.

I was informed of Casino's burger prowess by a film crew member of mine in Austin, John Spath, who begged me to give it a shot. In a town whose burger culture is dominated by Hut's and Dirty Martin's, and in a state enormously burger-proud, I was skeptical. Even John commented, "It's not the kind of place you'd expect to find good food."

I approached the tiny opening in a dark back corner of the bar to place my order. The small kitchen is manned by a staff of one. A solitary chef takes orders, preps buns, and grills the burgers. When the chef on duty that night, Orestes, was through tending to burgers on the grill, he reluctantly sauntered over to take my order. I waited over half an hour, but for my patience I was rewarded with a heavenly burger.

The burgers at Casino el Camino start as fresh-ground 90 percent lean chuck that's hand formed into 3 quarter-pound patties. They are cooked on an open-flame grill, placed on a bun, halved, then the two halves are placed back on the grill again, cut side down, to achieve a decorative grill brand on the cross section of your burger. It should be noted that cooking over a flame and achieving decent results don't often go together. Most grill cooks, especially those working from a Weber in their backyards, manage to overcook and ruin burgers. Every time I've been to Casino, the burger has been cooked perfectly. Casino el Camino cooks their burgers to temperature. If you ask for rare, get out the napkins and listen for that mooing sound. The cooks know what they are doing. Even a medium-well comes out juicy.

The menu lists burger concoctions that use the three-quarter-pound burger model and add condiments. There's the "Buffalo Burger," which is not actually buffalo beef, but a regular burger topped with hot wing sauce and blue cheese. Or try the "Amarillo Burger" with roasted serrano chiles, jalapeño cheese, and cilantro mayo. My favorite is the standard bacon cheeseburger with cheddar, listed as the "Chicago Burger."

Casino el Camino is both a bar and a person. Casino el Camino, the stage name for this rocker and bar owner, came to Austin for the famed South by Southwest Music Festival in 1990. He was impressed with the forward-thinking Texas town and told a friend back in Buffalo, New York, that it would make a great spot for a bar. "Before I went I thought Texas was all tumbleweeds and fucking cowboys," the Long Island, New York, native admitted. Casino el Camino, the bar, became a joint venture between Casino and the Buffalo restaurateur, Mark Supples.

Expect to wait for your burger, sometimes forever. Casino told me, "The grill only holds fifteen burgers at a time so we are limited in what can come out of that small kitchen." On busy nights the wait can be over an hour. But so what? Enjoy the music, gawk at the crazy piercings, and get a drink. If you complain, you may make it worse. Just remember, this is not fast food. It's slow food at its best.

CHRIS MADRID'S

1900 BLANCO RD I SAN ANTONIO, TX 78212

210-735-3552 I WWW.CHRISMADRIDS.COM

MON–SAT 11 AM–10 PM I CLOSED SUNDAY

Chris Madrid is like no other hamburger icon that I've met. If you are searching for him in the vast, sprawling 34-year-old burger joint, just look for the guy with jet black hair who is smiling and hugging customers. Chris has been hands-on since opening day in 1977 and can still be found moving briskly from kitchen to dining room to bar checking constantly on every moving part of the restaurant. And it seems that every customer in the place knows Chris. "That just means I'm getting old," Chris told me with a chuckle.

In the late '70s Chris bought a tiny burger stand in San Antonio on the corner of Blanco Road and Hollywood called Larry's Place. Fresh out of college, he saw potential in running a taco and burger stand. He renamed the place Chris Madrid's Tacos & Burgers but dropped "tacos" from the name (and menu) in 1980. "The burgers were selling so well and we had so many things on the menu," Chris told me. "We needed to simplify."

Originally, there were three burger sizes to choose from—the Baby, the Mama, and the Papa, but Chris streamlined that as well. In 1980, inspired by the Village People's hit song "Macho Man," Chris decided to call his larger eight-ounce burger "macho" sized. The smaller four-ounce "regular" sells well, but the macho is hard to resist. You can keep it simple and order the Old-Fashion Hamburger, a Texas classic with mustard, pickle, lettuce, onion, and tomato, but there's a better reason to eat at Chris Madrid's—the "Tostada Burger."

The Tostada Burger at Chris Madrid's is legendary. Chris did not invent this staple of San Antonio burger culture but he most definitely made improvements on the classic. The original version, called the "Beanburger," was supposedly invented at the now-defunct Sill's Snack Shack in San Antonio in the '50s and was soon copied by many other burger joints. A traditional Beanburger consists of only four basic elements—a hamburger, refried beans, Fritos, and Cheese Whiz. That's it, with no lettuce, pickle, or anything else to get in the way. Chris changed the name and altered the ingredients slightly for his version but has kept the basic integrity of the original intact. The Tostada Burger uses refried beans, but replaces the Cheese Whiz with cheddar and uses house-made corn chips instead of Fritos.

The macho Tostada Burger is a sight to behold. As you contemplate how to eat this enormous pile of heavenly goo, take a moment to appreciate what is in front of you. The bun, toasted on the grill, can barely contain the brown-and-yellow hues of its contents. The burger patty itself, a thin-pressed wonder made from fresh 75/25 beef, is hidden beneath a layer of refried beans and cascading cheddar.

The burger is impossible to pick up. I found

that cutting it in half made things slightly easier. My first bite of this legend sent me soaring. As I easily made my way through the macho I wondered why this burger was not replicated in every corner of America. The beans and chips worked so well with the beef, and the cheddar tied it all together. Chris said it best when he told me, "It's like a hamburger and an enchilada plate in one." What an amazing invention.

Chris Madrid's is enormous and has grown slowly over the years. Chris bought the icehouse (the Texas version of a deli/package store) next door and eventually put an awning over the large gravel parking lot between the two buildings and added more tables. The awning was replaced by a glassed-in structure and seating capacity increased to over 300. "We had to. It was too hot under there," Chris explained of the connecting addition. Today, the core of the restaurant is the connecting structure, a high-ceilinged dining room filled with mismatched tables and chairs. The icehouse side of the restaurant contains a beautiful recycled bar that Chris bought from a closed convent in the '80s and the original thick refrigerator doors from the icehouse are still functioning.

Every once in a while a mariachi group will wander through the restaurant entertaining customers downing their Tostada Burgers. Chris doesn't hire the musicians. "They just come in," he told me. Grab a local Texas favorite beer, Shiner Bock, while you wait for your burger. It'll come wrapped in "pickle paper," or waxed paper,

to keep your hands dry from the bottle sweat. "That's the way they used to do it back in the icehouse days," bartender of 24 years Jimmy told me. Jimmy is not the longest-running employee at Chris Madrid's. That honor goes to Chris's sister, Diana. "She's seen it all," Chris told me. "She was here on day one."

I heard a woman say in a singsong voice to Chris as she left with her family, "I just had another wonderful hamburger!" You'll be singing too.

CHRISTIAN'S TAILGATE BAR & GRILL

7340 WASHINGTON AVE | HOUSTON, TX 77007

713-864-9744 | WWW.CHRISTIANSTAILGATE.COM

(2 OTHER LOCATIONS IN HOUSTON)

MON–FRI 10 AM–9 PM | SAT 11 AM–9 PM

BAR OPEN TO MIDNIGHT

Imagine walking into an open mike night at a Texas roadhouse and finding Billy Gibbons, front man of ZZ Top, on stage. At Christian's this once was entirely possible because Billy's good friend Steve Christian owns the place. "He used to come in, put his name on the board," Steve told me. Christian's no longer hosts an open mike night but when the Texas rocker comes to town, Christian's is still his first stop for drinks and one of the best burgers in Houston.

Steve Christian is the third-generation owner of this roadhouse burger joint just off I-10 west of downtown Houston. Steve's grandfather opened Christian's Totem in the early '40s as a convenience store and icehouse. Before refrigeration and air conditioning, icehouses were integral to daily life in warm climes. Steve told me, "Guys would come down here to get ice for their wives and end up staying and drinking beer for a while." The beer fridge used to sit in the parking lot with a padlock on it. "My grandfather would leave for the night and toss the guys the key. Eventually, Christian's became a bar."

Steve's grandfather and father ran Christian's as a convenience store and a roadside bar for over 50 years. Steve told me, "In the '40s this was a dirt road out here," pointing to the impossibly busy Washington Avenue, large trucks rumbling in every direction. After a stint as a DJ in a topless club and a job as a crane operator, Steve told his dad he wanted to be the third-generation owner of Christian's. When he took over the business he had plans for expansion. Part of his plan was to put a great burger on the menu, and that burger wins "Best of Houston" awards annually.

The burger to get is the jalapeño cheeseburger—a fresh-ground, half-pound, griddled two-fister that comes in a plastic basket on a toasted white bun with lettuce, onion, tomato, pickle, mustard, and mayo. The jalapeños are snappy and hot and complement the large portion of meat well. "I only buy cold-packed jalapeños from Cajun Chef. They are the only ones that have a crunch," Steve explained. "I've spent years getting the ingredients just right." Recently, Steve has been experimenting with the deep frying of bacon. "It's awesome!" he said as he dragged me into the kitchen the last time I was there. He takes a strip of bacon, dips it into a batter, and tosses it into the fryer. "We've been putting them on the burgers now, on a burger we call the Fried Bacon Burger."

The crowd at Christian's is mixed. It's common to see construction workers, businessmen in suits, and tourists all enjoying their burgers. Former employee Kim, once told me, "There's such a variety you'd be amazed. See those guys over there? Undercover cops."

In 2004, Steve changed the longtime name of the bar from Christian's Totem to Tailgate Bar & Grill for purely logistical reasons. "We were not really a 'totem' any longer (Texas vernacular for the convenience store) and we were getting too many calls from people thinking we sold religious books." The Tailgate in the new name conjures up images of face-painted football fans in parking lots eating buffalo wings. Not so here. Steve has modified and welded actual pickup truck tailgates that serve as wall sculpture, and one supports a large plasma TV next to the bar. *Guy Art* to the extreme.

This burger joint will be around for a while. Steve plans to turn the business over to his son eventually. "We'll see. He's only nine years old now!"

DIRTY MARTIN'S KUM-BAK PLACE

2808 GUADALUPE ST | AUSTIN, TX 78705

512-477-3173 | WWW.DIRTYMARTINS.COM

OPEN DAILY 11 AM–11 PM

Dirty Martin's does not serve thick, gourmet burgers. Dirty Martin's serves excellent, greasy, thin-patty

burgers to Austin locals and students from the nearby University of Texas. Alongside these famed grease bombs, Dirty's also serves a guilty pleasure of yours and mine—the deep-fried tater tot.

Opened in 1926 as Martin's Kum-Bak Place by John Martin, the burger counter earned the nickname "Dirty's" for the dirt floor that remained until 1951. The original counter had just eight stools inside and most of the business was conducted in the parking lot with carhops. Today, the carhops are gone and the dirt floor has been covered for half a century, but Dirty's is still cranking out great burgers over 80 years from opening day.

The menu at Dirty Martin's is loaded with great bar food geared to pre- and post-party revelers in search of nourishment. The lunch crowd looks to be on the other end of the spectrum, nursing hangovers. There are many choices on the menu, but the burgers are king at Dirty's.

The burgers start as fresh ground, thin patties. They are cooked on a flattop griddle and slid onto waiting, toasted sesame seed buns. It seems that the thinness of the patty allows the grillman to cook burgers faster.

Have fun trying to interpret the somewhat cryptic burger options on the menu. Ask for a hamburger and you'll get a single patty with mustard, onion, pickle, and tomato. Ask for a large hamburger and get the same but twice the meat (two patties). Then there's the infamous "Sissy Burger," which replaces the mustard and onion with mayonnaise. I asked the grill team about the definition of a Sissy Burger and was directed to a man named Wesley sitting at the end of the counter. Wesley Hughes, retired from the grill, flipped burgers at Dirty's for 45 years. He bluntly explained to me, "Mustard is strong and not for sissies." I deduced that mayo is for sissies and left it at that. If you need a double-patty burger with mayo, be prepared to tell your waiter you need a "Big Sissy."

Few restaurants in America have the guts to put tater tots on their menus. This trashy little potato treat somehow has the ability to get crispier than fries and retains more grease (or flavor). You can go to the freezer aisle of your supermarket, buy a bag of tots, and cook them in your oven, but we all know how that tastes. Tater tots are best enjoyed deep-fried at places like Dirty Martin's. And what could be better than tater tots? How about the ultimate guilty pleasure—cheese tots.

If you find yourself hungry and near the University of Texas, don't hesitate to stop at the oldest burger stand in Austin. Order some cheese tots and a double burger and look for Wesley at the end of the counter during lunch. He's Dirty Martin's unofficial Head of Public Relations and knows how to spot a sissy, so order yours with mustard.

GUY'S MEAT MARKET

3106 OLD SPANISH TRAIL I HOUSTON, TX 77054

713-747-6800

WWW.DIRECTORYOFHOUSTON.COM/GUYS

TUE–FRI 9 AM–5:30 PM I SAT 9 AM–4 PM

CLOSED SUN & MON

Every once in a while I come across a place where the beef used for burgers is ridiculously fresh. Case in point, Guy's Meat Market in Houston where a full-service butcher shop doubles as one of America's best places to find a hamburger. Second-generation owner Brad Dickens put it in the simplest terms: "Everybody else buys their ground beef from somewhere. We are butchers. We do all of our own trimming and grinding right here."

But this is not your ordinary thick, juicy patty or even a classic griddle-smashed burger. Nope, this is the only place I've discovered in America where you can sink your teeth into a smoked hamburger. You read that correctly, at Guy's the burgers are cooked in a barbeque smoker.

"This must be what heaven is like!" a woman exclaimed as the screen door closed behind her. I could have blurted out the same and clearly understood her joy. The hickory smoke that envelops the place is intoxicating. Cashier Dee told me, "A woman was in here yesterday who said, 'I wasn't even hungry when I walked in here.'" Guy's will do that to you.

Guy's is a classic Texas butcher shop. Three journeymen butchers and ten other employees create a flurry of activity behind the counter. The sound of the butcher's band saw is ever present, the long glass cases are filled with fresh cuts of beef and sausage, and the thick essence of smoke completes the scene.

Not all burgers are created equal and a burger at Guy's is the perfect example. I know you are thinking, how can burger meat be cooked for more than 4 minutes without drying out? I was skeptical to say the least. The machine-pattied eight-ounce burgers are made from fresh ground chuck and cooked in a rotating barbeque smoker for just over an hour. The duration the patties spend in the smoker allows them to still be fairly juicy and gain the coveted "smoke ring" that barbeque aficionados seek, the red ring on the exterior of the beef that can only be produced by smoking meat.

A visit to Houston would not be complete without grabbing a meal with my good friend and food writer Robb Walsh. He had not been to Guy's in awhile and I was glad he agreed to meet me there. He taught me a secret to the smoked burger that I am forever grateful for. If you ask for your burger with everything you'll get pickles, lettuce, tomato, and a cold piece of American cheese. This is not the way Robb orders his burger. "This is a smoked burger," he reminded me. "You need barbeque sauce." He was absolutely right. Robb ordered his with raw onion, pickles, and Brad's house-made tangy barbeque sauce. There was no comparison between the two burgers. The burger with everything was pretty good but the burger with barbecue sauce was explosive. "See, I told you," Robb gloated. The flavor profile of the beef, sauce, and smoke

Brad Dickens

cradled in a soft white bun was phenomenal.

Guy's has been open since 1939 but the smoked burger only made its first appearance in the mid-eighties. "I tried it and it went crazy," Brad explained of the burger's swift popularity with his regulars. There are no tables at Guy's and most burger consumption is done in the parking lot. Dee explained, "Everybody tailgates." There are a few spots inside where you can stand and eat. Brad motioned for Robb and I to shove a few packages of buns out of the way and plop down on a counter in the grocery section of the market. "Just shove that bread outta the way—I don't care."

Today, expect a line of customers that starts at 11 a.m. on the nose and does not abate until the last burger has been wrapped. And there's always a shortage because Brad only makes 200 burgers a day. He almost always sells out. Why only 200? "That's all we have time for." I think I like this logic.

HERD'S HAMBURGERS

400 NORTH MAIN ST | JACKSBORO, TX 76458

NO PHONE | TUE–SAT 10:30 AM–4 PM

CLOSED SUN & MON

About an hour and a half northwest of Fort Worth, deep in rolling Texas ranchland dotted with oil rigs and cows, is a family-run burger joint in the tiny town of Jacksboro. They have no phone and the place is only open five-and-a-half hours a day, five days a week. But if you hit it just right (for lunch only) you'll get to experience one of the more unique burgers in Texas, the amazing "Herdburger."

What you won't get at Herd's is a big, juicy, classic Texas-sized burger, one that you can barely lift to your face and, like so many other Texas burger joints serve up, a thick patty weighing in at over a half pound. Instead what you'll find at Herd's Hamburgers is definitively the flattest burger in America, cooked to perfection by the third-generation owner, Danny Herd.

When I say flat I mean flat. The method for cooking burgers at Herd's is one that I've never witnessed anywhere else in America. When I told the forty-something, moustached Danny this he replied, "Others don't do this?"

Erase any notion that a burger should start as a patty. Picture a beautifully seasoned flattop griddle from the '40s that has a 3-pound pile of ground chuck sitting on the upper left corner. To make a burger, Danny slices an appropriately sized wad of beef from the pile with a concrete trowel, and then with a lightning-fast move, under the weight of the trowel, turns that wad into a flat patty 6 inches wide that is so paper-thin you could see through it. Danny works fast to fill, empty, and refill the griddle every few minutes, warming the buns on the flipped patties. The finished product is transferred to a station where most burgers are dressed "all the way," which is mustard, pickle, chopped onion, tomato, and let-

tuce. If you ask for a "double meat, double cheese," expect a glorious burger that weighs in at just under a half pound and whose loose, crumbly meat is falling out of the waxed paper bursting with a jumble of ingredients.

There are no plates at Herd's. There are also not many seats (except for a few upside-down soda crates and a strange, long row of old school desk chairs). And thankfully there not many other food options, either. Burgers are the focus at Herd's so don't come here looking for things like fries or malts. Danny's father, Claude, who owned and ran the place with his wife, Orlene, from 1971 to 2008, told me, "This was the way it was back in 1916 when my aunt started. I thought about [adding fries] but it's easier to pull a bag of chips off the rack." I asked Danny why there was no phone and his answer was perfect. "We really don't need it. That way we don't have to take phone orders." He's absolutely right—why take phone orders when the line is out the door most days by noon? And why close by 4 p.m.? It was Claude who started that practice. He explained flatly with a smile, "I wore out my patience, my back, and my knees at about the same time."

Claude and Orlene moved Herd's to its current location just north of downtown Jacksboro. They bought a small two-story apartment house and turned the garage downstairs into the restaurant. But this was not the only move in Herd's nearly 100-year history. From what I could glean from conversations with Claude and from inspecting photos on the walls Herd's may have

320

actually moved over seven times. Claude's first response when I asked about the moves was, "Gosh. I don't know." What we do know was that Herd's started as a tiny canvas shack downtown by Claude's aunt Ella Gafford. Apparently, in almost 100 years the method for making burgers at Herd's has never changed.

When Danny got word that his dad was planning to retire he knew he was the only one who could continue the tradition. "I worked here as a kid," Danny explained, and after 21 years in Denton, Texas as an employee at UPS he moved home to run the business. Danny likens the twenty-seven-and-a-half-hour workweek at Herd's to a vacation compared to his life with the delivery giant. "I think I'll get more mileage out of my body here than I would at UPS."

HUT'S HAMBURGERS

807 WEST 6TH ST | AUSTIN, TX 78703

512-472-0693 | WWW.HUTSFRANKANDANGIES.COM

OPEN DAILY 11 AM–10 PM

Hut's Hamburgers is not on the party drag in downtown Austin, Texas, where the crowds migrate to East 6th Street. This out-of-the-way burger restaurant is on the quiet west end of 6th Street, identifiable from blocks away by its vintage green and red neon sign. Follow the arrow on the sign to the odd-shaped 1930s red, white, and blue building.

The history of Hut's is so convoluted that I'll spare you the details and give you the skinny version. Basically, Homer "Hut" Hutson opened Hut's Hamburgers on South Congress in 1939. Across town the same year, Sammie Joseph opened Sammie's Drive-In on West 6th Street. In 1969, after numerous owners, Sammie's became Hut's.

The Memorial Day Flood of 1981 devastated downtown Austin. A witness to the aftermath described it as looking like a week of hurricanes had rambled through town. The west side of town, particularly where Hut's is situated, was destroyed. A local newspaper noted that through all the death and destruction, Hut's remained standing, prompting the phrase "God Bless Hut's."

Since 1981 Hut's has been owned and run by Kim and Hutch Hutchinson. Kim told me, "Since we bought Hut's very little has changed. We make everything from scratch." The Hut's they purchased was still selling burgers and chicken-fried steak, but the Hutchinsons updated the menu. The restaurant now offers salads and daily blue-plate specials like fried catfish on Fridays, but every time I've been to Hut's, I'm there to consume one of their award-winning burgers.

If you are looking for variety, you have come to the right place. Hut's serves high-quality, fresh-meat burgers with just about any topping you can think of. The menu is loaded with cute names for the burgers like the "Alan Freed" (with hickory sauce) and the "Beachboy" (with pineapple). Stick to the basics like the "Hut's

browse the flood photos on the wall. By the time you bite into your burger, you'll be glad Hut's was saved too.

KELLER'S DRIVE-IN

6537 E. NORTHWEST HWY | DALLAS, TX 75231

214-368-1209 | OPEN DAILY 10 AM–MIDNIGHT

The sign in front of this aging relic of Dallas hamburger culture says it all— "Keller's Hamburgers Beer." That's what you'll find here and not much more. Personally, I don't require much else and at Keller's I was in heaven.

During the day Keller's doesn't look like much. The low, faded green, beige, and brick central structure that houses the kitchen sits in the middle of a huge parking lot surrounded by long parking shelters that can accommodate up to 100 cars. Lunch seems to be moderately busy but at night, Keller's comes alive. The parking shelters light up with flashing neon and pickup trucks line the drive-in with tailgating Texans. On most Saturday nights, owners of classic cars still cruise into the drive-in to stage impromptu shows and beer flows more than soda. At Keller's, they'll not only bring your burger to your car seat, they'll bring you a beer too.

But Keller's is not just another roadside hamburger joint. Jack Keller opened his first drive-in in 1950 after working for the Big Sam Company.

Favorite," a bacon cheeseburger, and be rewarded with an unforgettable burger experience.

A rarity in the burger world, Hut's gives you the option to choose the type of meat for your burger. Hut's offers traditional fresh ground beef, buffalo, or Texas Longhorn. "We added buffalo and Longhorn to the menu for health reasons," Kim told me. Both Texas Longhorn beef and buffalo meat are superlean, and in the case of Longhorn beef, low in the type of fat that causes bad cholesterol. The one-third-pound patties are cooked on a well-seasoned flattop griddle. The Longhorn beef and buffalo meat come from a nearby ranch, and the traditional cow beef comes to Hut's as 90 percent lean ground chuck.

By noon most days, the restaurant is packed. On game days (the University of Texas is nearby) expect to be waiting on line or at the bar surrounded by fans decked out in UT orange. Use the time you'll spend waiting for a table to

Big Sam developed drive-in restaurants and is credited with opening the first in America, the Pig Stand in Dallas in 1921. Jack wanted to open his own drive-in and saw that there was a need to serve beer with the burgers. As Jack explained in his gentle Texas drawl, "Beer, hamburgers . . . that's all you need really." Cheers to that.

My first visit to Keller's was around 4 p.m. on a Tuesday and I was a little shocked to find people pulling up in pickups and motorcycles ordering beer and skipping the burger. Most seemed to just have one and move on, a post-work cold one before the ride home that made perfect sense to me. "Some come for the beers because they are only $1.75 here!" carhop Rachel told me. Rachel, a sweet, salt-of-the-earth, sun-baked Texan wearing an oversized T-shirt, told me she has been at Keller's for over 21 years and loves her job. "The tips are excellent. That's why I started here."

The burger selection is totally confusing with random, specially numbered burger combinations that are strangely out of sync. The #9 is a double meat with chili and the regular cheeseburger gets no number. I asked Jack about the reasoning behind the numbered burgers and he replied, "Lack of a good sign painter, I guess." Avoid confusion and order the #5, a double meat and cheese with tomato, shredded lettuce, and "special sauce," which my taste buds identified as Thousand Island dressing. Tater tots are on the menu at Keller's and when tots are on the menu I always skip the fries.

The thin-patty burgers at Keller's are cooked on a large flattop griddle and served on toasted, soft, white poppy seed buns. The drive-in gets a shipment of fresh beef daily and they come in as patties just over 3 ounces each. The burgers are delivered to your car wrapped in waxed paper, creating a perfect package of cheesy, beefy, greasy deliciousness. I can eat one of their doubles in three bites and go back for more.

The carhops are all female and range in age. There doesn't seem to be an enforced dress code for the carhops at Keller's and the outfits go from baggy tees to tight tank tops. One flirty carhop sported a straw cowboy hat and only worked the side of the drive-in that was frequented by the bikers, affectionately known as the Zoo Side. This section of the parking lot, to the left of the main structure, also has a few mismatched benches that look like church pews. Here, the bikers can rest, have a burger, and sip a beer. "These guys are mostly weekend bikers, you know, doctors, lawyers," Rachel pointed out. She didn't want me to get the impression that the Zoo Side was a hangout for some dangerous biker gang. From what I've seen there day and night, Keller's attracts a pretty docile biker crowd.

To order at Keller's, find a spot, check the menu posted on the main structure, and put on your hazard lights (or as the window says, "turn on your blinkers for service.") Soon after, a carhop will approach to take your order. Your meal will arrive on the classic drive-in tray that

hooks on your window and your beer will be wrapped with a napkin to prevent beer sweat— a nice touch.

If it were not enough that you can get an amazing burger, tots, and a beer brought to your car, you can also buy cases of beer to go. Keller's doubles as a package store, which means you can go on a beer run and reward yourself with a burger at the same time.

In a follow-up phone call, Jack told me, "Next time you are through Dallas come on by and I'll fix you an 'original.'"

"An original?"

"Yeah, that's me fixin' your burger."

So if you find yourself around Dallas in need of a beer break head over to Keller's. You'll be able to chase that beer with one of the tastiest burgers in America. And if Jack's on the griddle, you may be able to score an original.

KINCAID'S HAMBURGERS

4901 CAMP BOWIE BLVD | FORT WORTH, TX 76107

(VARIOUS OTHER LOCATIONS AROUND FORT WORTH)

817-732-2881 | MON–SAT 11 AM–8 PM

SUN 11 AM–3 PM

A visit to Kincaid's is a must on the burger trail in America. The restaurant is a revamped corner grocery that today is profoundly dedicated to the American hamburger. Most burgers found in Texas fall into the half-pound category and a hamburger at Kincaid's is no exception. The good word spread in the early 1970s that Kincaid's was serving up a stellar burger in the rear of the store. It was only a matter of time before burger sales eclipsed grocery sales and the rest is history. Today, Kincaid's grinds and patties up to 800 pounds of fresh beef daily (you read that correctly). For groceries, you'll have to go elsewhere.

Kincaid's is located on a corner on the edge of a quiet residential neighborhood in Fort Worth, and the atmosphere inside and out is laid-back and comfortable. Inside, the long, original stock shelves remain in place, their tops sawed off to act as surfaces to stand at, unwrap your burger, and dig in. It was O.R. Gentry, a meat cutter and manager at the grocery store, who bought the business from the ailing Charles Kincaid in 1967. It was O.R. who cut down those shelves and created countertops out of old doors he found for $1. And it was O.R. who created one the greatest burgers in America, a burger whose fame is so widespread that it can claim fans from every corner of the globe.

"He started with a $25 grill," Lynn Gentry said of her father-in-law. "O.R. would take the prime meats that didn't sell and grind them to make hamburgers the next day," Lynn explained. As the need for the corner grocery faded in America in the 1970s (spurred by the proliferation of the supermarket), O.R. began to focus more on burgers and less on groceries. When his

son, Ronald, took over the business in 1991, he and wife, Lynn, did away with the remaining groceries for good. "We pulled out all of the produce bins and refrigeration in the front and replaced them with picnic tables," Lynn told me. "We needed the space."

Kincaid's is a gigantic place. Today it's a clean, functional, bright restaurant where the integrity of the old grocery has been preserved. The concrete floors are polished to a high shine, and the original neon grocer's sign continues to glow red over the front door. The interior walls are still painted sea-foam green and Lynn told me, "The local hardware store calls this color Kincaid's Green." The restaurant can accommodate up to 280 burger enthusiasts, either standing or sitting, in over 3,500 square feet of space.

Every day Kincaid's grinds on premises the meat for their half-pound burgers. They use only chuck steaks from organic Texas beef that is free from hormones and steroids. The burgers are cooked on two six-foot flattop griddles. You can cook a lot of burgers with 12 linear feet of griddle space.

The burger is served on a white, seeded, toasted bun with tomato, shredded lettuce, pickles, yellow mustard, and thinly sliced onions. The elements of this burger are so well balanced that, taken as a whole, they create a nearly perfect burger experience and in turn a euphoric first bite. Curiously, the burger's condiments are placed underneath the burger instead of the standard above-the-patty placement. "We do that for speed," Lynn explained, pointing out that the buns are prepped before the burgers come off the grill. The inverted burger actually allows the juices from the meat to drip into the condiments and Lynn told me, "We think it makes the burger taste better."

Kincaid's is a family business. The Gentrys two sons work at the restaurant and Lynn's father retired from American Airlines and has been the manager of Kincaid's for over a decade. In the last few years, the Gentrys have opened a few new locations around Fort Worth including a 5,000-square-foot replica of the original complete with sawed-off grocery shelves and "Kincaid's green" painted walls.

Many refer to the burger at Kincaid's as the best in Texas. That's a mighty claim in this burger-proud state. It is a claim that the Kincaid's burger lives up to and a challenge the Gentry family takes in stride.

LANKFORD GROCERY

88 DENNIS ST I HOUSTON, TX 77006

713-522-9555 I MON–SAT 7 AM–3 PM

CLOSED SUNDAY

"There's nothing better than a good burger," was the first thing out of Edie Prior's mouth when I told her about the book I was working on. Edie is the owner of Lankford Grocery, a breakfast-and-burger destination opened by her parents, Nona and Aubrey Lankford, in 1939. From 1939 to 1977 the Lankfords operated the business as a grocery store before turning it into the café it is today. The only visible evidence of the store's past are the original Coca-Cola grocer's sign out front and the large enameled steel meat case separating the kitchen from the dining area. "I don't have the heart to pull it out," Edie said of the case. "We use it for storage now."

Lankford's is a funky place with a lot of heart and soul. There's a wall with pegs where locals hang their personal coffee mugs, the floor is impossibly slanted and creaky, the ceiling is low, and each table has a roll of paper towels in lieu of napkins. Edie heavily decorates the restaurant depending on the season. My first visit was just before Halloween so you can imagine the décor. "We just took down our summer theme," Edie's brother Jimmy told me, "We had beach balls and stuff hanging from the ceiling."

Jimmy, who has since passed away, used to work at Lankford making change and small talk

at the end of the counter. He said to me once, referring to the much-debated *GQ* magazine hamburger list, "What do these swanky men know about good hamburgers anyway?" True. A real man would do well to put one of these burgers down—a Texas-sized, fresh meat, two-fister.

Burgers at Lankford's are cooked to perfection on a flattop griddle, juicy on the inside and crisp on the outside. They start as hand-pattied fresh ground meat and are roughly eight ounces. Order a double and you are getting a pound of meat. The burger to order is the Bacon Double Cheeseburger (the bacon single works just fine, especially if you plan on eating again that day). The burgers come with shredded lettuce, red onion, pickles, tomato, cheese, mayo, mustard, and copious amounts of crisp bacon. All of this is served on a large toasted bun with a single toothpick straining to keep the contents vertical. I'm a hamburger professional and can deftly maneuver the sloppiest of burgers with ease, but this one got the better of me. "Uh, would you like a fork?" Jimmy said, sensing my struggle with the unruly pile of ingredients.

There are other burgers on the menu that sound excellent, like the "Soldier Burger," explained best by waitress Robin. "A man walked in one day and asked for a burger with an egg on it, so I did it!" Or try the "Fire House Burger" that contains a homemade habanero paste. "It is REALLY hot!" Edie warned me as she approached with a mason jar containing an orange paste. "Just try a little . . . do you have water?" The paste contained radishes, onion, mustard, and habanero peppers and was hot as hell. It was a deep-down hurt though, not a sharp pain, with lasting heat. Would I spread this on a burger? Absolutely. And recently a new burger creation has become a big seller, the "Grim Burger," which is topped with mac and cheese, bacon, an egg, and jalapeños. "One of our customers dreamed that one up," Edie told me.

Lankford's is only open for breakfast and lunch, so don't plan on having dinner there. Burgers are served all day though, starting when they open at 7 a.m. "People order burgers for breakfast, right when we open," Edie told me.

The small, sleepy café looks slightly out of place in this neighborhood very close to down-town Houston. "We used to be able to see the buildings downtown. These were all vacant lots," Edie pointed out. Those lots are being quickly transformed into condos and other large construction projects. Edie plans to be around for a while though. She wants to leave the business to family one day but told me, "I plan on being here as long as I can flip that burger."

LONGHORN CAFE

17625 BLANCO RD | SAN ANTONIO, TX 78232

210-492-0301

(5 OTHER LOCATIONS IN THE SAN ANTONIO METRO AREA)

WWW.THELONGHORNCAFE.COM

SUN–THU 11 AM–9 PM | FRI & SAT 11 AM–10 PM

CLOSED MONDAY

Don't look for this burger destination near the famous Alamo in downtown San Antonio. There are now six Longhorn Cafe locations and they all cater mostly to locals and any visitor willing to venture to the outskirts of the city. The 25-year-old burger chain is a beloved Texas roadhouse serving burgers, beer, and many other favorites and is totally worth the drive.

One of the keys to the success of the Longhorn Cafe is the amazing attention to the quality of the ingredients. Everything that goes into the burgers at the Longhorn is visible in a bank of glass-front coolers behind the counter. The

burgers are cooked on a flattop griddle in a big, open kitchen and prepped at a station adjacent to the griddle. It is all out in the open and as employee José Penado told me with a wave of his arm, "Everything we do is right here."

What they do is burgers and they do them expertly. The original griddle from opening day in 1984 is still in place and sees thousands of burgers a week. Longtime manager Uko Equere told me that the beef is always fresh, never frozen. "If someone brings in frozen I'll have to slap them!" he proclaimed. Uko is on your side.

The sign outside of the restaurant exclaims that the Longhorn Cafe is the "Home of the Big Juicy." I asked José what was on the "Big Juicy" and he explained, "All the burgers are Big Juicys," which is basically a one-third-pound, wide, flat patty on a large, toasted, white squishy bun. There are many burger options at Longhorn Cafe but the most popular, Uko explained, "is the double meat, double cheese." Ask for everything, and you'll get a burger piled high with shredded lettuce, raw onion, mayo, mustard, and pickles—a true Texas classic.

The kitchen area is an incredible study in efficiency. Everyone has a task to complete and during peak times the kitchen works like a well-oiled assembly line. A griddleperson slaps patties on the flattop and toasts buns alongside the burgers while another employee preps buns with condiments. Completed burgers are delivered to the counter in plastic baskets lined with waxed paper.

One employee spends his time only at the deep fryer. Get the "Half & Half" with your order and choose 2 of the 3 deep-fried sides: onion rings, fries, or tater tots. The onion rings are not to be missed (they are cut and battered in-house) but it's also hard to pass up on tater tots.

At Longhorn Cafe, you place an order at the counter, then find a seat and wait for your name to be called. Grab a pickled jalapeño at the counter to munch on while you are waiting. At the Blanco Road location you can sit in either the large dining room filled with booths and picnic tables, or check out the equally large outdoor patio with its big homemade slide for kids to play on. When things get crazy Uko opens up the private party room to handle overflow.

It's a big, clean, easygoing place that caters to all types. The first time I was there it was lunchtime and the place was mostly filled with dudes in auto mechanic uniforms and families, a mixed clientele that changes as the day progresses. Nighttime brings local high school and college students (and sometimes players from the San Antonio Spurs). "There is usually a line out the door," Uko explained. The place is packed on game day weekends.

The restaurant apparently opened in the '50s as a taco stand at what is now the Blanco Road location. In 1984 a Sooner (a graduate of the University of Oklahoma) and an Aggie (a graduate of Texas A&M) bought the stand, started selling hamburgers, and changed the name to the Longhorn Cafe. Two high school buddies, David Wynn and Paul Weir, came along and purchased the business in 1995. The duo is responsible for the Longhorn's expansion into a six-store chain.

What I also love about the Longhorn Cafe is that my favorite Texas beer, Shiner Bock, is available by the pitcher. I couldn't think of anything better to do in Texas than eat a roadhouse burger while drinking one of the best beers in Texas at a picnic table. What more do you need?

Directly across the street from the Blanco Road location (the original) is a Sonic Drive-In that is obviously not affecting business in the slightest. "We've been here so long that our customers are pretty loyal," Director of Operations Karen Turner told me. Be smart and go where the locals go.

37

UTAH

CROWN BURGER

118 NORTH 300 WEST | SALT LAKE CITY, UT 84103

801-532-5300 | WWW.CROWN-BURGERS.COM

(MULTIPLE LOCATIONS)

MON–SAT 10 AM–10:30 PM | CLOSED SUNDAY

Behold the "Crown Burger." At first you see what appears to be a pastrami sandwich, then, upon closer inspection, realize that your wildest fantasies have just come true—you are gazing at a cheeseburger stuffed to bursting with warm, thinly sliced pastrami.

Unique to Salt Lake City and its neighbors, the pastrami cheeseburger is a beloved Utah burger that, according to some locals, is best represented at the Greek-owned Crown Burger chain.

The Crown I visited was the second built (in 1979) in Salt Lake City. I was assured that the other six Crowns were similar, which is hard to believe given the almost indescribable décor of the interior of this restaurant. "Back in the '70s my family was in the Greek nightclub business," Mike, son of owner Manuel Katsanevas, tried to explain. Gargoyles, stuffed quail in flight, large chandeliers, Greek statuary, lush wallpaper, and a huge working fireplace round out the phantasmagorical setting. "We know we are fast food but we wanted to create an upscale dining experience," Mike told me.

It's true—don't be put off by the large staff in uniform behind the counter working at warp speed, multiple registers, numbers being called over a loudspeaker, and a general feeling of ordering food at one of the superchains. As you wait for your number to be called you stand between an ancient nine-foot-tall ornately carved wooden hutch and a grandfather clock, both salvaged from a hotel in France. "People ask all the time if this stuff is for sale," Mike said, pointing to the clock. "No, it is not."

The genius behind Crown is their business plan, which could only be pulled off by an intensely proud Greek family (they are actually from Crete). Each restaurant in the chain is independently owned by a family member. They share recipes and suppliers to maintain sameness and quality.

The burgers come in fresh as quarter-pound patties "every morning," Manuel explained. The menu is large and eclectic and includes hot dogs, tuna sandwiches, a fish burger, and, you guessed it, some of the best souvlaki and gyros in town.

The Crown Burger, char-broiled over an open flame, comes wrapped tightly in waxed paper and includes lettuce, tomato, chopped onion, American cheese, and of course, gobs of pastrami. My warning to you—do not remove the waxed paper prior to hoisting this beast to your lips. It will explode and the pastrami will end up in your lap.

The idea for pastrami on a cheeseburger was imported from Anaheim, California, by a relative of the Katsanevas family. "Uncle James had a restaurant called Minos Burgers and served a pastrami burger," Mike explained. When he moved to Salt Lake, he brought the idea to his family.

The burger also includes a Utah curiosity called fry sauce. For those unfamiliar with the fast-food habits of Utahans, fry sauce is basically ketchup and mayo mixed together. Mike told me, "We make our own fry sauce in house, made of seven ingredients, most of them secret." The sauce is mainly used as a dip for fries.

The Katsanevases have been approached more than once with offers to franchise but have resisted. Fear that the quality of their product would decline was not their only reason. "We make a comfortable living and we're happy with the way things are," Mike told me. "We have worked very hard for everything we have. Besides, this couldn't be a franchise; everything is made to order!"

38

VERMONT

DOT'S RESTAURANT

3 EAST MAIN ST | WILMINGTON, VT 05363

802-464-7284 | WWW.DOTSOFVERMONT.COM

SUN–THU 5:30 AM–8 PM | FRI–SAT 5:30 AM–9 PM

CLOSED MONDAY

Dot's is hard to miss as you roll into the picturesque downstate Vermont town of Wilmington. Just look for the only neon sign in town, thanks to a local ordinance that has banned neon signage on businesses. Fortunately, the neon sign over the door at Dot's has been grandfathered in.

Dot's is not a burger joint. It's a classic New England diner that serves comfort food favorites like pancakes, chili, and sandwiches but also happens to serve one of the best burgers in Vermont. Locals and tourists alike frequent Dot's, which sees healthy crowds year round. Nearby Mt. Snow attracts thousands of skiers and snowboarders on winter weekends, many of them looking for burgers.

The name of the restaurant goes back half a century but the actual building dates to 1832, making it the oldest structure in town. For its first 70 years, the building was a post office and in 1900, became a general store. In 1930, the store became a restaurant and had many names over the next few decades. In 1952, a man named Dude Sparrow bought the restaurant for his wife, Dot. When the Sparrows sold the diner to John Reagan in 1980 the name stayed.

The burger at Dot's starts as a hand-formed patty of fresh ground 80/20 Angus chuck. A mayo lid is used for portioning and the 5-ounce patty is cooked to temperature over a flame grill with lava rocks. It's served on a toasted, seeded white bun and nothing else but potato chips and a dill pickle spear. "They come plain," Mitch explained, "but we do not shy away from special requests." Cheese selection is American, Swiss, pepper jack, and Vermont cheddar and the usual condiments are available, including lettuce, tomato, and sliced red onion.

The burger at Dot's is best chased by a chocolate malt. Make sure to try the tasty fries, hand-cut daily. I asked waitress of 30 years Shirlee what drink would go best with this juicy

burger. She responded with a straight face, "A beer." She's right, and Dot's does have a selection of beer and wine, but I was there at 10:30am and had just finished my coffee.

The restaurant has been updated recently and the clean décor has a sort of cozy country feel with wood tables and chairs, pale blue floor tiles, and fireplace that no longer functions. Dot's is not large and the counter can only seat nine at swivel stools. There are tables with room for about forty people but try to snag the single booth at the front, in a nook out of the way.

Even though John and Patty Reagan have owned and run Dot's for over 30 years people still walk in and ask, "Where is Dot?" The friendly staff gets a kick out of the question and reply by jokingly pointing to longtime manager Mitch Soskin saying, "There's Dot!" "We get asked that at least three times a day," counterperson Cindy told me. Cindy is one of the most upbeat waitresses I've ever met and for good reason. Years ago she escaped corporate America and an executive job in Hartford, Connecticut to serve coffee to regulars at Dot's. "And I'm happier than ever! This is it!" she shouted down the counter.

WHITE COTTAGE

462 WOODSTOCK RD I WOODSTOCK, VT 05091

802-457-3455 I SEASONAL (MAY TO OCTOBER)

SUN–THU 11 AM–9 PM I FRI & SAT 11 AM–10 PM

CLOSED MONDAYS

"A lot of people come here thinking it's that great rock-and-roll town in New York," manager Norm Corbin told me, and added with his New England accent and a smile, "Well, it's nawt." This Woodstock is deep in the mountains of Vermont complete with covered bridges and gentle streams. Downtown is a destination with tour buses dumping happy shoppers onto the quaint main drag all summer long and well into foliage season. White Cottage is not here, though. Head a mile west out of town and you'll find a 54-year-old snack bar that has not changed much since its opening day in 1957. "Look at this picture, that says it all," Norm pointed out. Sure enough, a large, faded black-and-white photo taken in the early 1960s hangs in the counter window. With the exception of the period cars in the photo the White Cottage looks virtually unchanged a half century later. "We've put up a few layers of paint, that's it," Norm says.

"Everything is made in house, the sauces, the coleslaw, everything," the second half of the managerial team, Scott Noble, told me. All of the dairy used at White Cottage is from local farms and the beef for the burgers comes from Vermont cows. A local meatpacker in Burlington supplies the snack bar with fresh 6-ounce Angus chuck patties. The burgers are cooked on a flame grill and served on toasted, classic, white squishy buns. The bacon cheeseburger is the favorite at White Cottage and the standard call is to order one with "the works": lettuce, tomato, diced onion, pickle, mayo, mustard, and ketchup. This

is an amazingly juicy burger so don't let it sit around. Within minutes the juices will disintegrate the bun. I asked for one medium and it was cooked to temperature perfectly.

To order at White Cottage, step up to one of the windows. Pick up your burgers when your name is called over the loudspeaker. There's a tendency to go back to the window where you paid, but the pickup window is actually around the corner to the right. There's plenty of seating on the porch and out by the river that runs behind White Cottage.

Burgers aren't the only thing on the menu and you'd be a fool to walk away from White Cottage without a side of deep-fried clam bellies. In fact, even though the onion rings are amazing, order a side of these clams with your burger. Norm and Scott get the clams from Ipswich, Massachusetts and have a legion of fans. "Some people come from Ipswich to have the Ipswich clams here," Norm told me. Ipswich is two-and-a-half hours away. They're that good.

White Cottage is a seasonal snack bar and locals look forward to the opening every year. "Come spring, they are so excited to see us open," Norm told me and says that he's constantly harangued about opening day, which is usually the Friday before Memorial Day. "People are jonesing for clams and burgers." The busiest time of the year, though, is around Fourth of July when the tourists show up in force. The locals know better and avoid the snack bar when it gets crazy. "They stay away on weekends. They're smart," Norm explained.

Ice cream is king at White Cottage and in the peak of the summer the place is overrun by families looking for one of the snack bar's thirty-three flavors and soft serve. Ice cream is scooped behind a large picture window and kids can watch the action by climbing a two-step platform. Scott explained, "Parents were always lifting the kids up to watch us scoop so I made the steps from some scrap wood." How thoughtful is that?

White Cottage closes for the season the Monday of Columbus Day during the first week of October. Peak foliage has happened at that point and I imagine it starts to get pretty quiet in that part of Vermont. "It's also not winterized—there's no heat here," Scott explained. But the nice thing about a seasonal place like White Cottage is that you can't always have it. You'll have to wait, and what could be better than the expectation of good things to come?

39

VIRGINIA

TEXAS TAVERN

114 W. CHURCH AVE | ROANOKE, VA 24011

540-342-4825 | WWW.TEXASTAVERN-INC.COM

OPEN 24 HOURS A DAY,

7 DAYS A WEEK (EXCEPT CHRISTMAS)

"I hope you plan on having a Cheesy Western" were the first words out of Matt Bullington's mouth after I had introduced myself. I was thrown, because I thought I had come to the Texas Tavern for a straightforward hamburger, possibly a thin patty on a white bun. What Matt was selling me was actually the most popular burger at his over-75-year-old hamburger stand.

The "Cheesy Western" is a glorious combination of fried egg, thin hamburger patty, cheese, pickle, onion, and relish on a soft white bun. "We sell hundreds of Cheesys a day, especially to the late-night crowd," Matt told me. How late? "We're open all night." In fact, the only time the Texas Tavern closes is for part of Christmas Eve and day.

Matt is the great-grandson of Nick Bullington, the man who opened the tiny hamburger stand in 1930. "My great-grandfather saw Roanoke as a boomtown and decided to build his restaurant here." In the 1920s Roanoke had a vibrant locomotive construction industry. Nick, an advance man for the Ringling Brothers Circus, had collected recipes from his extensive travels around the United States. He had observed the best ways to make hamburgers (no doubt gleaning what he could from the success of White Castle at the time), had adopted a mustard-based relish from a circus recipe, and most importantly had borrowed a chili recipe from a hotel in Texas.

Curiously, the chili and burgers are sold separately as they have been for over seven decades. A chili burger is absent from the menu, though Matt said "A few people order them, but not many." The chili is so popular at the restaurant that it can be taken away by the gallon if necessary. That may be because the chili is more soup than condiment.

The grill area is just inside the front window, which was typical of burger joints of the era. The cook's station is a testament to efficient food prep. A hot dog steam box sits in front of a deep canister of chili. Next to that is the impossibly small 12-by-18-inch griddle. To the right of the griddle are two small burners for frying eggs and a box containing burger buns, relish, pickles, and

onions. The entire complement of ingredients and cooking apparatus to prepare everything on the menu occupies a mere six square feet—absolutely amazing.

The Texas Tavern is a rare specimen of a bygone era because nothing has changed since it opened. "Everything is original," Matt told me. The dented countertop, worn footrest, and ten lumpy red leather stools all feel so real. Some repairs to the griddle in 1975 are the extent of any "renovations," outside of the frequent paint jobs that keep the place looking as fresh and inviting as it may have in 1930.

A quote posted in the restaurant calls the tiny burger counter "Roanoke's Millionaire's Club." Matt explained, "We get all types in here. Whether you are the governor or a hobo, you'll be treated like a millionaire at the Texas Tavern."

40

WASHINGTON

DICK'S DRIVE-IN

111 N.E. 45TH ST | SEATTLE, WA 98105

206-632-5125 | (MULTIPLE LOCATIONS AROUND SEATTLE)

WWW.DDIR.COM | OPEN DAILY 10:30 AM–2 AM

At first glance Dick's looks like it might be a tired old drive-in serving frozen hockey pucks for burgers. But Dick's is anything but tired, and as the locals know, it's as vibrant as ever, serving excellent fresh-beef burgers, addictive fries, and hand-dipped milkshakes. The '50s have come and gone, but Dick's remains over five decades later, proving that simplicity and good food are the keys to longevity.

Dick's is a drive-in. There are five locations around town and only one has indoor seating. It's the sort of drive-in where you park your car and walk up to the window to order and pay. General manager Ken Frazier told me, "Dick's has always been a walk-up. Originally there were three separate lines, one for shakes and ice cream, one for burgers and soft drinks, and one for fries." In the '60s Dick's streamlined the system selling, all products at all windows. At the 45th Street location there's no seating anywhere and Maria, the longtime manager, told me, "In the summertime people bring picnic tables and chairs and set up in the parking lot. It's really cute."

The first Dick's was built in 1954 in the Wallingford neighborhood of Seattle just west of the University of Washington. On my first visit to the popular burger stand I arrived 15 minutes before opening to find workers inside scurrying to ready the griddle and cook the fries. There was no one in the parking lot. But within five minutes a hungry mob had gathered. When the first window called, "May I take your order?" I counted 45 people waiting to get their "Dick's Fix," a phrase a regular left me with.

The efficiency of Dick's is mind-boggling. Twenty-four employees, all wearing crisp paper caps and clean aprons, are set to repetitive tasks, such as weighing the fresh ice cream that goes into the shakes or prepping the buns with their secret sauce.

The menu is simple—hamburgers, cheeseburgers, fries, shakes, and soda. The thin patties of fresh beef are delivered to all locations in the chain every morning. The burgers, cooked on a flattop griddle, can be ordered plain or as the preferred Dick's Deluxe. The Deluxe comes with two quarter-pound patties, cheese, lettuce, mayo, and their special chopped pickle and mustard sauce. The sauce, a tangy, sweet, and creamy proprietary blend, should not be missed. All burgers are served on the perfect, white squishy bun wrapped in waxed paper.

If you love fries, you'll be in French fry heaven at Dick's. The fries are lightly greasy, thin, and fresh, not frozen. The shakes, also incredible, only come in the three classic flavors of chocolate, vanilla, and strawberry.

If you ask for extra sauce for your burger or ketchup for the fries you'll get a little serving in a small condiment cup, but expect to pay. Ketchup and other condiments are five cents

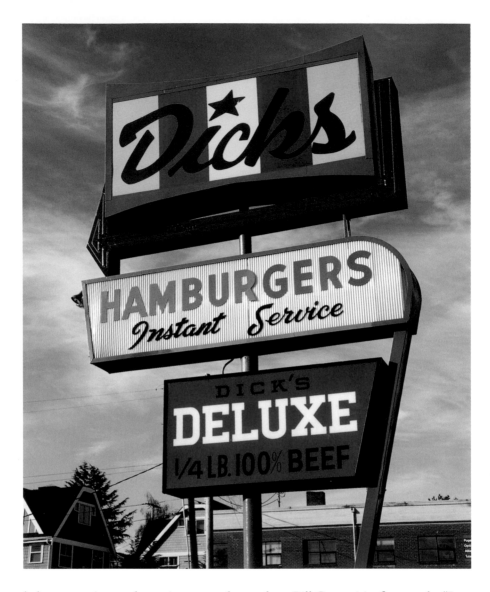

extra and the reason is mostly environmental, not financial. "We feel that the cup is much nicer to use for dipping than some foil pouch," Ken explained, "and by charging a nominal amount we feel we are minimizing waste." Gotta love a burger joint with a conscience.

The people of Seattle love Dick's. I was hard-pressed to find a carnivore that didn't frequent the place. Bill Gates visits frequently. "Last week he had a Deluxe, fries, and a shake," Maria told me. Even Sir Mix-A-Lot, Grammy Award winner and Seattle native, immortalized the Broadway location in his first hit song. In the lyrics, his posse skips Taco Bell for Dick's. The truth is, if there were more places like Dick's, serving wholesome, fast food, we'd all be skipping Taco Bell.

EASTSIDE BIG TOM

2023 EAST 4TH AVE I OLYMPIA, WA 98506

360-357-4852 I WWW.EASTSIDEBIGTOM.COM

MON–SAT 10:30 AM–8 PM I SUN 11 AM–6:30 PM

Big Tom could easily be the most nonde-script burger stand in America. If it were not for the large menu on the street side of the building, you'd think you had arrived at a construction trailer that had been haphazardly dumped in a parking lot. But the long lines of cars on each side of the structure are a hint that something good is happening inside. Indeed there is. Big Tom daily sells over 500 fresh thin-patty won-ders to loyal drive-up customers. But that's not all. Big Tom's trademarked "Goop" is dispensed here, a salad-type dressing that, in varying forms, is a Pacific Northwest mainstay for burgers.

"Goop is essentially mayo, mustard, and pickle relish with a secret salad dressing mixed in," longtime owner Chuck Fritsch told me. "What's the saying? 'If I told you I'd have to kill you'?" he said with a laugh. "It's really not a big secret," he admitted, "But if you are not making it in huge batches it doesn't taste the same." I can see why someone might want to copy the recipe—the taste is addictive. Besides adorning the Big Tom special double-double, Goop is also offered as a dip for the tater tots and fries. What could be more appealing or more American than "Tots 'n Goop"?

In 1948 Millie and Russ Eagan opened a burger stand east of downtown Olympia and called it (coincidentally) In and Out. Millie took her inspiration for a drive-thru from a popular motor court across the street. For the original stand the Egans relocated a minuscule barber-shop from another part of town. Since then, the stand has been rebuilt and changed names more than once, but has always been on the same spot. Through the decades the Egans expanded to nine stands in and around Olympia, but today only one remains.

Big Tom was the son of Millie and Russ Eagan. Overweight and inventive, he was known to help himself at the griddle and created a large burger that was not on the menu. Today it's a best seller at the burger stand that bears his name, a double meat, double cheese-burger with lettuce, tomato, chopped onion, and the famous Goop. Be prepared for the inevitable dripping Goop as you take your first bite. Chuck told me,

"We are known for making a sloppy burger." Chuck buys fresh ground 18 percent fat thin patties for the burgers at Big Tom. They are cooked on a flattop griddle that is usually filled to capacity with the sputtering patties.

The interior of Big Tom, which is all kitchen, is a lesson in functionality. An astounding amount of prep and cooking is done in the 288 square feet that is populated by up to seven employees at peak times. Every square inch is utilized—think submarine galley.

Chuck started working at the tiny burger stand in the '50s when he was 15 years old peeling potatoes. "It was warm and dry and sitting in a cubicle did not appeal to me," Chuck said about his longevity in the business. He is a true entrepreneur. The diesel pickup truck that makes the 90-mile round-trip to and from work each day is fueled by fry oil from Big Tom. "I used to have to pay to dispose of it." Now he drives down the road smelling like burning French fries.

Chuck, closing in on 53 years at Big Tom, is slowly turning the business over to his son, Michael, who literally grew up in the stand. Chuck pointed to a small space between the employee bathroom and slop sink. "We had the crib right there." Michael jokingly describes the transition as "indentured servitude." He told me, "I never thought I'd wrap myself around a hamburger joint," but he seems to enjoy the life. Michael plans to run the burger stand for a long time, or as he put it, "At least until I reach dad's age."

RECICE FROM
THE HAMBURGER AMERICA TEST KITCHEN

GOOP SAUCE, MY WAY

Goop is the sauce that adorns just about every burger in the Pacific Northwest. All of the goop sauces I've had taste pretty much the same, yet all contain highly secret ingredients. I've attempted to re-create goop sauce here, but remain fully aware that the best place to try this heavenly condiment is at places like the Eastside Big Tom in Olympia, Washington, and Dick's Drive-In in Seattle.

MAKES ENOUGH FOR 12 BURGERS

½ cup mayonnaise

¼ cup sour cream

4 teaspoons sweet relish

4 teaspoons yellow mustard

Mix contents. Spread on your favorite burger. The color should resemble a stock canary yellow Plymouth Barracuda. Tell your friends it's not the real thing, but pretty damn close. I can hear Chuck from Big Tom laughing as he reads this recipe.

41

WISCONSIN

AMERICAN LEGION POST #67

133 NORTH MAIN ST | LAKE MILLS, WI 53551

920-731-1265

OPEN FRIDAYS ONLY, MAY–OCT, 10 AM–8 PM

I had to make a special trip to Lake Mills, Wisconsin for a hamburger and timing was everything. When I discovered that this 85-year-old burger stand is only open on Fridays in the summer the planning began. I had only 23 Fridays to choose from.

The American Legion Post #67 Hamburger Stand is a gem. It's wedged between two larger buildings in the heart of downtown Lake Mills and has been there since 1950. For 24 years before that, the American Legion had a portable stand set up across the street. The stand today is walk-up service only with a severely limited menu, my kinda place. Hamburgers, cheese-burgers, and sodas are all you can spend your money on (with the exception of a must-have t-shirt that depicts a burger, or "slider," midway down a playground slide). Your only option for condiments is with or without onions. Ketchup and mustard are available on an old typewriter table on the sidewalk. "The most popular burger is one 'with,'" stand operator Randy told me, which is a burger with stewed onions. Typical for an old-time stand, cheese takes a backseat and makes up only a third of all burgers ordered.

I squeezed into the tiny stand while my burger was being made and immediately recognized a cooking method that is rapidly disappearing throughout the Midwest—the deep-fried burger. That's right, the one-fifth-pound burgers at Post #67 are deep fried in a huge, shallow tank filled with canola oil. The fresh pattied meat comes in every Friday from Glenn's Market in nearby Watertown and over 2,500 burgers are plopped in the hot oil on a busy day. Not too long ago the tank was filled with rendered lard and for health reasons they have switched to canola. These burgers are great but I can only imagine how sublime a lardburger must have been.

The first went down fast so I ordered another. The hot oil soaks the soft, white-squishy bun and becomes a condiment to the peppery burger. If you ask for cheese, a slice is placed on the bottom half of the bun so the hot oil from the burger melts it on contact.

The stand is run by a rotating crew of five, members of the American Legion Post #67 just down the street. Most of the crew members are in their seventies and eighties; each is a veteran who served in Korea or Vietnam. They have a great system worked out for delivering hot and tasty burgers to waiting customers. Someone takes your order at the tiny window and writes a code on a paper bag. The bag is passed back to another who shouts out the order. The cook pulls a burger out of the oil and hands it to another vet, who puts it onto a bun and wraps it up. The wrapped burger is then slid to the bag man who matches the wrapped burger to the code on the bag. When things heat up and the orders start pouring in, this system hums like a well-oiled machine.

There was an awesome note near the tank of oil and onions that read, "On the first, third, and fifth Fridays take a minimum of 50 burgers to Post 67 for bingo at 7:30 p.m." What a perk for those bingo players!

Everyone seems to have a great time on their shift and no one minds that they are not getting paid. Most of the volunteers are retired military and are compensated in burgers and beer. Not the kind of beer you take home, the kind you enjoy on the job. Intrigued, I asked past Commander Don Hein, "When does the drinking start?" He told me bluntly, "Whenever we start working." I gathered from the other vets hard at work that in most cases they are way too busy bagging burgers to drink themselves into oblivion. And as Don pointed out, "You really can't come down here and get hammered."

ANCHOR BAR

413 TOWER AVE | SUPERIOR, WI 54880

715-394-9747

WWW.ANCHORBAR/FREESERVERS.COM

MON–THU 10 AM–2 AM

FRI & SAT 10 AM–2:30 AM | SUN 10 AM–2 AM

Turn off your cell phone, grab a pitcher of beer, and disappear into the Anchor Bar for a few hours. You'll thank me later.

That's the type of place the Anchor is—a very comfortable, dark bar that is blanketed in the most amazing collection of nautical ephemera that you will find anywhere. The stuff is everywhere. Floor, walls, ceiling. "We have more stuff in the basement but there's no room to put it up," Adam Anderson, part owner and the son of the man that opened the place, told

me. "It's like a museum in here." Superior, Wisconsin is a shipping town and a bar like the Anchor fits right in.

Grab the table just inside the door on the right if you can. "We call that the library," Adam said of the table, which is actually a tiny, semi-private nook lined with books, board games, and more than one globe. Sitting here, separate from the rest of the bar, you actually feel as though you are enjoying the captain's quarters on a tall ship.

The centerpiece of the bar is a lifebuoy from the famous SS *Edmund Fitzgerald*, a Great Lakes freighter that met its demise one cold winter night in 1975. The tragic event was popularized in a song by Gordon Lightfoot, "The Wreck of the *Edmund Fitzgerald*." A violent storm and a failed radar caused the ship to sink taking with it twenty-nine crewmembers who were never found. "There's a group that comes in every year on the anniversary to toast the dead," Adam told me.

Adam's dad, Tom, worked at the Elk's Club in town and bought the bar when he heard it was for sale. His first move was to add food to the menu and started serving burgers. He and his manager of over 30 years collected from garage sales over the years the many rope nets, ships gauges, running lights, portholes, and shipping photos that make up the décor. That manager, Bean Pritty, continues to run the Anchor with Tom's sons, Adam and Aaron. Tom passed away in 2008 and Adam decided to move back home and leave his job as a successful sous-chef near Minneapolis to run the Anchor. Thanks to the dedication of Bean Pritty, in Adam's words, "The place kinda runs itself. If I'm here I'm just in the way."

There are more than a few burger options at the Anchor, seventeen to be exact. All start with a griddled, hand-formed, one-third-pound patty made from fresh ground 83/17 chuck. The beef comes to the bar from a local butcher and Adam told me, "If I run low during the day, they'll bring us more." Most of the burgers sound pretty wacky but good (like the "Sour Cream and Mushroom" or the "Oliveburger," the most popular). I opted for another favorite, the "Cashewburger," topped with Swiss cheese and a copious amount of whole, roasted, salted cashews that have been warmed on the griddle. A young grill person named Tom (who incidentally is named after the former owner and is the son of Tom's best friend) explained, "They get a

little softer when you put them on the grill." Naturally, the idea for the Cashewburger was born over beers. According to Adam, "My dad liked cashews so he put them on a burger one day." When a friend asked why, Tom responded, "Don't you like cashews?" The texture of the Cashewburger is unusual but amazing. No other condiments are necessary. The grease from the burger mixes with the chunky nuts and the Swiss cheese creating a salty, cheesy, beefy flavor profile. And hey, cashews are good for you! The fries are also really good. There's a French fry press next to the deep fryer and when an order comes in the grillperson grabs a potato, slams it through the press and tosses the fries in the hot oil. The fries are that fresh.

The Library

There are a few easy-drinking beers on tap (like Keystone Light and the local beer, Grain Belt) that can be purchased by the pitcher ($2.50 pitchers all day Monday) but don't miss the Anchor Bar's amazing selection of micro-brews. There are over 90 flavors to choose from. "That's our dessert menu," Adam joked, pointing to a box of candy bars behind the bar.

"It's a likable dive," a longtime regular named John told me sitting at the bar. "It doesn't pretend to be anything that it isn't."

DOTTY DUMPLING'S DOWRY

317 NORTH FRANCES ST | MADISON, WI 53703

608-259-0000

WWW.DOTTYDUMPLINGSDOWRY.COM

MON–WED 11 AM–11 PM

THU–SAT 11 AM–MIDNIGHT | SUN NOON–10 PM

Dotty's is in its fifth location in over 35 years. "Goddamn eminent domain was the reason for the last move," Jeff Stanley mumbled when I asked him about the moves. It seems the latest incarnation of Dotty's is working for him though. The exterior resembles a working-class Irish pub complete with black paint, small-paned windows, and the bar's name in gold. The interior is impressive—quality-crafted dark wood, large inviting bar, and an astounding collection of model aircraft dangling from the ceiling.

There is even an eight-foot scale model of the Hindenburg positioned over the grill area.

Friend and columnist Doug Moe, who referred to Jeff as "The Hamburger King of Madison" directed me to Dotty's. Jeff's bigger-than-life persona is infectious, and he is a well-liked underdog around town. He is damn proud to hold the title of king and knows his burgers. The first time I walked into Dotty's, Jeff announced without warning, "Hey everybody! This is the guy who made that hamburger film!"

"We only use the highest-quality ingredients," Jeff said as I took a big swig from my beer. His burgers are made from six ounces of fresh-ground chuck, pattied in-house. They are grilled on an open flame in plain sight of all customers and placed on specially made local buns that

have been warmed and buttered. Grill master David explained, "Jeff requests that the buns are not cooked fully so they remain soft." David is a bit of an anomaly in the burger world. Not that other burger chefs don't have his love of the craft, but none to date have been comfortable quoting celebrity chef Anthony Bourdain. "Have you read his stuff on kitchen cleanliness?"

This attention to detail and Jeff's public persona have put Dotty's on the top of local hamburger polls for decades. Being a stone's throw from the University of Wisconsin's Kohl Center and Camp Randall Stadium doesn't hurt either.

The name Dotty Dumpling's Dowry comes from an Arthur Conan Doyle short story, the same writer who brought us Sherlock Holmes. Dotty's menu is extensive, including an ostrich dish and the bar has an impressive twenty-four beers on tap. But please don't leave Dotty's without trying their excellent deep-fried cheese curds—they are indeed a necessary evil.

★ ★ ★ ★ ★

KEWPEE HAMBURGERS

520 WISCONSIN AVE | RACINE, WI 53403

262-634-9601 | WWW.KEWPEE.COM

MON–FRI 7 AM–6 PM | SAT 7 AM–5 PM

CLOSED SUNDAY

When the first version of this book came out, I went on a book tour and did lots of promotion. On a talk show in Wisconsin, a deejay surprised me and announced live on the air, "Go ahead, give us a call and tell George what he left out of the book!" One of the overwhelming responses was that I had omitted a Racine, Wisconsin favorite, Kewpee Hamburgers. Needless to say, I was on my way to Racine almost immediately.

At one time Kewpee Hotel Hamburgs were all over the Upper Midwest. The first Kewpee opened in Flint, Michigan and was one of the first hamburger chains in America. Like many of the great burger chains of the '30s and '40s, Kewpee downsized during the Great Depression and saw further decline as the owners experimented with franchising. Today, only five Kewpees in three states remain and are all privately owned. The Racine location is the sole surviving Kewpee in the Dairy State.

On my first visit to Kewpee I sat at one of the low horseshoe counters and was happy to see that at 10 a.m. the griddle was already filled with burgers. The place is huge and could easily seat fifty people. This version of the restaurant is relatively new, but over the last nine decades the building has been replaced three times.

Kewpee does not use a patty machine like its sister restaurant in Lima, Ohio. In fact, there are very few similarities between the two Kewpees. Owner and lead grillperson Rick Buehrens told me, "Here, you'll get a totally different burger than at the Ohio Kewpees." For starters, Rick has eschewed the original Kewpee method of forming square patties in favor of the even more traditional method of smashing balls of beef. He uses an ice cream scoop to form loose balls of fresh-ground beef and can produce six balls to the pound. In the morning, trays are filled with the balls and kept cold in the back. During a busy rush, Rick will take an entire tray, dump it onto the large flattop griddle, then sort and smash the mess into perfect patties.

An entirely separate flattop nearby is used to toast the buns. Ask for a cheeseburger and watch what happens. Rick does not sully the burger side of the griddle with cheese. Instead he'll toss a cold slice on the left side of the flattop for a few seconds to melt. Like magic, the cheese doesn't stick to the surface (or the spatula) and is transferred smoothly to your cheeseburger.

The burger options at Kewpee are basic—a single or double, with or without cheese, served on locally made, soft white buns. A burger with everything has pickle, chopped onion, mustard, and ketchup. I couldn't help but notice that the ketchup was clearly more prominent than the mustard. "That's based on what customers were telling me," Rick explained. "It seems like I put less mustard on these days."

Rick should know about changing tastes over time. He started working at Kewpee in 1976 as a dishwasher and became the owner after 27 years of sweat equity.

While waiting for your burgers, make sure to check out the enormous display case that contains hundreds of vintage Kewpie dolls of all shapes, sizes, and colors. The inspiration for the restaurant's name came from the popular turn-of-the-century doll. The display lends a touch of history to an otherwise modern diner. Though the space has been updated, the burger has remained faithful to its roots and is made with the freshest ingredients. Sink your teeth into a classic and slip back in time with a Kewpee burger.

PETE'S HAMBURGERS

118 BLACKHAWK AVE | PRAIRIE DU CHIEN, WI 53821
NO PHONE | WWW.PETESHAMBURGERS.COM
OPEN MID-APRIL THROUGH MID-OCTOBER
FRI–SUN 11 AM–8 PM
CLOSED MONDAY THROUGH THURSDAY

"Don't tell mom we stopped here," I overheard a woman say to her brother. When I asked why, she told me, "We are heading to our family reunion." That's the kind of place Pete's is—a 101-year-old institution that makes you want to stop even though you shouldn't. The draw is too great, the burgers amazing.

Pete's is a tiny, neat burger stand right in the center of the quaint southwestern Wisconsin town of Prairie du Chien. Little has changed at Pete's in the last century, except for the size of the place, which has gone from very small to small. "In 1909, Pete Gokey started selling burgers from a cart at fairs and circuses," his granddaughter Colleen explained. He then set up a table to sell

burgers on a corner only a few feet from where the stand now sits. Colleen is one of many Gokeys that work at Pete's, which is still owned and operated by the Gokey family. The tiny stand is filled with Gokeys. When I was there great-grandson Patrick Gokey was working the griddle.

The burgers at Pete's are not your standard American hamburger. A visit to Pete's is a must because the burgers at Pete's are cooked in a way that I've never seen anywhere else. They are boiled. I know that sounds strange, but local hamburger expert and friend Todd McElwee told me once, "I like to think of them as 'poached.'" And poached they are. Most have never had a burger quite like this.

A large, flat, high-lipped griddle or "tank" is filled with about an inch of water and a pile of quarter-pound balls of beef are dumped into the tank. In the center sits a mountain of thinly sliced onion, stewing in the hot water. The beef balls are pressed into patties that bob in the water like little boats and are flipped and ready in 15 minutes. The griddle can hold up to 70 patties and remains completely silent as the patties boil, bubble, and bob. I can only imagine that if this had been a standard griddle with that many burgers on it and no water, it would be a loud, sizzling mess.

The buns, soft white squishies from a local bakery, are not toasted. If you want onions, the grillperson scoops a bunch from the pile and transfers to a bun taking a moment to drain any remaining water. Cheese? Not at Pete's. In 101 years a burger has never seen a slice of cheese at Pete's. In fact, a burger with or without onions is your only option.

As you've probably surmised, this burger is not a big, charred, grease bomb. Quite the opposite, the burger at Pete's is moist, ridiculously hot, and not greasy. The limp onion, soft bun, and steamy hot beef package is surprisingly tasty.

Your options for toppings are ketchup, mustard, and horseradish mustard.

Although Pete's is small, the stand employs a dual window system to service customers. One Gokey makes burger magic at the griddle while two others work the windows, wrap burgers, and make change. The dual window setup makes for an excellent study in line dynamics. Most of the time both lines have an equal number of patient customers. But every once in a while a line grows with over 25 tourists and newbies that don't realize there's a second window. Without fail, a regular spots the imbalance and goes for the empty window. When I saw a regular named Ernie Moon briskly approach the empty window I asked why. "If they want to stand in line," gesturing to the opposite window, "that's fine with me!" He then explained, "I guess that's what you'd call having 'experience.' I've been coming here for 60 years." The reality is that the lines move very quickly. Assuming the griddle is full of burgers ready to go, you can step up to place your order and be walking away in 30 seconds with a steaming bag full of hamburger history.

One curious item I spotted for sale at the stand was "Pete's Secret Ingredient," a clear liquid in a bottle bearing the image of Pete himself. Rumor has it that years ago a Chicagoan passing through town asked Pete what he was cooking his amazing tasting burgers in and Pete told him, "Hamburger oil." He then proceeded to sell him a gallon of water. The bottled water for sale at the stand today is a prank that still gets chuckles

today but the tiny bottles of water sell for $2 with all proceeds going to a Gokey family charity that supports cancer and mental health research.

Don't make the mistake of showing up in Prairie du Chien in the cold months looking for a burger at Pete's. The tiny stand is seasonal and only open for six months of the year. And even during that time they are only open three days a week, Friday, Saturday, and Sunday.

"This stand put all the grandkids through college," Mary told me, which numbered fifteen. "I think my grandfather would be amazed that it's still here." And how fortunate we are that Pete's thrives.

THE PLAZA TAVERN

319 N. HENRY ST | MADISON, WI 97213

608-255-6592 | WWW.THEPLAZATAVERN.COM

OPEN DAILY 11 AM–10:45 PM

The sauce is the draw and its ingredients are most definitely kept secret. Only a handful of insiders know the 40-plus-year-old recipe. "A bunch of restaurants claim they serve a Plaza Burger but they don't," grillman Mick told me with assurance. "Hey, I don't even know the recipe!" Which is a little strange for a guy who probably made over a thousand of the thin patty wonders that week alone. Owner Dean Hetue sequesters himself in a locked room in the kitchen to concoct the creamy white, tangy sauce the Plaza has been putting on their burgers since the mid-1960s. "All I can tell you," Mick went on, "is that it's a sour cream and mayo-based sauce, and the rest is a secret." Whatever it is, this unique topping is good. Very, very good.

The Plaza is a tavern first, so the burgers at this popular watering hole seem like an afterthought. Cooked on a tiny griddle next to the long rows of hard booze, their unique arrangement of elements suggests that this is more than just another bar burger (fresh beef, wheat bun, and salad dressing). And regardless of the Plaza's standard collegiate look and feel, the burger is anything but standard. Fresh, thin quarter-pound patties are grilled in plain sight of bar patrons, placed on incredibly soft wheat buns, and served with a dollop of the secret dressing/sauce. The presence of a wheat bun actually makes it feel like you could have one or two more, guilt-free.

The bar feels like an enormous romper room for adults, complete with endless diversions for the buzz-addled, ranging from darts to pool and with pinball and video games for the solo drinkers. There are TVs everywhere and The Plaza's sheer size suggests that large, boisterous crowds can fill the place (with the University of Wisconsin around the corner that's not difficult to imagine, and it's been rumored that Joan Cusack was once tossed from the bar). But the few times I've been there (during lunch), I pretty much had the place to myself.

The Plaza has been a bar for over a century, with a stint as a speakeasy during Prohibition. In 1963 Mary and Harold Huss bought the bar and introduced their burger. Mary concocted the now-famous sauce and placed her burger on a half-wheat bun that is still used today.

Dean started working at the Plaza in 1980 in hopes that one day he might own the place. "I figured that if I stuck around long enough . . ." His patience paid off, and in 2003 the second generation of the Huss family sold Dean the tavern—and the recipe for the secret sauce. "I have a great photo of me handing Tom Huss the check and he's handing me the recipe," Dean told me laughing. "It almost looks like we are in a tug-of-war." That recipe now rests in a safe deposit box, and in Dean's head. "My wife knew the recipe, but it's been five years since she's made the sauce. I'll bet she forgot."

The menu at the Plaza is limited to things you might eat while drinking, i.e. "bar food." Hot dogs and a fishwich are available, but you'd be wise to indulge in a few Plaza Burgers. They also serve one of my favorite sides, a not-to-be-missed treat of the upper Midwest, the fried cheese curd. Imagine a rustic, homespun version of the processed mozzarella stick and you'll get the picture. Impossibly good, these deep-fried, random-sized wads of breaded fresh cheese are worth every calorie.

The Plaza sits on a bizarre little street near the state's capitol building and among the bustling stores catering to Madison's large student population. "There's so little parking out front," Dean mused, "so it's amazing that so many people find their way here." Dean has noticed, in his nearly three decades at the tavern, students turn into alumni and continue to patronize the Plaza. "It's the sauce that brings them back."

SOLLY'S GRILLE

4629 NORTH PORT WASHINGTON ROAD

MILWAUKEE, WI 53212

414-332-8808 | MON 10 AM–8 PM

TUE–SAT 6:30 AM–8 PM | SUN 8 AM–4 PM

For the burger purist and lover of the things that make America unique, a visit to Solly's is imperative. Pure and simple, Solly's serves one of the last real butter burgers in the nation. When I say "real" I'm referring to the copious amounts of creamy Wisconsin butter that is used on their burgers, as opposed to what their surrounding competition calls a butter burger. To everyone else who peddles this great Wisconsin treat, the burger bun is coated with a thin swipe of butter, much in the way you might butter your toast if you were on a diet. Solly's dramatically bends the rules and treats the butter as a condiment. In other words you actually won't believe how much butter goes on the burger. The first time I visited Solly's, I stood and watched that which I had only heard about from disbelieving past patrons. Could they really use upwards of two to three tablespoons of butter on one smallish cheeseburger? Oh yes,

they do, and have been for over 70 years.

I kid you not when I say that a butter burger at Solly's, as gross as it may sound, is an absolutely sublime experience in the gastronomic fabric of America and should be experienced by all. You may also catch yourself doing what I did subconsciously on my first visit—dipping the last bite of your burger back into the pool of butter on your plate. You quickly discover that whatever guilt you harbored while taking your first bite has dissolved by your last.

In 1936 Kenneth Solomon bought Bay Lunch in Milwaukee a clean sixteen-stool diner that served coffee, hamburgers, and bratwurst, and changed the name to his own. In 1971, he relocated Solly's Coffee Shop a few miles north to the Milwaukee suburb of Glendale. He left the restaurant to his second wife, Sylvia, and she in turn sold the business to her son and current owner Glenn Fieber.

The cheery and cherubic Glenn, fresh from a successful construction business, was faced with an unusual dilemma early in his ownership—move or perish. In 2000, the city government actually assisted Glenn in moving the entire restaurant a few hundred yards south to make way for, of all things, an outpatient heart clinic.

The interior of Solly's is a comfortable blend of yellow Formica horseshoe counters, swivel stools, and wood paneling. As they have been for decades, the burgers, fries, and shakes are all prepared in view of the counter patrons.

The fresh-ground 3-ounce thin patties show

up at Solly's daily and are cooked on a large flat-top griddle. The toasted buns are standard white squishy, but a soft "pillow" bun is also offered. There are many burger combinations and sizes (like the impressive two-patty "Cheese Head" that an ex-Navy Seal friend of mine devours with ease), but I suggest doing what my good friend and butter burger devotee Rick Cohler has been doing for over 50 years at Solly's—just order a butter burger.

Rick introduced me to Solly's. On our first visit together he begged me to try a burger "without" which is a burger on a bun with butter only, no onions. I obliged and immediately understood what all the fuss was about. As you bite into a freshly built butter-burger you actually have the opportunity to experience the texture of soft butter before it melts into a pool on your plate. Unlike Rick, my "usual" at Solly's is a burger with onions. The stewed onions at Solly's are like none other I have experienced. They are both sweet and salty, and full of flavor. I could eat a bowl of them with a spoon.

Glenn is one of my truest allies in the burger world. He understands his place in American history and his duty to supply hungry burger lovers with a treat as unique as the butter burger.

WEDL'S HAMBURGER STAND AND ICE CREAM PARLOR

200 EAST RACINE ST | JEFFERSON, WI 53549

920-674-3637 | MON–SUN 10:30 AM–9:30 PM

FRI & SAT 10:30 AM–10:30 PM

Somewhere south of Route 94 on a lonely stretch of highway between Madison and Milwaukee sits a gem of a burger stand. I was tipped off to Wedl's by good friend and burger icon himself, Glenn Fieber of Solly's Grille in Glendale, Wisconsin. He told me, "Ya gotta go out there, they are making a great little burger."

The stand at Wedl's is actually 8 x 8 feet, which is 65 square feet—small for a place that can move up to 600 burgers on a busy day. When I asked former owner Bill Peterson the size of the minuscule, nearly century-old stand, he went inside the larger adjacent ice cream parlor and produced a tape measure. The parlor, formerly a grocery store and at one time a hat shop, is over 800 square feet larger than the separate stand that sits proudly on the corner. In 1999 the stand was leveled by a reckless drunk driver while two kids were inside flipping patties. Miraculously, the employees survived with only grease burns but parts of the stand were scattered for blocks. The original griddle, a perfectly seasoned, low-sided, cast-iron skillet was recovered

from the debris two blocks away. A small hole was patched and it was put back into service. After much cajoling the stand was rebuilt on the same spot. I asked former owner Bill Peterson why he wouldn't just move the burger operation into the larger ice cream parlor but I knew the answer. "The people of Jefferson won't allow me to change anything. I can't break tradition."

In 2007, Eric and Rosie Wedl became the eighth owners of the burger stand and ice cream parlor after buying the business from the Petersons. As Bill was looking to sell, he asked his faithful 20-year-old burger flipper Bert Wedl if he was interested in buying the place. Bert in turn talked his parents into it, and in doing so he secured his own job and possibly the future of the historic burger stand. And he told me recently, "I hope to take over one day."

The burger at Wedl's is a classic one-sixth-pound patty griddled and served on a white squishy bun. Bert grinds chuck steaks in the basement of the parlor, throws in some "secret seasonings" (tastes peppery) and rolls the grind into small golf ball–size balls. The balls are smashed thin on the 90-year-old griddle and cooked until the edges are crispy.

Bert is barely 25 now and has flipped burgers at the tiny stand since he was 15. I couldn't help but notice that when things got slow behind the grill Bert would step out of the stand and sit on the steps of the ice cream parlor. Do you think he was subconsciously trying to avoid being the next victim of a hit and run? I do.

ZWIEG'S

904 EAST MAIN ST | WATERTOWN, WI 53094
920-261-1922 | MON–THU 5:30 AM–8 PM
FRI 5:30 AM–9 PM | SAT 5:30 AM–7 PM
SUN 7 AM–2 PM

The first time I visited Zwieg's, the McDonald's down the street had just suffered a bad fire. "I swear I didn't do it!" Mary Zwieg joked. Mary is married to Glenn Zwieg and Glenn's parents opened this local favorite burger counter in a defunct Bartles-Maguire filling station. It is positioned perfectly at the east end of town and still looks a lot like a vintage gas station, minus the pumps.

Grover and Helen Zwieg (pronounced like "twig") saw opportunity in converting the station into a hamburger joint to feed the late-night revelers when the bars let out at 1 a.m. "We used to be open until two thirty in the morning, though I don't know if they remember eating here." Glenn told me. "Every Sunday night there was a Polka fest in town and they'd all end up here afterwards, still Polka-ing!" In the 1950s, Glenn's parents added a dining room to the twelve-stool counter and pretty much nothing has changed since. "We did replace the griddle in 1998," Mary pointed out, but it had been in use for 50 years, since the beginning. It was such a big deal that the replacing of the griddle made the local newspaper.

The Zwiegs are not big on change and their customers are happy about that. They've been using the same butcher for their patties forever and Mary told me, "If they go out of business I don't know what we'll do." The burger starts as a thin one-sixth-pound patty that is cooked on the flattop in full view of the counter patrons. Sliced onion is placed on the patty. When the burger is flipped, the onion is grilled between the griddle and the patty. The patty, with its onion, is transferred to a soft white bun that has been toasted with butter on the griddle. The most popular burger (and the best beef-to-bun ratio) is the double with cheese. Many are ordered with pickles and ketchup, but everyone gets theirs with onions.

The burger has been on the menu since the beginning. "That's ALL that was on the menu!" Glenn joked. Today, Zwieg's actually has an extensive menu with soups, sandwiches, and fish-fry Fridays. "I have forty-five sandwiches on the menu but most people order the burgers," Mary told me. One tasty curiosity is the hamburger soup, which is basically a chicken soup with browned hamburger meat in it. When I asked what was in the soup Mary told me with a laugh, "I can tell you, but I'd have to kill you! It's a secret."

Glenn, now 67, started working at his parent's restaurant when he was in seventh grade. "I used to run down, empty the dishwasher, and eat," he told me. From that point on he has always worked at Zwieg's. He bought it in 1976, and has dedicated his entire life to the restaurant. He told me, "This is what I know."

Thank God there are still places like Zwieg's around. It's a comfortable, happy place where a counter full of regulars are really just friends waiting to be met. I'll never forget walking into Zwieg's the first time. By the time I left I knew everyone. That kind of hospitality is what makes great burgers taste even better.

Joe

EXPERT BURGER TASTERS

In the past few years, a small group of dedicated fans of *Hamburger America* has emerged hailing from every corner of the country. Some wrote e-mails to me saying they would do anything to have my job and, not surprisingly, they all wanted to help me with future research. Most were already established food bloggers in their respective cities and dedicated local hamburger addicts. I found this new network of burger experts to be unquestionably indispensible and saw them as first responders to new discoveries. It may sound silly, but they became my EBTs, or Expert Burger Tasters, a job they all took very seriously.

My EBTs thanklessly entered questionable dumps, long forgotten drive-ins, and sometimes drove for hours to sample burgers and gather information. Their advance work made my research easier and more focused. I no longer blundered into a town eating burgers I thought would be worthy of the book only to find frozen patties and questionable practices. With the help of these EBTs my goal was clear. In the process I also made great new friends and burger allies, most of whom joined me on the road when I showed up at their favorite burger joints.

If it were not for Sef Gonzalez (aka. Burger

Todd

Kris

Beast) in Miami I never would have been able to translate what El Mago in Little Havana was saying, not a chance. EBT Wayne Geyer led me to burger greatness in Dallas and Indianapolis, and the wanderer Jeff Moore set me straight in Tennessee. EBT Jim Ellison in Ohio not only knew where to get great burgers but also the rich histories behind them (he also sent me on my way once with excellent cookies from a local bakery). Joe Price not only knew ALL of the hot burger joints in Tulsa, he also ended up asking all of the questions in the Tulsa interviews. Jay Castaldi confirmed my favorites in Chicago and has joined me for burgers at all of them. Kris Brearton, the first EBT, has logged more miles with me on far-out burger journeys than anyone, including an insane 670-mile, 18-hour journey into New England. And my wife Casey left behind 17 years of vegetarianism to join me on the road for this edition of the book (finally, she got to eat some amazing burgers). But one EBT stands out above them all: Todd McIlwee from Waunakee, Wisconsin. His dedication is beyond comprehension and his love of the traditional American hamburger is enormous. He has driven hundreds of miles in pursuit of hamburger knowledge and firmly believes there is much more out there to discover.

There are others that have led me to the burgers of my dreams and I'm indebted to you all. Thank you for reminding me that I'm not alone out there in my passion for greasy goodness.

ACKNOWLEDGMENTS

I'm not really a writer. I'm a filmmaker, a photographer, and a nostalgic American. My quest to find America's greatest burgers and the people who make them started with a film I made many years ago called *Hamburger America*. As a result of that project, and the research for this book, I have amassed an absurd amount of hamburger knowledge. I owe an enormous debt of gratitude to dedicated food experts in many parts of the country for pointing me in the right direction and filling my brain and belly with unforgettable burger experiences.

Many thanks to Rick Kogan for being the president of the George Motz Fan Club and smelling success in hamburger reportage far before anyone else could. To columnist Doug Moe who has hosted and written about me in Madison, Wisconsin, and food writer Robb Walsh who made sure I was on the right track in Houston, Texas more than once. To Ed Levine from Serious Eats and Jim Fusilli of the *Wall Street Journal* for giving me tips on writing. To columnist Marshall King, my host in Indiana, and Tom Palmore and Bill Peterson, who introduced me to great burgers in Oklahoma. To friend Greg Ennis, who led me to burger greatness in Montana and protected me from drunken rugby players. And Rick Cohler who will never say no to a Butter Burger (or three) at Solly's Grille. To Kacy Jahanbini for venturing into Ann's Snack Bar before I did, and to Mac Premo for flying all the way to Meers, Oklahoma just to be nearly killed by a buffalo. To Vernon Schwarte for organizing motorcycle rallies to various places in *Hamburger America* (in the name of breast cancer awareness) and to all of the fans that have taken this book on the road to have it signed by my hamburger heroes (this small gesture goes a long way and shows these hamburger icons that their life's work is meaningful). Also to NYC Mayor Mike Bloomberg who is, without a doubt, hamburger obsessed. Thanks also to all of the butchers and meat people in my life, like Joe at United Meat in Brooklyn, Pat LaFrieda, Mark Pastore, SuSu Strassburger, and Jamie Schweid at Burger

Maker. To Brett Reichler, Paul Sale, and Steve Hanson at Bill's Burgers, Scott Smith and Andrew Fischel at RUB, and Randy Garutti at Shake Shack.

Thanks also to Nick Solares, Josh Ozersky, Melena Ryzik, Jeff Ruby, Jason Perlow, Stacy Perman, The Rev, and Adam Kuban, all food and culture writers of the highest order. To Seth Unger for attempting to manage all of this hamburger craziness in my life and to Nancy Meyers, always my host in LA. To Izabella, Kris, Diane, and Mitchell at James Beard and to Dan Appel and Rob Knox from danAppelcreative. Thanks also to Martha Stewart and Gayle King for having me on their shows, and to my amazing in-laws Sally and Jon for watching the kids while the wife and I powered through hamburger country. And of course to all of the tipsters who gave me advice about their favorite hamburger joint, whether they were driving the airport rental car shuttle, at the hotel bar, or sending me endless amounts of e-mail (keep sending that e-mail!). I'd also be quite lost without my core

EBTs Kris, Jim, Sef, Joe, Wayne, Jay, and Todd (aka #2). I also need to thank my food photography mentor, Greg Ramsey, who taught me a whole new way to look at food.

This book never would have seen the light of day had it not been for my agent, Laura Dail, and my patient editor, Jennifer Kasius, at Running Press. Thanks also to everyone else at Running Press, especially designer Joshua McDonnell.

The cooperation of the restaurants involved made writing this book a pleasure (with the exception of Ann's Snack Bar and Dirty Martin's). Enormous thanks is due as well to my close friends and family who have supported me and my burger mission for the last decade. And most importantly, to my wife, Casey, who ate her first burger in 17 years at the Bobcat Bite last year and to my children, Ruby and Mac who love hot dogs (I'm working on it). After enduring tens of thousands of miles of traveling and writing about everyone else's family, it's great to come home to my own.